HUMANITARIAN INTERVENTION AND CONFLICT RESOLUTION IN WEST AFRICA

For my son James Alex,
Thanks for the happiness you've brought into our lives

Humanitarian Intervention and Conflict Resolution in West Africa
From ECOMOG to ECOMIL

JOHN M. KABIA
The Tim Parry Johnathan Ball Foundation for Peace, Warrington, Cheshire, UK

ASHGATE

Published by
Ashgate Publishing Limited
Wey Court East
Union Road
Farnham
Surrey GU9 7PT
England

Ashgate Publishing Company
Suite 420
101 Cherry Street
Burlington, VT 05401-4405
USA

www.ashgate.com

British Library Cataloguing in Publication Data
Kabia, John M.
  Humanitarian intervention and conflict resolution in West
  Africa : from ECOMOG to ECOMIL
  1. Humanitarian intervention - Africa, West
  2. Peace-building - Africa, West 3. Peacekeeping forces -
  Africa, West 4. Africa, West - Politics and government
  5. Africa, West - Foreign relations
  I. Title
  341.5'84

Library of Congress Cataloging-in-Publication Data
Kabia, John M.
  Humanitarian intervention and conflict resolution in West Africa : from ECOMOG to
ECOMIL / by John M. Kabia.
      p. cm.
  Includes bibliographical references and index.
  ISBN 978-0-7546-7444-3
  1. Conflict management--Africa, West. 2. Conflict management--International
cooperation. 3. National security--Africa, West. 4. Peace-building--Africa, West. 5.
Humanitarian intervention--Africa, West. 6. Regionalism--Africa, West. 7. Economic
Community of West African States. I. Title.

  HN820.Z9.C73K34 2008
  363.2'32--dc22

2008031180

ISBN 978 0 7546 7444 3

Mixed Sources
Product group from well-managed
forests and other controlled sources
www.fsc.org Cert no. SA-COC-1565
© 1996 Forest Stewardship Council
FSC

Printed and bound in Great Britain by
MPG Books Ltd, Bodmin, Cornwall.

Contents

List of Tables

Acknowledgements

First and foremost, I thank the Almighty God for making this work possible. I owe a great debt of gratitude to the Bishop of Makeni, Sierra Leone, George Biguzzi, whose financial and moral contribution to this project has been very remarkable. Rev. Fr Piero Lazzarini deserves gratitude for his unceasing moral and spiritual support and inspiration in my pursuit of knowledge. Thanks for helping me realise my potential and giving me the opportunity to utilise it. Big thanks are due to my loving wife, Fatmata, whose constant reminders and loving support have helped me through the writing of this book. Thanks also to my mother, Madam Hawa Kargbo and my late dad, Mr James Kabia for their support and parental love. I am grateful to my close friends who have been the inspiration for this project: Peter Swaray, Patrick Hassan-Morlai, Ahmed O. Bangura and Nathaniel Sesay.

Profound thanks and appreciation also go to Professors David J. Francis and Malcolm Chalmers for broadening my horizon on the issues and dynamics of humanitarian intervention, West African security and conflict resolution. I am also pleased to acknowledge the support of Dr Kenneth Omeje of the Africa Centre, University of Bradford, whose critical comments and suggestions on earlier drafts of this book proved very helpful.

This note of gratitude will be incomplete if I fail to mention my colleagues at the Tim Parry Johnathan Ball Foundation for Peace – Clare White, Wendy Parry, Jo Dover, Rosie Aubrey, Lynn Hitchen, Val Barlow, Chanel Martin, Kerry Gibson, and Kelly Simcock – who have always been an indispensable source of encouragement since I joined the Foundation in March 2008. And to all who in diverse ways have contributed to the success of this book, I say a big thank you. I will ever be grateful.

List of Abbreviations

AAFC	Allied Armed Forces of the Community
ACC	Anti-Corruption Commission (Sierra Leone)
ACRF	African Crisis Response Force
ACRI	African Crisis Response Initiative
ACOTA	African Contingency Operations Training and Assistance
AFL	Armed Forces of Liberia
AFRC	Armed Forces Revolutionary Council
ANAD	*Accord de Non Aggression et d'Assistance en matière de Défense* (Non-Agression and Defence Aid Agreement)
APC	All Peoples Congress
ATU	Anti-Terrorist Unit (Liberia)
AU	African Union
BBC	British Broadcasting Corporation
BDF	Bong Defence Force
BMATT	British Military Assistance Training Teams
CA	Committee of Ambassadors
CDF	Civil Defence Forces (Sierra Leone)
CEAO	*Commununaute Economique de l'Afrique Occidentale* (West African Economic Community)
CFA	*Communaute Financiere Africaine* (African Financial Community)
CGG	Campaign for Good Governance
CIS	Commonwealth of Independent States
CPE	Complex Political Emergency
CPP	*Convention des patriotes Pour la paix* (Convention of Patriots for Peace)
CRS	Catholic Relief Services
CSM	Civil Society Movement (Sierra Leone)
DDR	Disarmament, Demobilisation and Reintegration
DPKO	Department of Peacekeeping Operations
DRC	Democratic Republic of the Congo
DSC	Defence and Security Commission
ECA	Economic Commission for Africa
ECOWAS	Economic Community of West African States
ECOMICI	ECOWAS Mission in Côte d'Ivoire
ECOMIL	ECOWAS Mission in Liberia
ECOMOG	ECOWAS Cease-fire Monitoring Group
ECSC	European Coal and Steel Community

EEC	European Economic Community
EO	Executive Outcomes
EU	European Union
GDP	Gross Domestic Product
GPA	General Peace Agreement (Mozambique)
HIPC	Highly Indebted Poor Countries
ICC	International Criminal Court
ICISS	International Commission on Intervention and State Sovereignty
ICG	International Crisis Group
ICJ	International Court of Justice
ICTR	International Criminal Tribunal for Rwanda
ICTY	International Criminal Tribunal for Yugoslavia
IFI	International Financial Institutions
IGNU	Interim Government of National Unity
IMATT	International Military Assistance Training Teams
IMF	International Monetary Fund
INGO	International Non-Governmental Organisation
INPFL	Independent National Patriotic Front of Liberia
IRIN	Integrated Regional Information Network
JCL	Justice Coalition of Liberia
LDF	Lofa Defence Force
LNTG	Liberian National Transitional Government
LPC	Liberian Peace Council
LURD	Liberians United for Reconciliation and Democracy
MAD	Mutual Assistance on Defence
MFDC	*Mouvement des Forces Démocratiques de la Casamance* (Democratic Forces of Casamance Movement)
MINUCI	*Mission des Nations Unies en Côte d'Ivoire* (United Nations Mission in Côte d'Ivore)
MODEL	Movement for Democracy in Liberia
MOJA	Movement for Justice in Africa
MSC	Mediation and Security Council
MSF	*Médecins Sans Frontières* (Doctors Without Borders)
NATO	North Atlantic Treaty Organisation
NCDDR	National Commission for Disarmament, Demobilisation and Reintegration
NCDDRRR	National Commission for Disarmament, Demobilisation, Reconstruction, Resettlement and Reintegration
NCDHR	National Commission for Democracy and Human Rights
NDVF	Niger Delta Volunteer Force
NGO	Non-Governmental Organisation
NPFL	National Patriotic Front of Liberia
NPRA	National Patriotic Reconstruction Assembly

NPRC	National Provisional Ruling Council
NTGL	National Transitional Government of Liberia
NUSS	National Union of Sierra Leone Students
OAS	Organisation of American States
OAU	Organisation of African States
ODL	Organisation of Displaced Liberians
OSCE	Organisation for Security and Cooperation in Europe
PAE	Pacific Architects and Engineers
PCASED	Programme for Coordination and Assistance for Security and Development
PDD-25	Presidential Decision Directive 25
PMC	Private Military Company
PoA	Programme of Action
QIP	Quick Impact Project
RECAMP	*Renforcement des Capacites Africaines de Maintien de la Paix* (Reinforcement of African Peacekeeping Capacities)
RENAMO	*Resistencia Nacional Mocambicana* (Mozambican Resistance Organisation)
RFDG	*Rassemblement des Forces Democratique de Guinee* (Rally of Democratic Forces of Guinea)
RUF	Revolutionary United Front
SADC	Southern African Development Community
SAP	Structural Adjustment Programme
SC	Security Council
SCSL	Special Court for Sierra Leone
SHIRBRIG	Standby High Readiness Brigade
SLA	Sierra Leone Army
SLPP	Sierra Leone Peoples Party
SMC	Standing Mediation Committee
SOD	Special Operations Division
SRSG	Special Representative of the Secretary-General
SSD	Special Security Division
SSS	Special Security Service
TRC	Truth and Reconciliation Commission (Sierra Leone)
UDL	Union of Democratic Forces of Liberia
UEMOA	*Union Economique et Monétaire Ouest Africaine* (West African Economic and Monetary Union)
ULIMO	United Liberian Movement for Democracy
UNAMSIL	United Nations Mission in Sierra Leone
UNDP	United Nations Development Programme
UNHCR	United Nations High Commissioner for Refugees
UNICEF	United Nations Children's Fund
UNMIL	United Nations Mission in Liberia
UNOCI	United Nations Operation in Côte d'Ivoire

UNOL	United Nations Peacebuilding Support Office in Liberia
UNOMIL	United Nations Observer Mission in Liberia
UNOMSIL	United Nations Observer Mission in Sierra Leone
UNSCOL	United Nations Special Coordinator for Liberia
UNSG	United Nations Secretary General
WAANSA	West African Action Network on Small Arms
WAEC	West African Economic Commission

Introduction

The end of the Cold War has been characterised by a wave of violent civil wars that have produced unprecedented humanitarian catastrophe and suffering. Although mostly intra-state, these conflicts have spread across borders and threatened international peace and security through mass refugee flow, proliferation of light arms and the rise of local mercenary groups. The UN coined the term Complex Political Emergencies (CPE) to describe these forms of conflicts. One of the most affected regions is West Africa which has been home to some of Africa's most brutal and intractable conflicts for more than a decade. Beginning with the Liberian civil war which erupted in December 1989, this 'bush fire that does not respect national boundaries' (Francis, 2000, 2) quickly spread to neighbouring Sierra Leone in 1991. In the 1990s, both Mali and Niger fought bitter wars with secessionist Tuareg rebels whilst Senegal is still battling Casamance separatists. Guinea Bissau erupted into full scale civil war in 1997 following a power struggle between mutinous sections of the army and the civilian government of President Nino Vieira. In September 2000, rebels from across the border in Sierra Leone and Liberia invaded parts of Guinea and in September 2002, an army mutiny in Cote d'Ivoire completed the vicious circle of conflict gripping the sub-region. However, West Africa, and indeed Africa as a whole is not unique in this respect. Following the collapse of the Soviet Union, conflicts in the Balkans and former Soviet republics destabilised Eastern Europe in the 1990s.

The optimism that followed the end of the Cold War brought about unprecedented international cooperation which allowed the United Nations to play a leading role in resolving such conflicts. As a result, UN peacekeeping and humanitarian intervention grew dramatically both quantitatively and qualitatively. The period between 1989 and 1996 alone witnessed the establishment of 29 peacekeeping operations (Woodhouse and Ramsbotham, 2001) with a sharp rise in the annual budget of peacekeeping from US$230 million in 1988 to US$3.6 billion in 1995 (Boutros-Ghali, 1998). The roles of humanitarian interveners also expanded considerably to include peacemaking and peacebuilding. The increased number of missions and expanded roles, however, seriously overstretched the capacity of the UN and posed complications in terms of logistics, inter-force relations, communications, financial resources and chain of command. The result has been a string of failures and humiliation of UN forces in places such as Somalia, Rwanda and Bosnia. Consequently, the UN was forced to scale down its intervention in intra-state conflicts in the mid-1990s. This led to the emergence of assertive regional/sub-regional bodies willing to take on board *ad hoc* security functions. From its inception in 1945, the UN anticipated the involvement of such regional organisations in the maintenance of global peace and security. Chapter VIII of the UN Charter acknowledges the importance of such groupings and urges member states to seek 'pacific settlement of local disputes through such regional arrangements or by such regional agencies before referring them to the Security Council'.[1] The changed international environment which followed the end of the Cold War allowed regional/sub-regional organisations in many parts of the world to fulfil this envisaged role. Among others, the Commonwealth of Independent States (CIS), Organisations of American States (OAS), The Economic Community of West African States (ECOWAS), Southern African Development Community (SADC) and the European Union (EU) all developed or are in the process of developing security, humanitarian and peacebuilding mechanisms to respond to the threat of civil conflicts. However, these regional/sub-regional efforts are fraught with problems including lack of resources, credibility and political consensus.

In Africa, ECOWAS has been at the forefront of developing humanitarian and peacekeeping response mechanisms. Officially justified on humanitarian grounds, ECOWAS deployed its military force, ECOWAS Monitoring Group (ECOMOG), in Liberia, Sierra Leone and Guinea Bissau in 1990, 1997 and 1998 respectively. In 2003 following the outbreak of conflict in Cote d'Ivoire, ECOWAS launched the ECOWAS Mission in Cote d'Ivoire (ECOMICI) and in August 2003, the ECOWAS Mission in Liberia (ECOMIL) was deployed following that country's relapse into violence. These interventions opened up new possibilities for the maintenance of international peace and security in Africa. They represent a significant shift in Africa's international relations, which was previously characterised by the traditional Westphalian principles of state sovereignty and non-interventionism in the internal affairs of states. *Humanitarian Intervention and Conflict Resolution in West Africa* seeks to locate these operations within an expanded post-Cold War conceptualisation of humanitarian intervention and examines the organisation's capacity in protecting civilians at risk in civil conflicts and facilitating the processes of peacemaking and post-war peacebuilding aimed at preventing a relapse into conflict. By using the empirical case of ECOWAS, this book seeks to examine the challenges posed by CPEs to humanitarian intervention. It also traces the evolution of ECOWAS from an economic integration project to a security organisation and examine the challenges inherent in such a transition.

This book is intended to contribute to the existing literature on ECOWAS interventions in West Africa, humanitarian intervention in general and the related debate on post-war peacebuilding. The distinctiveness of this study lies in its attempt at integrating the forcible and non-forcible nature of ECOWAS's intervention in West Africa. The conceptualisation of complex

---

1   UN, Charter of the United Nations, Chapter VIII, available online http://www. un.org/aboutun/charter/, accessed March 2005.

political emergencies also helps to contextualise ECOWAS peacekeeping operations and offers a fresh perspective to understanding the problems faced by the sub-regional body. Besides contributing to the literature on ECOWAS peace operations, this work also intends to contribute to the general study of humanitarian intervention and the wider debate of resolving complex political emergencies and rebuilding war-torn societies across the world. Such analysis will lead to a better understanding of the nature of these conflicts, and the motivations and roles of the various actors involved. The results of these findings will help policy makers develop sound and effective response mechanisms to Africa's protracted conflicts.

Theoretical Approach and Core Argument of the Book

This book defines humanitarian intervention as forcible or non-forcible actions taken by states, group of states, regional organisations or the UN, in situations of massive human suffering caused by repressive regimes or complex political emergencies, where the state has collapsed and law and order has degenerated into mass murder and anarchy. This intervention should seek to protect human rights and alleviate the suffering of victims in the short term; and address the underlying causes of the conflict by facilitating conflict resolution and peacebuilding in the medium to long term. Since the end of the Cold War, humanitarian intervention and post-war peacebuilding have received renewed interest with a vast array of publications and reports including works by Nick Wheeler (2000), Oliver Ramsbotham and Tom Woodhouse (1996), Oliver P. Richmond, David Chandler, Mike Pugh and Roland Paris among others. In their groundbreaking study, *Humanitarian Intervention in Contemporary Conflict*, Ramsbotham and Woodhouse (1996) argued for a broadening of humanitarian intervention to take on board both forcible and non-forcible strategies aimed at consolidating peace in post-war societies. This argument has been further developed when they called for cosmopolitan peacekeeping which will both be able to protect civilians and address the UN's emerging human security agenda (Ramsbotham and Woodhouse, 2005). In *Saving Strangers*, Wheeler reinforced this argument and posits that the success of an intervention is defined by 'how far intervention addresses the underlying political causes that produced the human rights abuses' (2000, 37). The report of the International Committee on Intervention and State Sovereignty (ICISS) also argued along these lines and called for a reinterpretation of sovereignty as a 'responsibility to protect'. It argued that the international community does not only have a 'responsibility to react' but also a 'responsibility to prevent' and a 'responsibility to rebuild' (ICISS, 2001). Since the end of the Cold War, the UN and other international organisations and aid agencies have responded to this challenge and developed a standard operating procedure involving power sharing arrangements, a new constitution and regular free and fair elections underpinned by Western liberal market economy. For Mark Duffield, this represents an attempt by the West to impose the *liberal peace* which he defines as 'a new or political humanitarianism that lays emphasis on such things as conflict resolution and prevention, reconstructing social networks, strengthening civil and representative institutions, promoting the rule of law, and security sector reform in the context of a functioning market economy' (2001, 11). The liberal peace thesis can be traced back to the era of the Enlightenment and Immanuel Kant's *Perpetual Peace* essay. It was popularised by Woodrow Wilson who presented it as the panacea for violent international conflict following the end of World War I (Paris, 2004). Proponents of this thesis argue that liberal democracy underpinned by a free market economy fosters peace in countries emerging from conflict. Within contemporary liberal peace discourse, poverty and underdevelopment are being linked to conflict and insecurity. This has led to the merging of the development and security policies of the UN and major donor countries and organisations. This convergence between development and security has been reflected in a number of high profile reports including DFID's *Fighting Poverty to Build A Safer World* (2005), the UN's *A Secure World: Our Shared Responsibility* (2004) and the Commission for Africa's *Our Common Interest* (2005). For instance, The Report of the UN High Level Panel on Threats, Challenges and Change observes that 'development is the first line of defence for a collective security system that takes prevention seriously ... Development makes everyone more secure' (UN, 2004). The Africa Action Plan of the G8 also argues that 'poverty, underdevelopment and fragile states create fertile conditions for violent conflict and the emergence of new security threats, including international crime and terrorism. There will be no lasting security without development and no effective development without security and stability' (G8, 2005, 4). However, the assumptions of the liberal peace thesis have come under attack by several analysts. For Duffield (2001), this merging of peace, development and security represents an attempt by the powerful to contain, stabilise and ameliorate the effects of violent conflicts in the third world. Drawing on the works of Cox and Duffield, Pugh argues that this emerging form of peacekeeping and humanitarian intervention is not value neutral but serves as a 'form of riot control directed against the unruly parts of the world to uphold the liberal peace' (2004, 41). In the same volume, Chandler argues that the *Responsibility to Protect* does not signal the emergence of new found humanitarianism but 'reflects the new balance of power in the international sphere'. He went on to argue that '[J]ustifications for new interventionist norms as a framework for liberal peace are as dependent on the needs of *realpolitik* as was the earlier doctrine of sovereign equality and non-intervention' (2004, 59). Richmond (2004) also questions the nature of the peace that is being implemented by UN and international peace missions and argues that this form of intervention allows outsiders to be in control over locals, drawing very close similarities to Western imperialism. Willett presents a more damning critique of the liberal peace project claiming that it has failed to secure sustainable peace in

Africa due to the failure of global institutions to realise the destabilising effects of their neo-liberal reforms. These reforms, including free trade, liberalisation and privatisation, according to her, 'have increased inequalities and the sense of social injustice which in turn has had the effect of intensifying levels of human security that feeds violence' (Willet, 2005, 570). Whilst acknowledging some of the arguments against liberal peace and humanitarian intervention highlighted above, a noticeable weakness of most critics is their failure to present effective and concrete alternatives. Inaction in the face of massive human rights abuses is not an option in today's interconnected world where state collapse in one remote part of the world has far reaching implications for international security.

This book adopts a solidarist approach and argues that humanitarian intervention for human protection purposes can be regarded as an acceptable 'breach' of international law, and emphasises the need for complimenting the short term aim of saving lives with the long term goal of building sustainable peace through institutionalisation of democratic values and the rule of law. The need for international support to peacebuilding is premised on the fact that parties to conflicts cannot effectively carry out these tasks due to institutional weakness, limited human and financial resources and economic problems. Reflecting this solidarist position, the following are the core arguments that underpin the analysis of this book:

1   ECOWAS interventions in West Africa are justified on humanitarian grounds and represent an acceptable 'breach' of international law. This justification is based on the emerging broader conceptualisation of humanitarian intervention and also reflects recent state practice and international acceptance of humanitarian intervention for human protection purposes.
2   ECOWAS' flexibility in shifting between forcible and non-forcible strategies represents a robust strategy of responding to the highly volatile security situation of, and unpredictable actors in, complex political emergencies. This duality goes beyond immediate civilian protection and alleviation of suffering to embrace ECOWAS' attempt at facilitating peace processes and implementing peacebuilding programmes in both countries.
3   However, the lack of an effective humanitarian policy, a coherent political plan and a well thought-out peacebuilding and exit strategy undermined the significant humanitarian gains of the ECOMOG missions in Liberia, Sierra Leone and Guinea Bissau and resulted in flawed peace processes and haphazard peacebuilding programmes.
4   In view of the above weaknesses, this book argues that cooperation between the UN and regional/sub-regional organisations represents the most viable response to complex political emergencies. Whilst regional/ sub-regional organisations may have the willingness to intervene, and the local knowledge of the conflict in question, most of them, with the

exception of NATO and the EU, lack the capacity, financial, human and military resources and credibility to mount an effective humanitarian mission in complex political emergencies. Notwithstanding its drawbacks and challenges, this evolving functional relationship presents real opportunities to future regional/sub-regional peacekeeping and humanitarian intervention. In the case of West Africa, this cooperation allows an overburdened UN and an ECOWAS in dire need of resources, capacity and credibility to maximise their comparative advantages.

Organisation of the Book

The book is presented in nine chapters. Chapter 1 provides a conceptual framework for humanitarian intervention in the post-Cold War era. A detailed analysis of complex political emergencies is used to understand the challenges and difficulties facing humanitarian interveners and form the basis for a re-conceptualisation of humanitarian intervention. The conceptual framework and definitions in this chapter also form the basis of analysis in the entire book. Chapter 2 analyses West Africa's intractable and interconnected conflicts with a view to understanding the context within which ECOWAS peacekeeping missions operated. It argues against the oversimplified analysis of West African conflicts as 'resource-based' or 'ethnic wars' and posits that the analysis of West African conflicts should be eclectic and take on board a variety of factors and actors. This analysis then form the background for an exploration of the sub-region's evolution from a primarily economic integration project to security regionalism in Chapter 3. By providing a historical perspective to ECOWAS regionalism, this chapter seeks to understand the problems that faced ECOMOG such as the Francophone-Anglophone rivalry, Franco-Nigerian tensions, and the roots of Nigerian hegemonic ambitions.

Chapters 4 and 5 focus on the ECOMOG interventions in Liberia and Sierra Leone respectively, highlighting the dual peacekeeping and peace enforcement strategy and co-deployment with UN missions. Chapter 6 examines ECOWAS interventions in Guinea Bissau and Cote d'Ivoire. These missions add a new dimension to the analysis of West African peace and security intervention. Besides being the only non-Anglophone countries for ECOWAS to intervene, they are also the only missions where the regional hegemon, Nigeria was not involved. Chapter 7 looks at the second ECOWAS intervention in Liberia and examines whether the lessons of the first intervention were learned. Building on the findings of the above chapters, chapter 8 takes a comparative insight into peacebuilding in Liberia and Sierra Leone and evaluates the efforts of domestic, regional and international actors in building sustainable peace. Although the focus of this book is on ECOWAS, however an analysis of the transitional period in these countries that does not take into account the contributions of other actors will be severely constrained. By integrating ECOWAS operations within the wider framework of peacebuilding activities in these countries, this chapter will provide alternative explanations for the difficulties and challenges faced by the sub-regional force. Chapter 9 assesses sub-regional efforts aimed at institutionalising security and conflict resolution mechanisms in the form of the ECOWAS Security Mechanism, arms control initiatives and various extra-regional programmes helping to build the capacity of West African militaries in responding to future complex political emergencies. The conclusion draws key lessons from the aforementioned discussions and analysis with a view to enhancing future humanitarian intervention in West Africa.

Chapter 1

Humanitarian Intervention in Complex Political Emergencies: A Conceptual Framework for Analysis

Introduction

The principles of sovereignty and non-intervention have long been bedrocks of the traditional Westphalian state system. Geared towards the maintenance of order and stability in the international system, these principles have frowned at foreign interference in the domestic affairs of states. In Africa, more than any other region, sovereignty and non-intervention became defining features of the Organisation of African Unity (OAU). Lacking popular sovereignty, most leaders in the continent depended on coercion and intimidation of political opponents to stay in power. The non-intervention norm of the Westphalian state system has therefore meant the protection of the status quo even in the face of massive human rights abuses. However, the end of the Cold War suddenly brought the issue of human rights and state collapse to the centre of international relations. Starting from the 1991 US-led 'Operation Provide Comfort' and 'Operation Southern Watch' to protect the Kurds of Northern Iraq and the Shi'a of Southern Iraq respectively from Saddam Hussein's intolerable repression, humanitarian intervention has emerged as a key policy option for international organisations, coalitions of states, regional organisations and big powers. However, the question of whether or not a state or group of states could legally intervene to stop massive human rights violations in another state remains a matter of great political and legal controversy.

With the proliferation of violent conflicts, the breakdown of state authority and the emergence of militia groups that have no regard for international norms and human rights in Africa and elsewhere, post-Cold War conceptualisation of humanitarian intervention has expanded from its nascent task of protecting victims of human rights abuses by repressive regimes in foreign countries to providing security to threatened populations caught up in the complex political emergencies (CPEs) that have come to characterise the end of the Cold War. It has also expanded to include non-forcible tasks such as the distribution of emergency relief to ameliorate the suffering of victims, securing the humanitarian space necessary for effective operations of aid agencies, and facilitating conflict resolution and post-war peacebuilding to prevent a relapse into conflict. These expanded roles and expectations have however placed serious difficulties on the part of interveners as the cases of Somalia, Rwanda and Bosnia demonstrate.

This chapter seeks to conceptualise humanitarian intervention in the post-Cold War era and examine the challenges it faces in today's complex political emergencies and post 9/11 era. It argues in favour of the solidarist approach to humanitarian intervention and posits that the challenges posed by CPEs warrants the broadening of its remits to include both forcible and non-forcible strategies aimed at safeguarding civilians in the short term and building sustainable peace in the medium to long term. Starting with a working definition of the concept, we then trace the origin and evolution of humanitarian intervention. Next, a detailed analysis of complex political emergencies will be used to understand the challenges and difficulties facing interveners and form the basis for a reframing of the debate on humanitarian intervention in light of current realities. The next section will develop a framework for analysis in the entire book which will be followed by definition of terms and concepts.

Humanitarian Intervention: A Working Definition

Wil Verwey (1992, 114) provided what is now considered a classic definition of humanitarian intervention,

> the threat or use of force by a state or states abroad, for the sole purpose of preventing or putting a halt to a serious violation of fundamental human rights, in particular the right to life of persons, regardless of their nationality, such protection taking place neither upon authorisation by relevant organs of United Nations nor with permission by the legitimate government of the target state.

Like other restrictionists' view of the term, Verwey stressed that the motive of humanitarian intervention should be 'solely' humanitarian. This strict stipulation disqualifies any intervention as 'humanitarian' considering the political interests and processes that are also certain to be involved in practice. Solidarists like Wheeler (2000) and Teson (2003) object to this strict emphasis on motive as they argue that this approach 'takes the intervening state as referent object for analysis rather than the victims who are rescued as a consequence of the use of force' (Wheeler, 2000, 38). This however leads us to two very controversial debates within humanitarianism: what counts as humanitarian and the question of the universality of human rights. Despite the frequent use of the term, 'a consistent and working definition of humanitarianism has evaded public and private authorities' (Nicholls, 1987, 193). This has prompted Adam Roberts to ask 'What on earth does humanitarian mean?' (Roberts, 1993, 13). Ephraim Isaac defines humanitarianism as 'a feeling of concern for and benevolence toward fellow human beings. It is a universal phenomenon manifested globally and through out the ages' (Isaac, 1993, 13). Ramsbotham and Woodhouse

(1996) link humanitarianism with international humanitarian law of armed conflict, international human rights law and emergency aid. But what level of humanitarian suffering requires outside intervention? Solidarists like Wheeler refer to a 'supreme humanitarian emergency' to describe a situation of extreme human suffering wherein 'the only hope of saving lives depends on outsiders coming to the rescue' (Wheeler, 2000, 34). However he admits there are no objective criteria for determining what counts as a 'supreme humanitarian emergency'. This work will define humanitarian emergency to mean a situation of excessive violation of human rights by a repressive government or cases of uncontrolled anarchy and mass murder caused by conflict and/or state collapse.

But reference to human rights also opens another controversial debate between universalists and cultural relativists. Proponents for the universality of human rights argue that human rights norms and standards are applicable to all human beings in all human societies, whatever geographical or cultural circumstances and whatever local traditions and practices may exist. The main challenge to the notion of universality of human rights comes principally from Asia, Middle East and Africa. Advocates of cultural relativism claim that most or some of the rights and rules about morality are encoded in and thus depend on cultural context. Hence, notions of right and wrong and moral rules differ through out the world because cultures in which they take root are different. To them international human rights instruments and their pretensions to universality may suggest primarily the arrogance of 'cultural imperialism' of the West. Practices considered violations of human rights in one part of the world may be viewed differently elsewhere. This work adopts a middle ground position between universalists and relativists. Whilst accepting the argument that human rights should be culturally sensitive, we however hold the view that there are minimum standards of human rights to be respected across the world. This includes the right to life, freedom of expression, association and movement.

Verwey's conceptualisation of humanitarian intervention also rules out intervention by the UN and confines the practice to action taken by individual states or groups of states without UN authorisation. Whilst this form of intervention is still prevalent as evidenced by the recent US/British led intervention in Iraq, recent interpretation of the concept has expanded the agents to include regional organisations and action taken by the UN (see Wheeler 2000; Ramsbotham and Woodhouse, 2006). From its inception in 1945, the UN anticipated the involvement of such organisations in the maintenance of global peace. Chapter VIII of the UN Charter acknowledges the importance of such groupings and urges member states to seek 'pacific settlement of local disputes through such regional arrangements or by such regional agencies before referring them to the Security Council'.[1] Ramsbotham and Woodhouse

---

1   Charter of the United Nations, Chapter VIII, available online www.un.org. aboutun/charter.

further expanded the agencies to include NGOs and UN aid organisations like the UN High Commissioner for Refugees (UNHCR) and UN Children's Fund (UNICEF). Whilst acknowledging the fact that non-state actors are now playing a prominent role in humanitarian intervention, this book, however, limit it to actions taken by states, groups of states, regional organisations and the UN Security Council. The action of aid agencies will be better understood as humanitarian assistance so as not to complicate analysis.

Verwey also rules out intervention undertaken with the consent of the target state. Post-Cold War understanding of the practice has, however included both consensual and non-consensual intervention. In fact in most of these missions, there is hardly a government with effective authority extending beyond the capital city. The 'threat or use of force' has also been a qualifying element of humanitarian intervention. The post-Cold War conceptualisation of the practice has, however expanded to include non-forcible strategies aimed at alleviating the suffering of those caught up in the middle of cross-fire and mechanisms to prevent a relapse into conflict. Ramsbotham and Woodhouse (1996, 115) offered a new typology of governmental humanitarian intervention as follows:

1 *Coercive (forcible) humanitarian intervention:*
   a) Forcible military humanitarian intervention;
   b) Coercive non-military humanitarian intervention.
2 *Non-coercive (non-forcible) humanitarian intervention:*
   a) Non-forcible military humanitarian intervention (eg. peacekeeping);
   b) Non-coercive, non-military humanitarian intervention.

The first category, coercive humanitarian intervention coincides with the classical definition. In the context of complex political emergencies, forcible military humanitarian intervention involves the provision and securing of humanitarian space for the work of aid agencies and conflict resolution workers as well as military enforcement action to safeguard safe havens for populations at risk. It also involves military action to overthrow repressive governments and compel warring factions to respect cease-fires and peace accords. Coercive non-military humanitarian intervention includes the imposition of sanctions in pursuit of humanitarian goals. The second category, non-coercive humanitarian intervention represents a dramatic shift from the traditional meaning of humanitarian intervention. Wheeler considers non-forcible humanitarian intervention to be 'the pacific activities of states, international organisations and non-governmental organisations in delivering humanitarian aid and facilitating third party conflict resolution and reconstruction' (Wheeler, 2000) This category also includes post-war peacebuilding programmes aimed at preventing a relapse into conflict and reconstructing the state.

For the purposes of this book and in light of the realities of post-Cold War conflict, humanitarian intervention will be defined as:

forcible or non-forcible actions taken by states, group of states, regional organisations or the UN, in situations of massive human suffering caused by repressive regimes or complex political emergencies where the state has collapsed and law and order has degenerated into mass murder and anarchy. This intervention should seek to protect human rights and alleviate the suffering of victims in the short term; and address the underlying causes of the conflict by facilitating conflict resolution and peacebuilding in the medium to long term.

Origin and Evolution of Humanitarian Intervention

The doctrine of humanitarian intervention owes its origin to the just war tradition. The doctrine as we came to know it today has been shaped through the ages by contributions of lawyers, philosophers, theologians and politicians dating back to Roman times. However, Christian conception of just war theory forms the nucleus of, and had a great influence on, present day conception of humanitarian intervention. Early Christians were predominantly pacifists. This position however changed dramatically during the era of Constantine which saw the Christianisation of the empire. The increasing political and social influence of the church led Christian theologians to work on justifications for the use of force – this eventually developed over time in the form of just war theory. Ian Clark succinctly puts it, 'while the early church had been strongly pacifists, its adaptation to post-Constantine 'establishment' brought with it a worldly acceptance of the need to defend the spiritual realm within the temporal and it is in this acceptance that just war origins are to be discovered' (Clark, 1998, 33).

Modern and secular conception of humanitarian intervention dates back to the seventeenth century and has been credited to the Dutch International Lawyer, Hugo Grotious. In *De Jure Belli est Pacis*, Grotious put forward the proposition that outside countries can legitimately intervene to stop human rights abuses in a neighbouring state. This proposition unleashed a heated debate among international lawyers of the eighteenth century. The first recorded case of humanitarian intervention however came in 1827 when Britain, France and Russia intervened to protect the Greek Christians in the Ottoman Empire. Again in 1860, France was authorised by other European powers to intervene in the Ottoman Empire to save the Maronite Christians in Syria against suppression in practicing their traditional religion. Other nineteenth-century cases include Russia in Bosnia-Herzegovina and Bulgaria (1877–30), and the United States in Cuba (1898).

The Cold War witnessed several instances of humanitarian intervention. The most cited cases are Tanzania's ousting of Idi Amin's despotic and tyrannical regime in Uganda in 1979, Vietnam's invasion of Pol Pot's Cambodia in the same year, and India's intervention in East Pakistan in 1971 to rescue its population from the intolerable repression of West Pakistan. International reaction was at best silent over such interventions as demonstrated in Tanzania's case and at worst openly opposed. Although the humanitarian outcomes of these interventions were apparent, the interveners were hesitant to declare them 'humanitarian interventions'. This reflected the prevailing international uneasiness with the practice.

However, at the end of the Cold War, there appears to be an international consensus in support of humanitarian intervention as evidenced by the unprecedented support to rescue the Kurds and Shiites in Iraq in 1991. Besides rescuing civilians from repressive regimes, the demands of the post-Cold War era have also drawn humanitarian interveners into the complex political emergencies devastating Africa, Asia and Eastern Europe which are characterised by the breakdown of government authority and massive human rights abuses. But the optimism generated by the end of the Cold War soon faded as failures in Somalia, Bosnia and Rwanda led many to question the effectiveness of the practice. The events of September 11 have also cast a big shadow of doubt on humanitarian intervention as focus of the US and other Western states appears to have shifted to the ongoing 'war on terror'.

Humanitarian Intervention in Complex Political Emergencies

As highlighted above, humanitarian intervention during the Cold War was mostly targeted at dictatorial regimes committing massive human rights abuses against their citizens. However, the devastating civil conflicts that characterised the end of the Cold War brought about a dramatic shift in the target and operations of humanitarian interveners. Of the nine cases frequently cited as examples of humanitarian intervention between 1991 and 2000, (Iraq, Bosnia, Somalia, Liberia, Rwanda, East Timor, Congo DR, Sierra Leone, Kosovo) six were in complex political emergencies. This new context posed massive challenges and real dangers to interveners. Consequently, the new context and challenges call for a broadening of humanitarian intervention from its classical conceptualisation of forcible action to include non-forcible strategies. This section will seek to understand the nature and dynamics of complex political emergencies – the new context for interventions – and the dangers they pose to interveners.

Nature and Dynamics of CPEs

During the Cold War period, International Relations theorists and Strategic Studies analysts were preoccupied with inter-state wars and the bipolar confrontation between the East and West. However, the post-Cold War period witnessed the eruption of new forms of conflicts, which do not fit into the traditional classifications. Terminologies to describe such conflicts include Protracted Social Conflicts (Azar, 1990), International Social Conflicts

(Ramsbotham and Woodhouse, 1996), and Complex political emergencies (CPEs). For Mary Kaldor (2001, 2), these '"new wars" involve a blurring of the distinctions between wars ... organized crime ... and large-scale violations of human rights'. However, Smith dismisses this 'new wars' thesis and posit that 'vicious civil wars sustained by identity politics, supported by diasporas and waged by paramilitary gangs ... have rumbled on from one decade to the next ... the end of the Cold War has been meaningless for most of these wars' (2003, 34). He went on to argue that post-Cold War interest in civil wars amongst international relations theorists 'was the product of Cold War displacement' (Smith, 2003, 34). Whilst agreeing with Smith that intrastate war is not a new phenomenon, however, we can see significant changes in the goals of, and tactics used by, warring groups in many parts of the world. Most intrastate conflicts during the Cold War period were either liberation struggles or proxy wars. However, at the end of the Cold War, we saw the emergence of new forms of conflicts that can best be described as factional wars based on intra-elite power struggles, coup d'etat, and warlordism. Despite their seemingly internal nature, they have regional and international dimensions and ramifications evidenced by the destabilising effects of small arms proliferation, mass refugee flow and cross border conflagrations (Francis, 2000). Whilst the *Human Security Report 2005* suggests that there is a general decrease in the number of armed conflicts around the world, it acknowledges the fact that Africa is the only continent where this number is on the increase with 'more people being killed by wars in this region than in the rest of the world combined' (Human Security Centre, 2005, 4). This disturbing trend makes the study and analyses of CPEs very crucial in our attempt to tackle the vicious circle of conflict in Africa and elsewhere.

The concept of CPEs was coined by the UN in the early 1990s to describe the emerging forms of conflicts in the post-Cold War era. Encompassing various types of conflicts, the term is not an analytical tool but a descriptive category lacking precision and distinctions.[2] Duffield defines CPEs as 'protracted political crises resulting from sectarian or predatory indigenous response to socio-economic stress and marginalization ... [They] have a singular ability to erode or destroy the cultural, civil, political or economic integrity of established societies' (Duffield, 1994, 38). This form of conflict is multi-dimensional as it combines overwhelming violence with large-scale displacement of people, mass famine, fragile and failing economic, political and social institutions. Although often exacerbated by natural disasters, the roots of CPEs can be located in political issues. Unlike classical conception of war which is fought

---

2   For an in-depth analysis of CPEs, see Jenny Pearce (1999), 'Peace-building in the Periphery: Lessons from Central America', *Third World Quarterly*, Vol. 20, No. 1; Jonathan Goodhand and David Hume (1999), 'From Wars to Complex Political Emergencies: Understanding Conflict and Peace-building in the New World Disorder', *Third World Quarterly*, Vol. 20, No. 1, pp. 13–26; M. Duffield (1994), 'Complex Emergencies and the Crisis of Developmentalism', *IDS Bulletin*, Vol. 25, No. 4

between armies, a shocking feature of CPEs is the fact that warring factions often deliberately target vulnerable groups of civilians and humanitarian aid workers. Nordstrom therefore observes that the safest place to be in today's 'dirty wars' is the military (Nordstrom, 1992, 271). Another feature of CPEs is the medley of fighting forces involved, all of which add to the complexity of the conflict. Kaldor (1999) identifies five types: regular armed forces or remnants, paramilitary groups, self-defence units, foreign mercenaries and regular troops under international auspices. To this list we will add local mercenaries like the ones roaming the West African sub-region offering guerrilla services to any disgruntled group. Considering their guerrilla type warfare, most of these warring groups use small arms which are relatively easy to carry and maintain. This has led to a proliferation of small arms in CPEs in Africa and elsewhere. Another feature of these fighting forces is the widespread use of child soldiers. In Sierra Leone and Liberia, all the conflicting parties used boys as young as eight to either fight or carry looted goods for them. Abducted girls were most often used as sex slaves of senior commanders. CPEs are often protracted and erupt in states where political authority is seriously contested or has virtually collapsed. The regional dimension of this form of conflicts also makes them a threat to regional peace and security.

Analysing CPEs: Causal and Intervening Factors

There is a wealth of literature focusing on the causal factors of CPEs.[3] This literature broadly identifies three levels of analyses for CPEs: international/ regional level, state level and community level. Though different conflicts have context-specific causal factors, there are common themes that have been identified by the theoretical literature.

(i) International/regional factors   Although CPEs are often regarded as 'internal' or 'civil wars', there are strong external linkages and causal factors. At the systemic level, several analysts point to the end of the Cold War, the policies of International Financial Institutions (IFIs) and the effects of globalisation as destabilising factors precipitating and fuelling conflicts and the process of state collapse in Africa and elsewhere. Most countries under the scourge of CPEs are former colonial territories unable to establish the essential institutions, processes and legitimacy required for effective governance. The East-West rivalry of the Cold War made it possible for these countries to receive economic and

---

3   See for instance Azar (1990), op. cit; Hugh Miall et al. (1999), *Contemporary Conflict Resolution*, Cambridge: Polity Press; Lionel Cliff and Robin Luckham (1999), 'Complex Political Emergencies, State Failure and the Fate of the State', *Third World Quarterly*, Vol. 20, No. 1; P. Collier (2000), 'Doing Well Out of War' in M. Berdal and D. Malone, *Greed and Grievance: Economic Agendas in Civil Wars*, Boulder, CO: Lynne Rienner.

military aid from either the US or the Soviet Union. At the end of the Cold War, these 'hand-outs' stopped coming thus plunging these states into severe economic and political crises. Shaw and Okolo perfectly sum up the situation, 'the demise of bipolarity ... has rendered obsolete Africa's strategy of playing off one side against the other in the quest for attention and assistance' (Shaw and Okolo, 1994, 6). The analysis of West African conflicts in Chapter 3 provides an empirical example of this international linkage.

The effects of globalisation and the policies of IFIs and Bilateral donors have also come under attack by conflict analysts (Kaldor, 1999; Miall et al, 1999; Francis, 2000). The underprivileged position of African states in the global economy means the continent receives no more than 1 per cent of the world's total investment. The few investors that venture into Africa are mostly interested in the primary sector. The unfavourable terms of trade imposed on African countries by Western trading partners are geared towards the marginalisation of the region. This perpetuates what Miall et al. regard as 'the deep and enduring inequalities in the global distribution of wealth and economic power' (Miall et al., 1999, 78), which will result into what Rogers and Ramsbotham (1999) call 'a crisis of unsatisfied expectations within an increasingly informed global majority of the disempowered'. The harsh and often confusing policies of International Financial Institutions like the World Bank and International Monetary Fund (IMF) further serve to compound the region's economic and political woes. The World Bank/IMF's Structural Adjustment Programme (SAP) for developing countries which calls for the implementation of severe austerity measures like the massive down sizing of the work force and extensive privatisation have had negative effects in 'third world' countries. Although the overall aims of the programme appear to be impressive on paper, its failure in most African states was inevitable owing to the lack of understanding of the nature of domestic politics. For instance, the proceeds from the sale of public corporations did not go to developing other sectors like health and education as envisaged by framers of the programme but instead went into the private bank accounts of politicians. Unemployment, which has been a perennial problem of developing countries, was aggravated by SAP and this led to frustration and social unrest. Idle youths can become a fertile recruiting ground for warlords as examples in Sierra Leone and Liberia have demonstrated over the past decade. At first glance, these systemic explanations of conflicts might seem far removed and irrelevant to local situations. But as the analysis of West African conflicts in Chapter 2 shows, research over the years has uncovered the effects of these global level policies on local realties and dynamics.

At the regional level, CPEs are caused by spill over or contagion effects, rogue states and leaders and the desire of neighbouring states to exploit and control the resources of others.

(ii) State failure and CPEs   The literature seems to have reached a consensus on the link between 'failed' states and CPEs. Empirical evidence has shown that

state failure is both a trigger and a consequence of CPEs. A failed state as defined by Carment (2001, 10) is one that 'does not fulfil the obligations of statehood. The leadership does not have the means and credibility to compel internal order or to deter or repel external aggression'. Zartman (1995, 1) defines state failure as 'a situation where the structure, authority, law and political order have fallen apart'. In 2005, the UK's Department of International Development (DFID) adopted the term 'fragile states' to describe a state 'where the government cannot or will not deliver core functions to the majority of its people' (DFID, 2005, 7). As the definition suggests, DFID's 'fragile states' concept is not new as it represents the same meaning as failed states.

A failed state is characterised by its increased inability to provide security and basic services to its people including health, education and food. The institutions of government are in a state of near-collapse and the capacity of the state to manage conflicts and tensions is drastically diminished. State failure is often preceded by years of dictatorship characterised by patron-client networks, massive corruption, intimidation and suppression of the opposition. These factors erode the legitimacy of the state and set the stage for disaffected groups to challenge its authority. The end of the Cold War has witnessed a growing number of states falling under this category and these include Sierra Leone, Liberia, Bosnia, etc. State failure is caused by a multiplicity of factors, including the international/regional factors discussed above in addition to the challenges posed by premature and unstable democratic institutions and ethnicity. As central authority disappears, failed states face increasing fragmentation and instability and exclusionist policies connected to ethnic and religious identities emerge as alternative sources of loyalty. This apparent absence of an effective central authority paves the way for the immediate rise of crime, massive loss of life and descent into chaos and all out war. In this context, humanitarian interveners are faced with the difficulty of determining who is in charge and who they need to work with. The resulting protracted conflict further erodes what is left of government institutions and infrastructure and leads to state collapse as in Somalia.

(iii) Greed or grievance? – the political economy of CPEs   Analysts like Collier link the outbreak of CPEs to greed and economic opportunism rather than structural inequalities and deep-rooted grievances. But as Francis (2001) argues, one will wonder why countries like Botswana and Ghana, rich in diamonds and gold respectively, remain relatively peaceful. Diamonds have been discovered in Sierra Leone since 1930 but why did it take more than half a century for war to breakout? Why did conflict erupt in Mozambique, a country without strategic resources? All these questions point to the inadequacies of Collier's greed based interpretation of African conflicts and stress the need for further research in understanding Africa's civil wars. Limiting the causal factors to economic opportunism certainly distorts a clear understanding of the underlying factors and further complicates the process of resolving conflicts. Whilst not outrightly

dismissing greed and economic opportunism as contributing factors to CPEs, however, the root causes of such conflicts must be located in the 'politics of decline' that is characteristic of failed states and the international and regional linkages discussed above. Greed can be better understood as a factor that fuels and further protracts a conflict. It is in this context that the study of political economies underpinning CPEs has attracted renewed interests over the past decade. These include the works of Goodhand and Hulme (1999); Kaldor (1999); Duffield (1997); Keen; and Pugh and Cooper (2004).

Though CPEs lead to the collapse of the formal and legal economy, they often result in the creation of a 'parallel economy' (illegal) based on predatory tactics and international or regional links. Duffield regards this parallel economy as 'the emergence of entirely new types of social formation adapted for survival on the margins of the global economy' (1997, 100). Examples of such parallel economies abound and include the Revolutionary United Front (RUF) and Taylor's trade in Sierra Leone's diamonds, the Khmer Rouge's smuggling of timber and gems across the Thai border and drug cartels set up by rebel groups in Central and South America and the Taliban in Afghanistan. These parallel economies create what Goodhand and Hulme (1999) call 'conflict entrepreneurs': people who benefit from the lucrative trade and are bent on prolonging the conflict. But as Miall et al. (1999) observe, the wealth accrued from this trade is not used to pay the rank and file of the fighters but they are instead let loose to fend for themselves by looting and pillaging. In the process, these fighters commit widespread human rights abuses. In their frantic efforts to loot and extort, opposing factions often collaborate with each other. In Sierra Leone for example, the collaboration between the RUF rebels and government soldiers produced what became known in local parlance as 'sobels'.

Humanitarian aid also becomes the target of warring factions in CPEs (Anderson, 1999). There are many instances of looting of humanitarian aid warehouses by warring groups. These groups even loot aid supplied to civilians. Some fighting groups force aid agencies to pay what Kaldor (1999) calls 'custom duties' for the passage of aid convoys through their areas of control whilst others solicit payment for providing security for NGOs. An example is the case of aid agencies in Somalia paying local armed security agents called 'technicals' to provide security (Jonah, 1993). The above analysis has shown that an understanding of the political economies of CPEs and their various beneficiaries and 'conflict entrepreneurs' is necessary in the drive to formulate effective response mechanisms to these conflicts.

(iv) Understanding violence in CPEs   CPEs are characterised by unspeakable acts of violence and brutality inflicted on the civilian population. The rape, amputation, torture and widespread burning and looting of property by Revolutionary United Front (RUF) fighters in Sierra Leone represent an extreme example of what takes place in these conflicts. In explaining the violence that gripped West Africa, Robert Kaplan (1994) interpreted it as 'new barbarism';

an expression of senseless and irrational convulsions of violence, and a return to medieval forms of tribal war and 'warlordism'. There has, however, been a systematic effort by conflict theorists and sociologists to find an explanation for what seems irrational violence in most of today's CPEs. In a study of the Mozambican and Sri Lankan conflicts, Nordstrom explains that what seems to be pathological violence is a deliberate strategy to undermine and destroy the daily and normal meaning of life and replace it with 'fundamental knowledge constructs that are based on force' (1992, 269). This can become an effective strategy of maintaining control on the civilian population. This holds true for the RUF in Sierra Leone whose failure to win 'hearts and minds' have caused them to resort to violence and fear as instruments of control. It can also be understood as a means of instilling fear on the enemy. In Liberia and Sierra Leone, rebel groups were known for displaying human skulls of their victims.

Francis (2001) attributes the atrocities committed by the RUF to what he termed the 'falamakata' culture prevalent in Sierra Leone. Falamakata is the linqua franca for imitation. He considers the majority of Sierra Leoneans to 'have a social predisposition to imitation' and a 'desire for perfection, i.e. to supersede the feat or expertise of the "originator"' (Francis, 2001, 118). This explains why the RUF imitated the brutality practised by their counterparts in Liberia and the *Resistëncia Nacional Moçambicana* (RENAMO) in Mozambique. Consequently, other groups in the conflict copied these terror tactics and applied them to perfection. In keeping with Francis' 'falamakata' culture, Richards (1996) regards this violence as dramaturgy of the Hollywood 'Rambo' war culture. Others link this brutality to the influence of drugs like marijuana and crack cocaine. Whatever the explanation for this form of violence, it appears to be a deliberate strategy to keep the civil populace under coercive control.

(v) CPEs and civil society   David Francis defines civil society as 'the realm of private sphere in which social movements become organised, representing diverse interests and agendas' (2005, 18). CPEs are very destructive of civil society. As noted above, warring groups often deliberately target civil society as a way of undermining and weakening its resolve to act as a check on predatory elites. These terror tactics are meant to destroy the social capital and the moral economy that underpin civil society. Swift (1989) defines the moral economy as, 'the range of redistributive processes which occur within communities'. This involves networks of exchange that are welfarist and reciprocal. Harvey (1997) identifies three main ways in which CPEs can impact on the moral economy. Firstly, displacement separates families and communities and removes people from places they can draw on reciprocal networks. Secondly, looting creates a general shortage of resources within communities which precludes even the richer members from assisting poorer ones. Thirdly, terror tactics employed by warring groups destroy social capital which is the basis for the moral economy. Although it has been a feature of the development studies literature, the

theoretical literature on Conflict Resolution has just recently started focusing on the link between conflict and social capital. Putman defines Social capital as 'features of social organization, such as trust, norms and networks that can improve the efficiency of society by facilitating coordinated actions' (1993, 167). The terror tactics of warring groups are meant to 'create legacies of embitterment and suspicion that are the opposite of the relationships of trust and confidence vital to social capital' (Harvey, 1997, 207). In Sierra Leone, warring groups were able to divide whole communities leading to accusations of 'collaboration' with one faction or the other. This deep-rooted suspicion and finger pointing led to many summary executions carried out by civilians on their neighbours. CPEs further undermine and weaken civil society by manipulating ethnic and religious differences.

It is not all doom and gloom however as stories from war zones show civil societies that are resilient in the face of terror. Francis has noted the positive role played by civil society in CPEs in taking over 'security and welfare functions of the weak and collapsed states' (2005, 19). This resilience strengthens community solidarity. In Sierra Leone, inhabitants of Bo defended their city against RUF fighters and formed Civil Defence Groups. At the height of the Rwandan genocide, Hutus and Tutsis in a particular neighbourhood of Kigali called themselves *Hutsis* and tried to defend each other in the community. In Somalia elders in Northwest Somalia played an active role in negotiating peace (Kaldor, 1999). These cases of resilience in the midst of anarchy and chaos characteristic of CPEs demand a new understanding of civil society in conflict. Contrary to the belief that civil society cannot thrive in CPEs, the above cases have indicated that in fact in some circumstances, such conflicts do actually galvanise and strengthen civil society.

(vi) The media and CPEs For better or worse, the media, both local and international, has considerable influence on the dynamics and outcome of CPEs. It has been at the forefront of international efforts to mobilise public support for humanitarian crises. The television pictures beamed into the living rooms of Western audiences lead to widespread calls for governments to 'do something'. However this show of humanitarian concern has the unintended effect of rushing into operations without adequate planning and thought – a recipe for failure in most humanitarian missions. The media can also play a negative role in fuelling conflicts either indirectly by acting as PR agents for warlords or deliberately by fanning hate messages. As most of the warring factions in CPEs lack effective communication capabilities, warlords often grant interviews to the media as a way of communicating with their units in the field. A case in point is the use of the BBC by former RUF Field Commander, Sam 'Mosquito' Bockarie to order his troops to burn Freetown after getting reports of an imminent UK intervention. Taylor in Liberia manipulated the BBC Africa Service's Robin White into selling his agenda to international audiences. By unwittingly acting as PR agents of these warlords, the media

has helped to legitimise warring factions in several parts of the world. In some other cases, they can play a deliberate and destructive role in fuelling conflicts. The most extreme case of the negative use of the media is in Rwanda where the Hutu government used a radio station to fan hatred against Tutsis and mobilise Hutus for what they euphemistically call the 'elimination of the cockroach'. However, with better understanding of the nature of CPEs, the media can play a more constructive role in managing and resolving CPEs and building the foundation for durable peace.

Humanitarian Intervention: The Post-Cold War Debate

The legality and legitimacy of humanitarian intervention has been the subject of heated debate over the centuries involving international lawyers, academics, diplomats and philosophers. The arguments for or against humanitarian intervention are classified in various categories. The ethical argument is divided between pluralists, realists and statists on the one hand, and solidarists and liberals on the other; whilst the legal debate is between restrictionists and counter-restrictionists. For pluralists, humanitarian intervention is a violation of the fundamental principles of sovereignty, non-intervention and non-use of force which guarantee order in the international system. States and not individuals are the bearers of rights in the international system. A right of humanitarian intervention, they argue, will jeopardise the delicate order and stability of the international society and unleash uncontrollable anarchy. Solidarists, on the other hand, argue that individuals are the rightful bearers of rights and support actions by states to protect and preserve these rights. States should be stripped of the protection of sovereignty if they use it to violate the human rights of their people. And for states to enjoy the protection which the principle of non-intervention accords them, they 'should satisfy certain basic requirements of decency' (Vincent and Watson, 1993, 126). The humanitarian intervention debate in legal circles is very intense and no near a consensus. The thrust of their disagreements border around interpretation of the UN Charter, UN General Assembly Resolutions, International Court of Justice (ICJ) judgements and customary international law (Ramsbotham and Woodhouse, 1995).

In light of the challenges posed by complex political emergences to humanitarian intervention, there is a need to revisit this debate in the context of post-Cold War realities and dynamics. In fact, this debate is as active now as it has ever been. Whist pluralists and statists continue to emphasise the threat of intervention to world peace and stability, realists are becoming even more vocal in calling for governments to withdraw from humanitarian missions. Representing the extreme side of this view are Robert Jackson, Edward Luttwak and Stephen Stedman. Jackson makes a forceful case against humanitarian intervention,

In my view, the stability of international society, especially the unity of the great powers, is more important, indeed far more important than minority rights and humanitarian protections in Yugoslavia or any other country – if we have to choose between these two sets of values. (2000, 291)

Stedman (1993) refers to advocates of the doctrine as 'moralists' who do not engage with the tough practicalities. Luttwak in a 1999 article, 'Give War a Chance' argues against intervening in civil conflicts until one side secures a definitive military victory. Doing the contrary, he contends, will only serve to prolong them. Luttwak's alternative seems to have gained many adherents in the UN Security Council, as well as in the foreign and defence departments of some of the big powers. There are many instances in which war seems to have been given a chance: Sudan, Burundi and the war between Eritrea and Ethiopia are just few examples. UN troops were only deployed in the later after Ethiopia had won a decisive victory over Eritrea (Jakobsen, 2001). What Luttwak however fails to realise is the nature of post-Cold War conflicts which are often protracted and do not end easily since no party has the capacity to win a decisive victory.

Others contend that UN Security Council action is only legal in cases that pose a threat to international peace and security. As such, the UN or regional organisations are not supposed to intervene in civil conflicts and cases of abuse of human rights by despots as these are purely internal matters to be dealt with by citizens of those states. They regard abuse of the principles of sovereignty and non-intervention to be the real danger to world peace and stability. This sort of analysis overlooks the interconnectedness of the post-Cold War world and the regional and global ramifications of CPEs. As noted earlier, CPEs are characterised by overlapping internal and external sources, actors and effects and do not show clear starting and terminating points. CPEs have widespread regional and international ramifications. At the regional level, neighbouring states suffer from the devastating effects of massive refugee flow, spread of light weapons, local mercenaries and economic dislocation. The refugee problem poses a serious crisis for not only developing states in Africa, Asia and Latin America, but also the industrialised states of the West. This massive influx of refugees stretches economies of developing countries to breaking point and causes serious social and political problems for Western governments. Armed groups and local mercenaries in West Africa and the Great Lakes Region also use refugees as a cover to launch cross border attacks. At the global level, neglected CPEs in remote corners of the world can have a negative impact on world peace and security. Recent media and intelligence reports have linked West African conflicts to the growing problem of international terrorism. In November 2001, a report by the Washington Post revealed the relationship between al Qaida and the RUF of Sierra Leone (Farah, 2001). These reports have underscored the need for concerted regional and international efforts to manage the growing menace of CPEs. Their potential threat to regional and international stability means they can no longer be regarded the 'internal' affairs of a particular state.

Pluralists and statists who continue to advance the argument of sovereignty and non-intervention as a bar to humanitarian intervention also fail to realise the fact that most target states of humanitarian intervention today are failed states lacking governments worthy of the protection of sovereignty. In a report to the Canadian government, the authors reconceptualised sovereignty as 'a responsibility to protect' (International Commission on Intervention and State Sovereignty (ICISS), 2001). A government that is unable or unwilling to offer such protection, it is argued, do not deserve the privileges and international recognition that comes with sovereignty. In calling for a unified stance on humanitarian intervention Kofi Annan poses this stark question: '... if humanitarian intervention is, indeed, an unacceptable assault on sovereignty, how should we respond to a Rwanda, to a Srebrenica – to gross and systematic violations of human rights that affect every precept of our common humanity?' (quoted in ICISS, 2001, vii).

Several responses to the above question and recent state and international practice have indicated an emerging international consensus on humanitarian intervention. Whilst defending the North Atlantic Treaty Organisation (NATO) action in Kosovo, British Prime Minister Tony Blair (1999) declared his 'Doctrine of the International Community' stating that the international community have both a right and a duty to intervene in cases of extreme human suffering. In a similar vein, the report of the High-Level Panel commissioned by the UN Secretary-General endorsed the right and responsibility of the international community to protect those caught up in extreme human suffering (UN, 2004). In fact many resolutions passed by the Security Council since the end of the Cold War have expanded 'threats to international peace and security' to include situations of intra-state conflict and complex political emergencies. And as highlighted above, the mandates of UN peacekeepers in these circumstances have also expanded from the traditional 'force protection' to including the protection of civilians, and facilitating the process of peacemaking and peacebuilding. Even the African Union (AU), successor to the OAU has enshrined in its Constitutive Act, the right of humanitarian intervention 'in respect of grave circumstances, namely war crimes, genocide and crimes against humanity' (AU, 2000). But some scholars doubt this so-called new found 'international solidarity' in light of developments since the 9/11 terrorists attacks in the US (Wheeler and Bellamy, 2004). There is growing evidence that the US is reverting to its Cold War policy of prioritising its strategic interests over concern for human rights and democracy. The Western preoccupation with the 'War on Terror' has led to inaction and neglect in cases of extreme human suffering but in which Western security interests are not at stake. The slow and ineffective response to the Darfur crisis is a case in point. However, other analysts have observed that the link between state failure and terrorism as established in Liberia and Sierra Leone is motivating Western intervention.

But as will be shown in Chapter 8, these interventions do not adequately address the root causes of CPEs.

Despite the gloom and pessimism surrounding humanitarian intervention, this book is in favour of the solidarist debate and accepts a re-conceptualised humanitarian intervention as ethically, politically and legally legitimate but like Wheeler (2000) and Ramsbotham and Woodhouse (1996), believe that the international community needs to develop an appropriate framework and principles governing its practice. For the purpose of this book, the legitimacy and success of humanitarian intervention will be measured according to the principles set out below.

A Post-Cold War Framework for Humanitarian Intervention

Many analysts and policy makers on humanitarian intervention have tried to develop appropriate principles and frameworks on which acceptable conduct of humanitarian intervention should be based. These attempts are not new as they represent a long quest by mankind to define acceptable uses of force and cross border intervention that goes back to the Just War era. In fact most of the principles are adapted and refined from Just War principles. Drawing from various analysts, this section will develop a framework upon which the ECOWAS/ECOMOG humanitarian intervention in West Africa will be assessed.

Ramsbotham and Woodhouse (1996) consider an intervention legitimate based on the following principles: humanitarian cause, humanitarian end in view, humanitarian approach, humanitarian means and humanitarian outcome. The Report of the International Commission on Intervention and State Sovereignty (ICISS) also reflects the above principles (ICISS, 2001). Drawing from the various principles and frameworks highlighted above, this work assesses the legitimacy, conduct and success of ECOWAS's humanitarian intervention in West Africa based on the following three principles: (1) was there a humanitarian cause warranting intervention? (2) Was the conduct of interveners in line with international human rights norms and international law? (3) Did interveners succeed in (a) alleviating the suffering of victims (b) put in place long term strategies aimed at preventing a relapse into the situation that caused the suffering? Like Wheeler (2000) this work objects to the sole emphasis placed on motives by restrictionists since we consider intervention to be inextricably linked to political considerations. Humanitarian cause will therefore be taken to mean a situation of extreme human suffering caused by a repressive government, or state collapse, requiring outside assistance. The legality of the intervention on the other hand will be based on Security Council Resolution. Where such a resolution is not available, a mission will only be considered legitimate where there is evidence that the Council failed to discharge its responsibility of maintaining international peace and security.

The second key principle is based on the conduct of interveners. Here, we will seek answers to a long list of sub-questions: (1) were there clear and unambiguous humanitarian objectives and mandate for the intervener? (2) Did the resources and logistics match the tasks laid out in the mandate? (3) Did the various contingents have a common military approach? (4) Was there a unified and effective chain of command? (5) Did interveners behave in a manner consistent with their declared humanitarian purposes? In order words did interveners respect the human rights principles they claim to protect? (6) Was there effective coordination between the mission and humanitarian organisations and other actors on the ground?

The principle of humanitarian outcome is gaining prominence in many academic and policy circles (Ramsbotham and Woodhouse, 1996; Wheeler, 2000; Keohane, 2003). In addition to the short term objective of providing security to threatened populations and distributing aid to deprived people, humanitarian outcome has now expanded to include economic and political reconstruction, in other words, a move from relief to long term development aimed at addressing the root causes of the suffering. This is the case for both contexts which require intervention: namely tyrannical governments, which violate human rights and weak and failing states which cannot guarantee the safety of their citizens. In the case of the former, the criticisms levied against the American-led coalition in Iraq in failing to devise an effective post-intervention reconstruction strategy underline the importance of this principle. This study therefore assesses humanitarian outcome based on the following: (1) short term relief of suffering, safeguarding of civilians and termination of human right abuses and mass murder; (2) a just and fair peace process that addresses the grievances and issues at stake in the conflict; (3) an effective peacebuilding programme that tackles the root-causes of the conflict and puts in place institutions, mechanisms and processes in order to prevent a relapse into conflict.

Definition of Terms and Concepts

The new context and challenges facing humanitarian interveners have warranted a rethinking of traditional meanings of some terms and concepts associated with the practice. These definitions will form the basis of analysis and discussion in the entire book.

Peacekeeping

A major problem in the discussion of peacekeeping is the absence of a common definition of the concept. This complication has further added to the problems of peacekeeping operations. The word itself is not mentioned in the UN Charter thus prompting journalists, diplomats, academics and practitioners to develop different interpretations of the term. *The Blue Helmets*, the UN's official peacekeeping manual, reflecting the traditional dimension of peacekeeping, defined it in a narrow sense as an 'operation involving military personnel, but without enforcement powers, undertaken by the United Nations to help maintain or restore international peace and security in areas of conflict' (quoted in Woodhouse and Ramsbotham, 1999, xi). In a similar vein, Johan Galtung (1981) in his famous pyramid conceptualised peacekeeping as an activity aimed at ending direct violence and creating what he termed 'negative peace'. However, such narrow definitions are problematic and do not reflect the broader dimension of present day peacekeeping. Contrary to *The Blue Helmets*' definition, contemporary peacekeeping now involves a wide range of actors including a large number of civilians and police personnel in addition to the traditional military sector. Peacekeeping can no longer be regarded as an exercise to restore 'negative peace' since missions now attempt to take on board both peacemaking and peacebuilding roles to complement their military function.

This work will adopt the definition of peacekeeping contained in our co-authored book, *Dangers of Co-deployment:*

> ... peacekeeping refers to complex or multi-functional operations in which impartial military activities are aimed at establishing a secure environment and facilitating long-term civilian peacebuilding activities. (Francis et al., 2005, 24)

As warring factions are known to have manipulated the UN's principle of impartiality, this work will adopt the Brahimi report's redefinition of impartiality as:

> Adherence to the principles of the Charter: where one party to a peace agreement clearly and incontrovertibly is violating its terms, continued equal treatment of all parties by the UN can in the best case result in ineffectiveness and in the worst case may amount to complicity with evil. (UN, 2000)

Peace Enforcement

The British Peace Support Operations manual, *Wider Peacekeeping* defines peace enforcement as 'operations carried out to restore peace between belligerent parties who do not at all consent to intervention and who may be engaged in combat activities' (HMSO, 1995). Peace enforcement can be located within Chapter VII of the UN Charter. This type of operation involves a predisposition to use force in order to restore a semblance of security or guarantee the implementation of a peace agreement or cease-fire. Whilst peacekeeping relies on the consent of warring parties, peace enforcement does not. However, in complex political emergencies, this divide between peacekeeping and peace enforcement can be very blurred. As warring parties in these conflicts are known for their intransigence and lack of respect for peace agreements, interveners are faced with the challenges of shifting between peacekeeping and enforcement. However, enforcement action within the context of CPEs should not be designed as a punitive measure but act as a means to induce compliance within the wider framework of long term peacebuilding.

Co-deployment

As defined by Francis et al., Co-deployment refers to United Nations 'military deployment or deployment of field mission in conjunction with regional peacekeeping forces specifically authorised by the UN Security Council with a mandate to assist in the restoration of peace and security to a country in conflict' (2005, 53). In light of recent developments, co-deployment can also be expanded to include the collaboration between UN and/or regional peacekeepers and the forces of developed Western nations. This will therefore include the case of Cote d'Ivoire where the ECOWAS Mission in Cote d'Ivoire (ECOMICI) collaborated with both the UN and French troops. Co-deployment covers a wide array of activities that go beyond traditional peacekeeping and includes protection of safe havens and humanitarian relief corridors, organising and monitoring elections, peace making and post-war peacebuilding and reconstruction.

Safe Havens

The term *safe havens* was coined in the aftermath of the first Gulf War in 1991 (Woodhouse and Ramsbotham, 1999). Following civil unrest in Kurdish and Shia parts of Iraq, Saddam Hussein responded with overwhelming force that led to the displacement of millions and large number of deaths. The international response to the carnage was the creation of a safe zone that extended from Iraq's northern border to the 36th parallel, where military activities were proscribed. The term itself reflects Western sensitivity not to infringe on Iraq's sovereignty. In May 1993, the UN declared six areas in the former Yugoslavia as safe havens, which will act as protective umbrella and safe zones for Muslims from all over the country to gather. In this context, safe havens mean a clearly demarcated area established through UN Security Council resolution and protected by UN or multinational forces with the consent or knowledge of warring parties. When applied to CPEs in Africa, safe havens take on a slightly different meaning. Unlike the traditional meaning of the term, safe havens in CPEs are not clearly demarcated areas with Security Council approval. These places acquire the status of *safe havens* by default due to the presence of UN, regional/sub-regional or multinational forces. The perceived security associated with the presence of these forces lures the vulnerable civilian population to drift to the so-called safe haven. Consequently, a key task of UN, regional and multinational forces in these settings has been the protection of civilians within these *de facto* safe havens.

Humanitarian Relief Corridors

As used in this book, humanitarian relief corridors refer to roads used by aid agencies for the purpose of reaching their target beneficiaries. In complex political emergencies, these roads are constantly under threat of attack from warring factions. The threat is heightened by the fact that some of these roads pass through frontlines. This volatile security situation therefore demands the provision of military escorts to humanitarian aid convoys.

Peacebuilding

Peacebuilding has received much attention and importance over the past decade. Major donors, international NGOs and academics have come to regard this concept as the best way of promoting peace and development in conflict torn societies across the world. However, the term itself has been the subject of a myriad of interpretations and definitions. In *An Agenda for Peace*, the then UN Secretary-General defined peacebuilding as 'comprehensive efforts to identify and support structures which will tend to consolidate peace and advance a sense of confidence and well-being among people' (Bouros-Ghali, 1992, 32). Like Lewer (1999), Boutros-Ghali views peacebuilding as inextricably linked to conflict prevention. Whilst preventive diplomacy is aimed at avoiding an outbreak of violence, 'post conflict peacebuilding is to prevent a reoccurence' (Boutros-Ghali, 1992, 33). In this regard peacebuilding involves both short term measures to prevent a relapse into conflict and medium to long term programmes to consolidate and build a culture of peace. Such programmes include disarmament, reintegration and resettlement (DDR), small arms control, institutional reform, security sector reform, human rights monitoring, electoral and economic reforms.

Security Sector Reform

Since the mid 1990s, the international donor community, aid agencies, policy makers and academics have increasingly underlined the importance of security sector reform to the overall success of peace processes. The security sector 'includes all those organisations which have authority to use, or order the use of, force, or the threat of force, to protect the state and its citizens, as well as those civil structures that are responsible for their management and oversight' (Chalmers, 2000). It includes a wide array of security actors ranging from military and paramilitary forces, intelligence services and police to judicial and penal services and civilian oversight mechanisms such as ministries of defence and executive and legislative organs.

Weak and ineffective security structures form part of the underlying causes of most conflicts in the developing world and also have negative development implications. In this respect, some analysts now argue that what is actually needed in CPEs is not 'reform' but overall transformation of the security sector (Le Roux, Dornelles and Williams, 2004). In this context, security sector reform or transformation therefore represents international and national efforts to rebuild the security sector within the wider framework of good governance and democratisation. Security sector reform projects include the following:

- training and capacity building of the security forces, including promoting respect for human rights and rule of law.
- strengthening the capacity of civilians to effectively manage and oversee the security sector.
- promoting transparency of budgetary allocation and financial management of security forces.

Disarmament, Demobilisation and Reintegration (DDR)

Since the end of the Cold War, DDR programmes have been at the centre of international peacebuilding efforts in war-torn societies. These programmes have formed part of comprehensive peace settlements signed by parties to the conflicts usually under the auspices of international and/or regional organisations. Like the name suggests, DDR programmes are divided into three phases. However, this categorisation is not rigid as the different phases are interdependent and do overlap. During the *disarmament* phase, combatants are assembled in designated cantonment sites. This is followed by the surrender of weapons and registration of ex-combatants. *Demobilisation* represents the disbanding of military formations and structures and the severance of the link between the fighters and their commanders. It involves practical steps such as pre-discharge orientation and counselling, discharge, health screening and transportation to resettlement sites. Reintegration refers to both medium- and long-term programmes designed to help rebuild the lives of former fighters, reabsorb them into society and ensure their sustainable livelihoods (Berdal, 1996). This involves projects such as the immediate re-insertion package (given most often in the form of cash payments), vocational training and job creation. Due to recent experiences involving civilian discontent with what is perceived as undue preference for ex-combatants, reintegration projects now increasingly cover host communities and victims of conflicts.

Conclusion

This chapter has reviewed the contributions of academics, policy makers and international lawyers in developing a conceptual framework for humanitarian intervention that meets the challenges of the post-Cold War era. Drawing from these contributions, we have attempted to re-conceptualise humanitarian intervention and outline principles to govern its practice. The changed context in which interveners are required to work in the post-Cold War era has brought with it fresh challenges. With failing and disintegrating state structures and authority, interveners are now faced with the difficulty of determining whom to deal with. Any choice made will more or less compromise the principles of neutrality and impartiality and pose serious security risks and operational difficulties. An ill-planned and poorly coordinated intervention will inadvertently intensify the suffering of the victims and serve to legitimise and strengthen the power structures of predatory warlords. The new context therefore calls for the broadening of the concept to include both forcible and non-forcible intervention strategies aimed at providing a long-term solution to the roots of CPEs. As these conflicts are multifactorial and multidimensional, they require an equally multifaceted and coordinated response. Considering the danger posed by CPEs to local populations and international peace and security, the debate on humanitarian intervention should move from its preoccupation on disagreements over legality to engaging with practical questions concerning its proper conduct and ways to make it more effective.

Chapter 2
Analysing Conflicts in West Africa: Causal Factors and Interpretations

Introduction

The West African sub-region is home to some of the world's most brutal and protracted conflicts. Since the end of the Cold War, many countries in the sub-region have been embroiled in conflicts ranging from intermittent low-intensity conflicts in Nigeria, Ghana and Guinea to devastating civil wars in Liberia and Sierra Leone. Senegal has endured more than two decades of secessionist warfare with *Mouvement des Forces Démocratiques de la Casamance* (MFDC) rebels over control of the Casamance region of Southern Senegal whilst Mali and Niger are still recovering from their own secessionist battle with the Tuareg rebels. Lack of political pluralism has caused deep-seated unrest in Togo, Benin and Burkina Faso. Frequent 'coup attempts' in Mauritania are adding to that country's problems between the Arab ruling class and the marginalised Black population. In 1997, Guinea Bissau became engulfed in a bitter struggle for power between mutinous sections of the army and the government of President Nino Vieira. In September 2002, Côte d'Ivoire, which used to be the oasis of peace in a troubled region, was plunged into a civil war.

What is responsible for these regional conflagrations? In Chapter 1 we established a link between state failure and complex political emergencies. In the case of West Africa, the causes of state failure and conflicts are diverse and can be traced as far back as the sub-region's colonial legacy, Cold War past and peripheral status in the world economy. At the centre of this analysis, however, is what Francis (2001) calls the 'politics of decline' characterised by clientelism and neo-patrimonialism which have produced weak and failing states across Sub-Saharan Africa and sowed a fertile breeding ground for insurgency.

Although different conflicts have context specific causal factors, this chapter will attempt an analysis of the main factors underlying most of West African conflicts. Starting with an overview of the political economy of West Africa, we will move to examine the impact of Colonialism on the sub-region and see how this has laid the foundations of authoritarianism, state collapse and conflicts. As historical legacies are not enough to explain the sub-region's widespread instability, the nature of post-independence domestic politics will also be analysed to highlight the devastating effects of neo-patrimonial and clientelistic politics and how these have produced failed states and complex political emergencies. Next we will examine the role of ethnicity and religion in

West African conflicts. Immediate and intervening factors that acted as catalysts for conflicts will then be examined. These are mostly regional in nature and include the role of local mercenaries and strategic resources, the proliferation of small arms, and regional support for dissidents. The chapter argues against the oversimplified analysis of West African conflicts as 'resource-based' or 'ethnic wars' and posits that the root causes of the sub-region's instability are deep rooted and can be traced as far back as the colonial period. In effect, analysis of West African conflicts should be eclectic and take on board a variety of factors and actors.

Political Economy of West Africa

The West African sub-region covers an area of 6.5 million square kilometres and consists of 16 states excluding Cameroon and Chad, which are usually categorised as Central African. With an estimated population of over 254 million people, the sub-region accounts for approximately 30 per cent of the entire population of Africa (World Bank, 2005). West Africa presents a wide range of ethnic, linguistic, cultural, political and religious differences. Nigeria alone has about 250 ethnic groups. Members of some ethnic groups are spread across borders. For instance, the Yorubas can be found in Nigeria, Benin, Ghana and Cote d'Ivoire; Hausas in Nigeria, Ghana, and Niger; Kanuris in Nigeria, Niger and Chad; the Wollofs in Senegal and the Gambia; Mandigos in Guinea, Guinea Bissau, Sierra Leone and Liberia; the Ewe in Togo and Ghana and the Fullanis in virtually all the states in the sub-region. As will be discussed in the next section, this has come about as a result of the arbitrary demarcation of West Africa by European colonial powers in the Berlin conference of 1884. European imperialism further worsened the ethnic and linguistic divide by imposing their own language differences. Thus West Africa is today divided into Anglophone, Francophone and Lusophone states. The next chapter shows how these linguistic differences continue to plague the project of West African integration. The partition in Berlin also resulted in vast differences in size, population and resource endowment of West African states. For instance, the size, population and wealth of countries like The Gambia, Sierra Leone, Togo and Benin is dwarfed by those of Nigeria, Ghana, Senegal and Cote d'Ivoire.

But despite the above differences, West African states share common features. Ten of the sub-region's 16 countries (no data for Liberia) fall within the Low Human Development category of the United Nations Development Programme's (UNDP) Human Development Index Report of 2008 (UNDP, 2008) due to factors such as low life expectancy, high infant mortality rate, high levels of illiteracy, low per capita incomes and abject poverty. All the states in the sub-region, except Liberia, are former colonies. It is therefore not surprising that most of the political and administrative systems are modelled on those of the former colonial masters. West African economies are based on the export of energy products (oil and petroleum products), minerals (diamonds, iron ore, rutile, bauxite, gold) and cash crops (coffee, palm oil, cocoa, piassava, pineapple and groundnuts). Francis considers this to be the result of the uneven way in which European imperialists incorporated West African economies into the capitalist world system, relegating them to the peripheral status of 'hewers of stone and drawers of water' (2001, 12). In a bid to diversify the economy after independence, West African states have sought to industrialise but these efforts are hampered by lack of capacity, capital, technological and infrastructural development.

Table 2.1   Basic indicators for West African states

Country	Population mid 2003 (m)	Land Area ('000 km²)	GNI per capita (US$) 2003	Life expectancy at birth	Adult literary(@ age 15) 2003
Benin	6.7	111	440	53	33.6
Burkina Faso	12.1	274	300	43	12.8
Cape Verde	0.5	4	1440	69	75.7
Cote d'Ivoire	16.8	318	660	45	48.1
Gambia	1.4	10	270	53	37.8
Ghana	20.7	228	320	54	54.1
Guinea	7.9	246	430	46	41.0
Guinea Bissau	1.5	28	140	46	39.6
Liberia	3.4	96	100	47	
Mali	11.7	1220	300	41	19.0
Mauritania	2.8	1025	400	51	51.2
Niger	11.8	1267	200	46	14.4
Nigeria	136.5	911	350	45	66.8
Senegal	10.2	193	550	52	39.3
Sierra Leone	5.3	72	160	37	29.6
Togo	4.9	54	310	50	53.0

Sources: The World Bank (2005), *African Development Indicators 2005*, Washington
DC: The World Bank; Data for Adult Literacy: UNDP (2005), *Human
Development Report 2005: International Co-operation at a Crossroads: Aid,
Trade and Security in an Unequal World*, New York: UNDP.

Colonialism in West Africa: Legacy and Impact on State Formation

Understanding the process of state failure and collapse requires an analysis of how these states were formed. Such an analysis will reveal the deep-rooted causes of West African conflicts and the impact of colonialism on state formation. With the exception of Liberia which was founded as a settlement for freed slaves by an American Charity, the American Colonisation Society, all the states in the sub-region share a colonial past. But even Liberia shares some of the legacies of colonialism as descendants of freed slaves resettled in Monrovia behaved like 'colonial masters' over the indigenous population. This section seeks to examine the impact of colonialism on the process of state formation in West Africa and the resulting conflicts in the sub-region. It is however necessary to give a brief background on colonialism in West Africa in particular and Africa in general.

Although parts of West Africa, and indeed Africa, were already under colonial rule by the beginning of the nineteenth century, it was not until 1884 that the process of acquiring colonies began in earnest. Upon the invitation of Von Bismarck, European powers assembled in Berlin in November 1884 to 'carve-up' Africa into colonial territories. This arbitrary partition never took into account the existing ethnic and natural borders in Africa. And as mentioned above, this resulted in the creation of countries with many different ethnic groups. Nigeria for instance has more than 250 ethnic groups with very different cultural and linguistic background. In some other cases, some ethnic groups straddle several countries. These artificial borders have caused and continue to cause serious social and political problems to post-colonial African states. In West Africa, arbitrary borders are partly responsible for the long running secessionist war in the Casamance region of Senegal. The decision to allow Britain to take control of a tiny strip of land (The Gambia) running through Senegal has made it very difficult for the Senegalese government to effectively control the southern part of the country. The amalgamation of disparate ethnic groups within state borders has also made the process of integration and nation building very difficult. As we will see later, these borders have also contributed to the regional spread of conflicts as members of the same ethnic group in neighbouring countries come to the aid of their kin.

The dominant colonial powers in West Africa were France and Great Britain. The Portuguese were also involved but to a minimal level. Although there were variations in the policies of the different colonial masters, the common underlying motives of all of them remained the subjugation and exploitation of the African continent. The French considered their territories as overseas provinces of France. To this end, they sought to integrate their territories closer to the metropole. This resulted in weakening of local authority structures through their policy of 'assimilation'. The British on the other hand opted for the cheaper option of governing their colonies through indirect rule. This involves delegating greater powers to local authorities. The Portuguese implemented the most draconian policies in their territories.

However, unlike the settler-dominated colonies of East and Southern Africa, decolonisation in West Africa was relatively peaceful except for the former Portuguese colonies, Guinea Bissau and Cape Verde, who had to wage a bitter war of independence. Nationalist agitation surfaced in West Africa following the end of World War I and the creation of the League of Nations. The League's principle of self-determination provided the impetus for the activities of the early nationalist leaders. The involvement of many West African soldiers in the liberation of Europe during the Second World War also galvanised support amongst natives for decolonisation. Furthermore most of the elites from these colonies have been educated in Europe and could now articulate their demands using the political language of the West. The creation of the United Nations also acted as a major catalyst towards independence. Founded on ideals of equality and self-determination, the UN message accelerated the move towards independence. In West Africa, Ghana led the way in 1957 followed by Guinea in 1958. Most countries had independence between 1960 and 1961 with Cape Verde the last to be free from foreign rule in 1975.

Although colonial rule lasted for a relatively short period (in some cases less than a century), its legacy on African politics and state formation is enormous. Whilst it is worth noting that there are slight variations in the legacies of different colonial masters, however, vast similarities can be found. Besides the problems created by the arbitrary borders, there are wide ranging political, economic and social problems caused by colonialism. As our analysis below will reveal, some of these problems are at the root of the region's incessant conflicts.

Politically, there was little done by colonial powers to prepare the colonies for independence despite the fact that nationalist agitation started nearly 50 years before. In fact most of the colonial masters were caught off guard with the speed of events after World War II. The French for instance were still thinking of creating a grand Franco-African Confederation in 1958. This lack of preparation meant that at independence, most West African and indeed African States have few educated personnel to take over the administration of these countries. Guinea Bissau for instance only had 14 graduates at independence and an illiteracy rate of 97 per cent (Lamb, 1984). It was not surprising therefore that 'the skills of the new civil servants were too few and their experience all too limited to master the many tasks of governance' (Chazan, 1999, 43). Not only were the new civil servants unprepared for the tasks they faced, the new political leaders also lacked the necessary skills and experience to govern. Most of these leaders gained their positions through their ability to organise anti-colonial protests and campaigns. Whereas 'the bulk of their own political understanding had been modelled in a centralised and authoritarian colonial context', at independence, they were faced with pluralist political institutions of alien origins (Chazan, 1999, 45). Kasfir is right when he noted that 'the political culture bequeathed by colonialism contained the notions that authoritarianism was an appropriate mode of rule and that political activity was merely a disguised form of self-interest, subversive of the public welfare' (Nelson Kasfir, cited in Naomi Chaszan et al., 1999, 43). In fact in most of these colonies, pluralist politics and universal adult suffrage was only introduced about a decade before independence. For Thompson, this represents the irony of colonial rule: 'Imperial powers sought to leave a legacy of constitutional liberal democracy. These were the liberties and political representation that imperial administrators had consciously withheld from Africans during their own rule' (2004, 21). As will be discussed in the next section, this legacy of authoritarianism laid the foundations of patrimonialism and clientelistic politics that undermined the economic and political development of post-colonial West Africa and sowed the seeds of state failure and complex political emergencies.

Besides failing to prepare the colonies politically, the colonisers also failed to bring meaningful economic and industrial development. No serious attempt was made at industrialisation. The few industries that were established were mainly focused on the primary sector. Infrastructural and development projects started late in the process. In keeping with their underlying economic motives, the few infrastructural projects implemented were geared towards facilitating the exploitation of the colonies' raw materials. Evidence of this incoherent and lopsided development policy can be seen in the way roads and railways were built to link only the major producing areas with the seaport. Consequently, young men were lured from rural areas lacking in amenities to coastal urban cities. Unfortunately, this trend has not been reversed by post-colonial governments. In search of livelihood and a better life, the majority of these youths have remained unemployed in the urban areas thus providing a fertile recruiting ground for would-be dissidents. The link between youth unemployment and rebellion will be further explored in latter sections of this chapter.

Nature of Domestic Politics in Post-Colonial West Africa

For the purpose of analysis, West African domestic politics will be divided into two periods: the first one being from 1960 to 1990 – the era of one party rule and military dictatorships within the context of Cold War politics. The next period started in the early 1990s after the end of the Cold War and represents the efforts at democratisation and economic structural adjustments. This period also witnessed the growing marginalisation of the entire African continent in economic and political terms. However, this periodisation is not rigid as political and economic developments in the sub-region overlap both periods.

A False Dawn: Post-Colonial West Africa and the Era of Dictatorships

The euphoria that greeted independence in the 1960s was short-lived as post-colonial regimes failed to deliver on their promises of economic development and political emancipation for the masses. Patrimonialism and clientelism are key concepts in trying to understand the crisis of legitimacy and governance that rocked several West African and indeed African countries. Thompson aptly defines patrimonialism as 'a form of political order where power is concentrated in the personal authority of one individual ruler ... The state is their private property, and the act of ruling is consequently arbitrary' (2004, 115). In West Africa, the politics of patrimonialism led to growing tendencies towards authoritarian rule. But as noted in the previous section, post-independence leaders inherited from colonial rule a highly centralised, undemocratic and authoritarian system of government. This has led some analysts to argue that the authoritarian rule of post-independence rulers was merely a continuation of what existed during colonialism (Thompson, 2004). Most post-independence leaders regarded their positions as rewards for their struggle for independence. Any opposition was branded as unpatriotic and considered ungrateful to the efforts of nationalists. Members of the opposition were suppressed, intimidated and jailed. In several countries such as Ghana and Guinea, crude sedition laws were formulated to suppress the activities of the opposition. The press was heavily censored and freedom of expression was curtailed. And as Chazan et al. observe, 'opposition itself was considered to be immoral. Unity was equated with uniformity, disagreement with treason' (1999, 49). Complete concentration of power on leaders was achieved with the adoption of the one party system, for example in Ghana, Cote d'Ivoire, Guinea and Sierra Leone. Even in countries where the system was not institutionalised, one party rule became *de facto* as opportunities for fair competition were absent. Senegal and Liberia can be classed under this category. Various reasons were used by leaders to justify one party rule (see Jordan, 1969; Thompson, 1999). Kwame Nkrumah considered multi-party politics to be divisive and a distraction from the goal of national development. Felix Houphouet-Boigny regarded one party rule as a manifestation of the unity that already existed whilst Sekou Toure saw opposition parties as undermining the national development goals. Siaka Stevens borrowed from Julius Nyerere of Tanzania when he opined that one party rule is in line with the traditional democratic African principles of unity and consensus. Notwithstanding the different justifications for adopting the system, the methods and strategies employed were similar. It resulted in the total concentration of power in the hands of the President and his closest allies. The role of national legislatures was reduced to rubber-stamping the decrees and wishes of Presidents. In these circumstances, there was no basis for the establishment of Max Weber's legal-rational source of legitimacy as the state was personalised and the divide between private and public became blurred. Leaders were immortalised, for instance, it was common to see presidents having titles like 'father of the nation'. In addition, important places were named after leaders like the Siaka Stevens Stadium, Kwame Nkrumah Institute etc. Some leaders went as far as declaring themselves 'Life Presidents'. Nkrumah of Ghana and Stevens of Sierra Leone are notable examples.

Closely linked to the politics of patrimonialism is clientelism. In the absence of political legitimacy based on legal-rational governance, support for patrimonial rulers was based on clientelistic networks aimed at buying off opposition and rewarding followers. Christopher Clapham describes clientelism as 'a relation of exchange between unequals' (1982, 4). It is a mutually beneficial relationship between the patron and client. Thompson (2004) refers to this relationship as a form of political contract: whilst the patron rewards the client with public office, security and resources, the client reciprocates with support that helps to legitimise the patron's position. Clientelism in West Africa resulted in a seriously flawed process of distributing the state's scarce resources. Most leaders succeeded in building strong patron-client relationships that meant that only supporters of the regime benefited from state resources. This guaranteed the support and loyalty of key institutions like the army and police on whose loyalty the regimes relied for survival. But it also led to inefficiency and massive corruption in the running of the state. Inefficiency permeated the entire state structure as appointment to public office was not based on qualifications or merit but on association with the ruling elites. The meagre resources available for nation building were diverted to sustaining the patron-client networks. As Reno aptly observes, political leaders 'convert wealth into political resources, buying the loyalty of some and buying weapons to coerce others and thus gather more resources and so on' (Reno, 1999, 1). In these circumstances, corruption became rife as clients used their positions for rent-seeking. This involves taking bribes for performing their 'official' duties, kick backs on contracts, fraudulently selling off government property for private gain or diverting large sums of money to private Swiss accounts. There was also an international dimension to clientelism as the extractive nature of most African economies enabled leaders to agree dubious deals with foreign businesses and individuals to serve their selfish interests. The consequence for the masses was a state of declining social services, dilapidated infrastructure, weak and collapsing economy and widespread poverty. The increasing 'informalisation' of the state also led to a weakening of state institutions and subsequently state failure and collapse. The political and economic discontent generated by this collapse sowed the seeds of most of the sub-region's conflicts.

But in the midst of this growing impoverishment, patrimonialism and clientelism ensured some sense of stability and legitimacy for the ruling elites. However around the 1980s and 1990s, patrimonial-clientelistic politics suffered a major crisis of legitimacy. Thompson (2004) observes that the economic crisis of the 1980s and 1990s including the negative effects of the Structural Adjustment Programmes (SAP) and global economic recession, and the drying up of aid money following the end of the Cold War resulted in the decline of resources available to ruling elites to sustain their patron-client networks. This in turn led to loss of legitimacy and widespread economic difficulties for patrons and clients alike. The resulting hardship brought about a spate of angry demonstrations across West Africa that were crushed with massive brutality by the authorities.

In the middle of this chaos and instability, and with no established means of peaceful political change, the military emerged as the only challenger to the dictators and as Lewis observes, 'where opposition is illegal, governments can be changed only by coup d'etat' (Lewis, quoted in Jordan, 1969, 105).

The first military coup in West Africa took place in Togo in 1963 when Eyadema overthrew President Olympio in a bloody coup. Since then, West Africa has been the most coup prone sub-region in Africa. Out of 16 countries in the sub-region, Senegal is the only one to have escaped the scourge of military rule (Thompson, 2004). From Sierra Leone to Ghana, the justifications given by the military for seizing power are similar: to stop the misrule and massive corruption and human rights abuses of civilian dictators and return the country to a sound socio-economic and political footing. But despite the rhetoric, the record of military leaders in West Africa is far more appalling than their civilian counterparts. Human rights abuses reach unprecedented proportions during military rule as the cases of Sani Abacha, Rawlings and Samuel Doe indicate. Opponents of the regime are intimidated or brutally murdered whilst freedom of the press is severely restricted. Corruption is rife. Most of these leaders end up transforming themselves into civilians, allowing them to contest and rig the elections that follow. This spate of military coups have retarded economic development in the sub-region and sowed a climate of deep instability.

Undesirable as the above developments are, the Cold War superpowers actively and consciously tolerated and supported the dictators, both military and civilians. This support for authoritarian regimes was meant to promote their political and strategic interests. Former US deputy assistant secretary for human rights acknowledged the fact that during the Cold War, 'Africa was viewed as yet another playing field on which the struggle between the Soviets and ourselves was to be waged' (Bishop, quoted in Diamond, 1995, 250). Brutal and corrupt as Doe was, the US made him a key ally and effectively turned a blind eye to his excesses. In other West African states, the US intervention was limited as long as British and French influence was enough to thwart Communism. Soviet role in West Africa was limited and only acted as a response to US and Chinese influence in the sub-region (Chazan, 1999). Nevertheless, with its anti-colonial and radical stance, the Soviet Union was able to win over a few revolutionary leaders like Guinea's Sekou Toure and Ghana's Kwame Nkrumah.

West Africa in the Post-Cold War Era: Between Democratisation and Marginalisation

At the end of the Cold War in the late 1980s and the subsequent withdrawal of superpower support, these regimes faced increasing internal and external pressures for reform. The internal pressures came in two forms. The first type was peaceful, civil society based campaign for democratic reforms whilst the second form was violent and aimed at taking over the state. Having being suppressed for a long time during Cold War politics, these dissident groups suddenly realised that there was no longer any backing for dictators; the lid was then opened for everyone to express their dissent. Without support from their erstwhile allies, states like Liberia, Sierra Leone, Guinea Bissau etc. all degenerated into a vicious circle of violence and instability.

The external pressures came from the Bretton Woods Institutions, the UN and major bilateral donors like the US, UK and France who tied the granting of aid to economic structural adjustment and democratisation. In its 1989 study, *Sub-Saharan Africa: From Crisis to Sustainable Growth*, the World Bank linked the problem of governance to the poor economic performance of the continent. Major Bilateral donors were blunter in warning African leaders that economic aid will be conditioned on satisfactory transition to democracy and the adoption of Western models of liberalised economy (Diamond, 1995). But as discussed above, these were the same institutions and governments turning a blind eye to, or supporting repressive regimes in Africa during the Cold War. Hoogvelt (1997) also noted the contradiction in the new democratic conditionalities and the way in which strong and authoritarian regimes in Asia have been credited for the region's economic success. What then, is responsible for this sudden change of policy? Some analysts have argued that these new conditionalities are geared towards 'focusing responsibility on governments of developing countries, both for past ills and for implementation of reform packages' (Hoogvelt, 1997, 174). Another plausible explanation for this sudden shift can be found in the fact that, after the end of the Cold War and the demise of communism, the West no longer needed the services of African dictators to help fend off soviet influence. With the battle of ideologies won, the US and its Western allies can now shift to promoting 'democracy' in the developing world.

With increasing internal and external pressure, governments across the sub-region were forced to accept reforms and a gradual move towards democracy. New political parties, human rights groups, pro-democracy movements, students, workers, market women, professionals and the unemployed all joined in the campaign for reforms. National Conferences were held in several states in the sub-region to discuss the new democratic constitutions. Multi-Party systems were adopted across the sub-region and freedom of the press and independence of the judiciary were enshrined in the constitutions. Elections were organised in Senegal, Mali, Benin, Cape Verde, Niger, Togo, Ghana, Guinea, Cote d'Ivoire, Burkina Faso and Nigeria. But the optimism that followed these events soon dissipated. In countries such as Nigeria, Sierra Leone and the Gambia, military coups reversed all the gains that were achieved by pro-democracy campaigners. Even in those countries were elections were held, their conduct and aftermath cast a big shadow of doubt on the sustainability and effectiveness of democracy. In Guinea, Ghana and Cote d'Ivoire, a large section of the opposition boycotted the elections citing the absence of a level playing field. In Togo, intimidation and targeted killings of members of the opposition effectively killed any meaningful challenge to the authority of Eyadema. Niger slumped back to military dictatorship in 1999. As the discussion so far illustrates, the military has been, and continues to be a perennial problem in West African politics.

The above bleak picture of the state of governance in West Africa and indeed the entire continent has been the subject of several scholarly debates, analysis and commentaries. Sola Akinrinade calls it 'democracy without democratisation' (1998, 79). He criticises the democratisation process in the entire continent for reducing democracy to the symbolic holding of elections rather than transforming the inherently undemocratic structure of the post-colonial state. This failure reduces elections to a mere exercise of choosing between two oppressors. It was only in Mali, Niger, Benin and Cape Verde that elections resulted in the ousting of incumbents. The failure to address the social and economic needs of the people is also a significant drawback for the democratisation process in West Africa. As Akinrinade succinctly puts it, 'when democracy is indifferent to the grinding poverty of the masses, giving the vote to the poor is virtually meaningless' (1998, 81). In short, democracy should not only bring about political liberalisation but also, and most importantly, economic and social welfare for the masses.

The inability of the pro-democracy movements in these countries to present a united front against dictators is also partly responsible for the difficulties in sustaining democracy. In most of these countries, so-called pro-democracy campaigners include former members of ruling parties and professionals who have fallen out of favour with leaders. These are the same people who have contributed to the subversion of democracy in their respective countries. Democracy for this group of people is purely about gaining power. This obsession with power has divided and seriously weakened the opposition. In Senegal, seven presidential candidates stood against President Diouf in 1993. 19 political parties contested the 1990 elections in Cote d'Ivoire. In Nigeria, prior to the annulment of the 1993 elections, 120 people aspired to be Presidential Candidates! (Akinrinade, 1998, 81). This apparent friction within the opposition is a big boost to incumbents. In addition to the friction within the opposition is its inability to present a credible and feasible alternative programme. This is not surprising as politics in West Africa revolves more around personalities than issues. However, the above shortcomings of the pro-democracy movement should not deny it the credit it deserves. Besides the small group of self-interested recycled politicians, there is an active and committed majority of activists, most of them ordinary people who have borne the brunt of bad governance in the sub-region. The sacrifices of these people in forcing political reforms and bringing a semblance of democracy should not go unnoticed.

The actions and policies of external actors (IFIs, private investors and foreign governments) should also be considered when analysing the democratisation process in West Africa. As mentioned in Chapter 1, foreign direct investment remains at a very low rate of 1 per cent of total world investment. The cynicism expressed by this business executive sums up the view of business leaders towards Africa: 'Who cares about Africa; it is not important to us; leave it to the IMF and the World Bank' (quoted in Callaghy, 2000, 46). Despite the promises of aid and economic assistance tied to democratisation, IFIs and Western donor countries have not matched their words with deeds. For instance, the US scaled down its development aid to the entire sub-Saharan Africa from $2 billion in 1985 to $1 billion in 1997 (Mburu, 2003). The Debt burden continues to take a heavy toll on already fragile economies. By 1992, African debt was over $180 billion which amounts to over 100 per cent of Africa's total GNP (Callaghy, 2000). As discussed in Chapter 1, the continent remains politically and economically marginalised. Democracy does not thrive in a situation of abject poverty as is in Africa.

There also appears to be a contradiction between democratisation and the economic conditionalities imposed on Africa by IFIs. Both new and old regimes alike have faced serious difficulties in implementing these directives. Because of their unpopular nature, elected governments have been forced to resort to draconian measures in implementing Structural Adjustment Programmes. In implementing such top-down directives, governments were required to ignore the views and opinions of the masses. This caused deep seated resentment in many countries across the region and led to a series of violent demonstrations and riots. Harbeson shares this view when he noted that 'the multidonor campaigns for simultaneous economic and political liberalisation risk becoming counterproductive, self-defeating, and accessories to the troubled political and economic circumstances of African countries in the early 1990s' (1995, 15). Former Executive Secretary of the UN Economic Commission for Africa puts it more bluntly: 'The donor countries that are encouraging Africans to take the democratic path are also the countries that are encouraging Africans to adopt economic policies that alienate the people' (Adediji, quoted in Callaghy, 2000, 46). In his study on Sierra Leone, William Reno (1999) also established a link between neo-liberal reforms and the outbreak of violent conflict. He argues that these economic reforms attacks the patrimonial state and undermines the basis of legitimacy of most leaders in Sub Saharan Africa.

The beginning of the twenty-first century witnessed a rekindling of the spirit and determination of West African civil society to put democratisation back on track. ECOWAS and the African Union (AU) have also shed their state-centric image to start engaging with civil society and putting democracy and good governance at the centre of their programmes. Notwithstanding these steps, the sub-region is still suffering from bad governance and the failure of leadership. These twin problems are at the heart of most of the political upheavals devastating the sub-region.

Ethno-Religious Factors

In West Africa and indeed across the continent, ethnic and religious differences have resulted in widespread violence and unrest. Niger, Mali and Burkina Faso are grappling with their Tuareg problem. Cote d'Ivoire has been brought to a standstill in the violence between the Muslim north and the mainly Christian south. Nigeria has suffered more than 100,000 deaths in more than 50 conflicts with an ethno-religious link since the inauguration of a civilian government in 1999 (Ebo, 200). But the region is not unique in this respect. In the 1990s, the Balkans was devastated by notions of ethnicity and in the European Union, Northern Ireland and Basque country in Spain are notable examples.

Ethnicity has a very contested definition but for the purposes of this work, we will adopt Alex Thompson's basic definition: 'a community of people who have the conviction that they have a common identity and common fate based on issues of origin, kinship ties, traditions, cultural uniqueness, a shared history and possibly a shared language' (2004, 60). When applied to Africa, 'ethnic group' represents a positive move from 'tribe' because of the latter's links with primitiveness and backwardness. The Western media is often quick to label African conflicts as ethnic or religious wars stemming from primordial animosities between different social and identity groups. Such an analysis regards conflicts in Africa as natural and inevitable due to the ethnic composition of the continent. Whilst not dismissing the ethno-religious dimensions of some African conflicts, the primacy given to ethnic and religious factors is an oversimplification and clearly distorts an understanding of the multiple and complex underlying factors at play. As the Carnegie Commission on Preventing Deadly Conflict succinctly puts it:

> The words 'ethnic', 'religious', 'tribal', or 'factional' – important as they may be in intergroup conflict – do not, in most cases, adequately explain why people use massive violence to achieve their goals. These descriptions do not, of themselves, reveal why people would kill each other over their differences. To label a conflict simply as an ethnic war can lead to misguided policy choices by fostering a wrong impression that ethnic, cultural or religious differences inevitably result in violent conflict and that differences therefore must be suppressed. (1997, 29)

Many other analysts have challenged the primordialist's position by claiming that today's ethnic groups are in fact modern social constructions. Thompson (2004) argues that pre-colonial Africa was organised around a loose set of ethnic groups characterised by flexibility of membership. This view is shared by Black who maintains that 'ethnicity, at least in its contemporary form, is a consequence of the creation of nation-states' (2003, 125). The driving force behind this 'ethnicisation' is partly the need to enhance administrative convenience and stem any resistance coming from the subjects through the so-called 'divide and rule' policy. The case of Rwanda stands out very clearly. Many writers have argued that ethnicity in pre-colonial Rwanda was not a divisive issue (Clapham, 1999; Utterwulghe, 1999; Sebahara, 1998). Both Hutus and Tutsis speak the same language, Kinyarwanda, share the same culture and lifestyle and often intermarry. Many writers also seem to agree that there is no record of pre-colonial conflict between the two dominant groups despite the patron-client relationship that existed by which Tutsis were the patrons and Hutus the clients (Clapham, 1999; Utterwulghe, 1999). In this regard, the theory of ancient hatreds cannot really account for Rwanda's genocide. The colonial system sharpened group differences and created ethnic consciousness. The Belgians, after World War I continued the German policy of 'divide and rule'. They tried to legitimise this policy by a theory differentiating a superior race of immigrant hamites from the so-called 'primitive indigenous Negroes'. This theory, though erroneous, regarded the Tutsis to be more civilised, physically closer to the Europeans and therefore deserve power, privilege and status than the Hutu (Sellstrom and Wohlgemuth, 1996, 26). This colonial policy therefore resulted in the monopolisation of power in the hands of Tutsis. Ethnic division was further accentuated by the classification of the population as either Tutsi or Hutu (to qualify as a Tutsi, a person had to own at least ten cattle) with no movement between the groups. Identity cards were introduced in 1933 to identify a person's ethnic group. This policy resulted in the discrimination of Hutus in education, employment and other social services and according to Sellstrom and Wohlgemuth proved a crucial element in 'firmly establishing ('structuring') the ethnic cleavage' (1996, 27). Whilst ethnicity in West Africa may have led to minor skirmishes in the pre-colonial and colonial periods, there is no evidence of sustained ethnic hatreds.

At independence, most African leaders who lack a popular political support base willingly exploited ethnic identities to further their political interests. In this context, 'the pursuit of political office, personal ambition and interests of the political elites are framed in ethnic terms to mobilise ethnic solidarity' (Francis et al., 2005, 81). This applies both to seating governments who focus a disproportionate amount of the country's resources to their ethnic groups; and opposition parties who campaign for support on the basis of alleged 'marginalisation of our ethnic group'. Devoid of political manipulation, most ordinary Africans live peacefully side by side with members of other ethnic groups. The problems arising from ethnicity can therefore be linked to the failure of governance and the 'politics of decline' discussed above. And as argued in our co-authored work, 'ethnicity is not so much the problem, but rather is the politicisation, exploitation and manipulation of ethnicism by the ruling and governing class' (Francis et al., 2005, 81). Instances abound in West Africa where politicians have played the ethnic card to maximise their political capital. Facing the real danger of losing elections, successive southern based politicians in Cote d'Ivoire have banned Alanssan Ouattara, a politician from the mainly Muslim north, from contesting presidential elections, on the basis of being a foreigner from Burkina Faso. The government saw this as an opportunity to propagate the doctrine of '*Ivoirite*' distinguishing between 'pure' and 'immigrant' Ivorians. The apparent government backed xenophobic and ethnic attacks at members of the opposition further complicated the situation. In Liberia, Taylor was able to exploit the feeling of victimisation by the Gio and Mano tribes to elicit their support. In Sierra Leone, efforts by the RUF to tap on the ethnic fears of a section of the society however ended in dismal failure.

Religion is a major part of life in West Africa with Christianity and Islam being the dominant faiths. A few others follow various traditional beliefs. Clashes between Christians and Muslims in Nigeria and Cote d'Ivoire have brought the debate about the role of religion in West African conflicts to the fore. However, like ethnicity, religion has also been manipulated for political gains. Thompson observes that 'religion enters politics not just for spiritual or moral reasons; often there are instrumental imperatives as well' (2004, 71). As with ethnicity, any analysis of so-called religious conflicts that focuses only on religious differences and fails to understand the underlying motives of the principal actors is misleading. In Nigeria, the conflict between Christians and Muslims go beyond religious differences to encompass attempts by both Southern and Northern Elites to win political power. Mention has already been made of the Cote d'Ivoire case. To underline the political nature of these so-called religious conflicts, the Sierra Leone case is relevant. After several frustrated efforts by both regional and international mediators, the Inter-Religious Council of Sierra Leone was able to initiate peace talks that culminated in the resolution of the Sierra Leone conflict. A coalition of religious communities, the Inter-Religious Council of Sierra Leone is based on respect of individual religious differences, working to promote cooperation among the religious communities on shared concerns, specifically working to end the war, to establish a just and sustainable peace, to advocate recognition and respect for human rights (Biguzzi, 2000). As noted earlier, religious and ethnic differences are not essentially a cause for conflict. These differences become lethal when politicians and self-interested groups decide to use them to further their objectives.

Understanding the Regional Security Complex and Conflict Formation

Whilst the above factors form the primary or underlying causes of the incessant conflicts in West Africa, they do not account for the actual outbreak of fighting. A mixture of triggering factors, most of them regional in nature, has succeeded in transforming these latent conflicts into violent and protracted wars. These factors do feed and reinforce each other to produce a set of intractable and interlinked conflict triggers. This section will situate the West African sub-region within Buzan's theory of security complex which is defined as 'a group of states whose primary security concerns link together sufficiently closely that their national securities cannot realistically be considered apart from one another' (1991, 190). It will therefore focus on the role of state sponsors of dissident groups, small arms, local mercenaries, civil militias, and strategic resources in triggering conflicts in the sub-region. It argues that these factors are intricately linked to each other and any meaningful attempt to solve the regional spread of conflict in West Africa should take cognisance of this fact.

State Sponsors of Conflicts in West Africa

Behind the rhetoric of regional integration and security regionalism of ECOWAS member states lies deep suspicion and mistrust. This can be seen in the pattern of cross-border support for dissident groups in neighbouring countries. It goes as far back as the Biafran War in Nigeria in 1967 when Cote d'Ivoire supported Biafran separatists. One area that has come to symbolise this practice is the Mano River Basin. In December 1989, Charles Taylor's NPFL used Cote d'Ivoire as a staging ground for their invasion of Liberia. In this project, they also received the support of Burkina Faso and Libya. Burkina Faso's Blaise Campoare is believed to have reciprocated the assistance he received from Foday Sankoh and Taylor in ousting Thomas Sankara (UN, 2001). There are also credible reports linking Liberia, Cote d'Ivoire, Burkina Faso and Libya in aiding the RUF. In return, Sierra Leone and Guinea actively encouraged and supported the formation of the United Liberation Movement for Democracy (ULIMO), an anti-Taylor faction. In September 2000, Guinean dissidents, *Rassemblement des Forces Democratique de Guinee* (RFDG) attacked Guinean border towns from Liberian territory with the support of Taylor and the RUF. In retaliation, Guinea supported the Liberians United for Reconciliation and Democracy (LURD) and allowed its combatants to launch attacks into Liberia using Guinean territory.

Away from the Mano River Basin, Cote d'Ivoire accused Burkina Faso and Liberia of providing support to Northern and Western rebels respectively. Burkina Faso in turn accused Cote d'Ivoire of being behind an attempted coup in 2003 (BBC, 2004). Senegal blamed elements of the Guinea Bissau Army of gun running with the Cassamance Separatists. An attempt to fire the Army Chief accused of being behind the deal resulted in a civil war. Mauritania accused Burkina Faso of being behind the series of attempted coups in that country (IRIN, 2005).

The above cases of state support for dissident groups clearly highlight the regional nature of conflicts in West Africa. But what is behind this pattern of cross-border support for dissidents? A combination of personal, economic and strategic foreign policy motives can be identified. In West Africa and indeed across Africa, personal ties play a significant role in international relations and diplomacy, what Adibe refers to as 'messy geopolitics' manifested through 'a complex web of personal ties and 'friendship' (Adibe, 1998, 81). The influence of this web of relationships involving sub-regional leaders must be brought into focus for a clear and comprehensive understanding of the causes, complexities and nature of the devastating conflicts in the sub-region. Personal reasons played a crucial role in motivating Houphouet-Boigny to give support to Taylor. The Ivorian President enjoyed cordial relationship with the assassinated President Tolbert and the latter's son, Adolphus Tolbert, was married to the former's daughter. Adolphus was jailed by Doe after the 1980 coup and subsequently murdered whilst in detention (Dunn, 1999). Houphouet-Boigny never forgave

Doe for this act of savagery against his family and was bent on revenge. Thus when Taylor approached him for support, he saw this as an opportunity to avenge the killing of his close friend and son-in-law. Personal motivations also played a key role in Blaise Campaore's decision to render support to Taylor. Campaore is son-in-law to Houphouet-Boigny (he married Adolphus Tolbert's widow). He is reported to have provided additional troops and material support to Taylor. He also allowed his territory to be used as a transit point for military supplies from Libya which are then transported to Liberia via Cote d'Ivoire (Ofuatey-Kodjoe, 1994).

Closely linked to personal and friendship ties is the ethnic factor discussed above. As most ethnic groups in West Africa straddle across borders, there has been the tendency for neighbouring states to assist their kinsmen and women on the other side. This is true for the conflicts in Cote d'Ivoire, Liberia and Cassamance. In Cote d'Ivoire, Burkina Faso is seen to be sympathetic with the demands of the dissidents, most of whom are immigrants from that country. The same applies to Liberia where Guinea's Lansana Conte is accused of supporting his Mandingo kinsmen in ULIMO and later LURD (ICG, 2003).

Strategic foreign policy calculations also play a part in the leaders' decision to lend support to dissident groups. For Houphouet-Boigny, in addition to the personal motive discussed above, he considered the Liberian conflict as a chance to reduce Nigerian hegemony in the sub-region. President Babangida of Nigeria was a very close ally of Doe. Replacing Doe with his protégé, Taylor would give him considerable influence in Liberia and seriously thwart Nigerian hegemonic designs. As part of his strategy to reduce Western influence in the region and promote his image, Qadafi of Libya provided Taylor with material support and training for his forces (Ofuatey-Kodjoe, 1994). This strategic foreign policy concerns also have economic undertones. The section on strategic resources will reveal the role played by Liberia and Burkina Faso in the Sierra Leone blood diamond trade.

This environment of cross-border support has sowed deep mutual mistrust and suspicion among West African leaders and resulted in a vicious circle of retaliatory support for the neighbouring country's dissident groups as the above instances indicate. This situation is exacerbated by the availability of young people in the sub-region, most of them veterans of past conflicts, who are prepared to fight for any group that can pay the right price. It is to this problem of local mercenaries that we will now turn.

'Soldiers without Borders': The Spread of Local Mercenaries

Mercenaries can be defined as foreign freelance combatants who offer their labour and skills to a party in a foreign conflict in return for money. Most of the literature on mercenaries in West African conflicts has focused on foreign private military companies from outside the sub-region (Musah and Fayemi, 2000; Francis, 1999). These groups include the South African Executive Outcomes

(EO) and the British Sandline International. Little, if any, research has been undertaken to study the devastating role of indigenous West African mercenaries roaming the sub-region in search of 'employment'. The only study came in the form of a 2005 Human Rights Watch Report. The scourge of local mercenaries is not a new phenomenon. A number of West African nationals were reported to be among the NPFL force that invaded Liberia in the early 1990s. Few years later, this same group, consisting of a mixture of Burkinabe and Liberian fighters, assisted the RUF dissidents in launching attacks on Sierra Leone. The use of mercenaries has increased dramatically since the beginning of the millennium as thousands of ex-combatants were released from their assignments in the Sierra Leone and Liberian conflicts following DDR programmes in those countries. An overview of mercenary activity over the past decade reveals the extent of the threat such groups pose to sub-regional security. There were credible reports of Liberian and Sierra Leonean combatants involved in the Guinea Bissau conflict. In 2000, RUF and Liberian fighters were also heavily involved in destabilising Guinea with a series of attacks in the Forest Region and the South of the country bordering Sierra Leone. Following a bust-up with the RUF Leader, Foday Sankoh in 1999, Sam 'Maskita' Bockarie defected to Liberia with a number of fighters loyal to him. This group became the nucleus of a sub-regional mercenary force. In Cote d'Ivoire, Bockarie's men fought on the side of the Western rebels (ICG, 2003). The use of mercenaries is however not only confined to dissident groups. Governments in the sub-region have also solicited the services of such groups as and when necessary. ULIMO in the mid 1990s openly fought with the Sierra Leone Army to repel RUF attacks. Cote d'Ivoire used a group of Liberian mercenaries called Lima in its war with the New Forces (Human Security Network, 2004). Taylor's use of foreign fighters has already been discussed. It is reported that Burkina Faso makes a provision in the budget to cover the salaries of the 400 Burkinabe soldiers fighting in Liberia (UN, 2001).

There are several factors behind this rise of mercenary groups in the sub-region. A key factor is youth unemployment. With a growing population, youths in West Africa account for a significant proportion of the entire population. This number is however not matched by employment and educational opportunities (UNDP, 2004). A direct link between a rise in youth unemployment and the rise in mercenary recruitment can be established. Unemployment in the major mercenary generating countries (Burkina Faso, Sierra Leone and Liberia) is among the highest in the sub-region. For Burkina Faso, the export of labour goes back to colonial days when thousands of young people moved to the relatively wealthy Cote d'Ivoire. Due to the lack of jobs and the danger this may cause, Taylor is said to have encouraged his former fighters to cross borders (ICG, 2003). The lure of fighting in foreign conflicts is very hard to resist for most of these young people who have very limited chances of a better life in their countries. Cash payments are reported to range from US$100 to US$400 (ICG, 2003). In addition to upfront cash payments, these recruits are also assured of the booty. As discussed in Chapters 4 and 5, the problems encountered by the demobilisation and reintegration programmes in Liberia and Sierra Leone also encouraged ex-combatants to go in search of 'employment'.

However, youth unemployment alone is not enough to explain the rise in mercenary recruitment. For most of these fighters, war has become a way of life. Some of these youths began fighting as young as 8 years old. Guns are treated as toys and war itself becomes a reality 'video game'. This is exploited by leaders who use mercenaries as proxy forces and unscrupulous businessmen who profit from the environment of insecurity created by such forces. The link between the strategic resources of the sub-region and conflict will be discussed later. Attempts to control local mercenaries are hampered by the porous borders, the availability of a large quantity of weapons and the covert support they receive from several sub-regional leaders.

Civil Defence Militias

In his groundbreaking edited work on civil militias in Africa, Francis (2005) distinguishes between first generation civil militias who are an organised group of civilians called upon in times of emergencies to provide supplementary military support, to second generation civil militias in complex political emergencies organised by diverse interest groups, with no constitutional or legislative legitimacy. Unlike first generation civil militias, second generation militias have little or no military training beyond the use of light weapons. Like home-grown mercenaries, civil defence militias have become key features of conflicts in West Africa. This is symptomatic of failed states which have clearly lost monopoly of the use of force. With ill-prepared and unmotivated armies, governments in the sub-region have turned to a variety of groups ranging from traditional 'hunters' to overzealous youths. Other groups have emerged that challenge the authority of governments. In Sierra Leone, pro-government civil defence militia forces consist of local hunters organised around four major groups based on ethnicity: the Kamajors are mostly Mendes in the South and East of the country; the Tamaboros consists of the Limbas, Korankos, Yalunkas and Susus of the North; the Kapras are Thamnes from the North and West and the Donsos are Konos from the East. Besides providing security for their localities, these groups, especially the Kamajors have steadfastly defended the fragile government in Freetown. These groups draw their motivation from perceived mythical powers of invincibility and heroism dating back several centuries. In Nigeria, Kenneth Omeje (2005) distinguishes between substitutionary militias like the Bakassi Boys who take on law enforcement functions in their local areas and adversarial militias who are resistant to the state and its neo-patrimonial and prebendal politics of exclusion. In the last category are groups like The Niger Delta Volunteer Force (NDVF) who are involved in violent campaigns against oil companies. In Cote d'Ivoire, pro-government militias are drawn from student networks and political party youth activists. These include units such as Bees, Gazelles, Ninjas and Panthers, all united under the umbrella of the *Convention des Patriotes Pour la paix* (CPP). In Guinea, following RUF and RFDG attacks in September 2000, the government mobilised young people into a vigilante group called the Young Volunteers Militia (Human Security Network, 2004).

Civil militias can be both a positive as well as negative influence on peace processes. As stated above, the Civil Defence Force (CDF) in Sierra Leone filled the vacuum created by the renegade army by providing security for the local population and defending democracy. In Cote d'Ivoire, vigilantes resisted Robert Guei's attempt to rig the elections and perpetuate himself in power. The Young Volunteers of Guinea, in collaboration with the Guinean Armed Forces, were able to forestall the RFDG advance on Guinea and virtually nipped the rebellion in the bud. But there is another side to civil militias. Most of these groups have been implicated in massive human rights abuses. In Sierra Leone, the tactics of the RUF and CDF were very difficult to distinguish as both groups resorted to terrorising anyone suspected of allying with, or sympathetic to, their enemies. In Guinea, the Young Volunteers indiscriminately targeted foreigners in September 2000. There are also fears that friction might surface between the constitutional army, law enforcement agencies and civil militias. This fear has already reared its ugly head in Sierra Leone where the stalemate arising from the Army and Kamajor friction gave birth to the AFRC coup of May 1997. These groups have also been heavily politicised and are most often exploited by conflicting parties. There is a well grounded fear that the civil defence militia of today will be the dissidents and rebels of tomorrow.

Small Arms and Conflict in West Africa

The devastating effects of small arms in West Africa cannot be overemphasised. The sub-region is awash with an estimated 7 to 8 million illicit small arms. From Nigeria to Mali, small arms have been used to inflict untold human misery and the loss of livelihoods. Since 1990, an estimated 2 million lives have been lost in conflicts involving small arms (Graduate Institute of International Affairs, 2003). In addition to exacerbating conflict in the sub-region, they have resulted in the breakdown of law and order, the weakening of democracy and the militarisation of daily life. Across West Africa, millions of small arms are carried by non-state actors including criminal gangs and bandits, rebels, mercenaries, vigilantes and civil defence militia. These groups wage a campaign of terror and cause widespread human rights abuses. One area that has come to epitomise the effects of small arms is the Mano River Basin where insurgent groups in Liberia, Sierra Leone and Guinea use such weapons with impunity.

The sources of small arms are varied and include both external and internal. Following the end of the Cold War, there was a need to get rid of the stockpile of weapons. For most states in Eastern and Central Europe, the weapons industry has become a key enterprise in the post-Cold War economy. A growing network of corrupt personnel and unscrupulous arms dealers smuggle such weapons to troubled spots around the world and most of these weapons end up in Africa. A large proportion of small arms transfer is also linked to sub-regional cross border support for dissident groups discussed above. Until 1997, rogue elements within the Guinea Bissau Army were involved in illegal trafficking across the border to arm MFDC separatists in Senegal. A UN panel of experts has also documented the network of arms transfer to dissident groups in the Mano River Basin involving Libya, Cote d'Ivoire, Burkina Faso and Liberia. This cross border transfer becomes very difficult to police because of long and porous borders between West African countries. This situation is exacerbated by poorly trained, unmotivated and corrupt border guards. In Nigeria, there are reports of weapons entering the Niger Delta region from the Great Lakes (Musah, 2002). Peacekeeping troops of ECOWAS also contribute to the proliferation. During the Liberian conflict, there were reports of gun running involving ECOMOG troops (Walraven, 1999). Dissident groups also acquire arms by overrunning government and peacekeeping positions and arsenals. The UN Panel of Experts documented cases in which the RUF was able to seize weapons from both the Sierra Leone Army and UNAMSIL troops. Small arms and conflict are closely interlinked and appear to form part of a vicious circle. Whilst small arms sustain and aggravate conflicts in the West African sub-region, these same conflicts contribute immensely to the proliferation of arms across borders to zones of relative peace.

Strategic Resources and Conflicts in West Africa

West Africa is endowed with a variety of strategic resources including diamonds, bauxite, iron ore, rubber, oil, gold and timber to name but a few. In relation to conflict in West Africa, the focus of attention has been on diamonds, timber and oil.

Contrary to the traditional view of diamonds as symbols of love, they have helped fund and fuel conflicts across Africa especially in Sierra Leone, Liberia, Congo DR and Angola. Their small size makes it possible for warlords, terrorists and unscrupulous business people to easily smuggle them across porous African borders. This has been achieved with the complicity of the diamond industry. The recent international focus on conflict diamonds started with the publication of Global Witness' report, *A Rough Trade* in 1998 which exposed the role of diamonds in financing the UNITA rebellion in Angola. This was followed in 2000 by The Partnership Africa Canada report, *The Heart of the Matter: Sierra Leone, Diamonds and Human Security*, and the Fowler Report on Angola (UN 2000). The campaign that followed brought together a number of NGOs, governments and the diamond industry in a forum called the Kimberley Process. But the link between diamonds and armed conflicts in Africa is not a new phenomenon as the cases of Congo and Angola in the 1960s and 1970s show.

In Liberia and Sierra Leone, diamonds have been at the centre of the warring factions' strategic plans and calculations. The RUF and Charles Taylor have used proceeds from diamond sales to purchase drugs, arms and ammunitions, and maintain strategic alliances both at home and abroad. Liberia, with fewer deposits than Sierra Leone, was used by the RUF as a conduit for diamonds mined in Kono. Reliable data is hard to come by but the following figures put the problem into perspective

- while the Government of Sierra Leone recorded exports of only 8,500 carats in 1998, the HRD records imports of 770,000 carats;
- annual Liberian diamond mining capacity is between 100,000 and 150,000 carats, but the HRD records Liberian imports into Belgium of over 31 million carats between 1994 and 1998 – an average of over six million carats a year;
- Cote d'Ivoire, where the small diamond industry was closed in the mid 1980s, apparently exported an average of more than 1.5 million carats to Belgium between 1995 and 1997 (Smillie et al., 2000).

There are very strong connections between diamonds in Liberia and Sierra Leone and the proliferation of small arms as the report of the Panel of Expert on Sierra Leone indicates (UN, 2001). In 2001, an overlooked dimension of conflict diamonds was also uncovered by the Washington post: its links with global terrorism. Douglas Farrah exposed the links between the RUF, Taylor and al Qaeda. In the months following 11 September, the report alleges that al Qaeda used diamonds to move and store their assets (Farrah, 2001).

Although little attention has been placed on timber, there is overwhelming evidence that warring factions are using it to help fund their campaigns. Global Witness has also been at the forefront of the campaign to raise awareness about what the UN terms 'conflict timber' (UN, 2001). In Cambodia, the Khmer Rouge and other factions used proceeds from the timber trade to sustain their conflict. In Liberia, Taylor's NPFL was able to set-up a parallel economy in its area of control involving timber-for-arms trade. In this trade, many countries have been implicated of complicity. Global Witness reports that France and China, P5 members, were the major importers of Liberian timber (Global Witness, 2002). It is not surprising then that both countries opposed attempts to impose a ban on Liberian timber exports. Such a ban was only agreed after years of lobbying by NGOs and civil society groups in 2003.

Recent findings by prospecting companies have revealed that countries along the coast of West Africa are rich in oil. Already, Nigeria is one of the world's major oil producers. These findings have the potential of turning around the economic fortunes of these poor countries as happened in the Middle East. However, recent disturbing events in Equatorial Guinea involving an attempted coup sponsored by a number of Western interests have raised fears that oil will be the next extractive industry to fuel conflict in the sub-region. Nigeria has already confirmed these fears. In the Niger Delta region, groups of militant youths are engaged in constant battles with the security forces and oil companies over allegations of regional neglect.

Conclusion

Whilst every conflict has its own context-specific factors, certain common themes can be identified across the sub-region. This chapter has traced conflicts in West Africa to flawed colonial policies, negative Cold War impacts, patrimonial and clientelistic politics, and political manipulation of ethnic and religious differences as the primary causes. The role played by immediate factors in turning latent conflict to overt and violent war has also been recognised. Most of these factors are regional in nature and any framework for conflict resolution in West Africa should recognise this fact.

Conflicts in West Africa have had devastating political, economic and social effects on all the countries of the sub-region. In addition to the contagion effect of conflict and the problems of small arms proliferation, mercenaries and conflict diamonds that go with it, the sub-region has suffered enormous damage. The forced displacement and generation of massive refugee numbers have stretched the fragile economies of host countries to breaking points. Besides, the security problems that go with this mass refugee exodus cannot be overemphasised. Conflicts in the sub-region have also been long associated with the use of child soldiers. Across warring zones in the sub-region, the sight of an 8-year old carrying a gun is common. With no education and the right to enjoy their childhood, the future of many of these children has been adversely affected.

Chapter 1 linked state failure and collapse to conflict and vice versa. Most countries in West Africa are failed states and require massive efforts by the international community to revitalise and restore them. But the process of negotiating civil war peace settlements, implementing peacebuilding programmes and initiating a feasible conflict prevention programme has been hampered by a lack of knowledge of the fundamental causes of conflicts in West Africa.

Chapter 3

From ECOWAS to ECOMOG: The Evolution of ECOWAS Security Regionalism

Introduction

ECOWAS was established in 1975 by developing West African states as part of their strategy to promote economic development and prosperity for their respective countries. However, following widespread conflict and instability in the sub-region, the leaders came to the realisation that economic prosperity cannot be achieved in the absence of peace and security. Beginning with a process that saw the adoption of nascent security protocols in 1978, the region has today developed and institutionalised elaborate conflict resolution, peacekeeping and security mechanisms.

This chapter seeks to examine the evolution of ECOWAS from an economic integration project to that of a security organisation and examine the challenges inherent in such a transition. This background is essential in understanding the regional dynamics underlying the ECOWAS peacekeeping operations. By providing a historical perspective to ECOWAS regionalism, this chapter forms the basis for understanding the problems that faced ECOMOG such as the Francophone-Anglophone rivalry, Franco-Nigerian tensions, and the roots of Nigerian hegemonic ambitions. This historical background is followed by a review of ECOWAS' aims and institutional framework. A conceptualisation of ECOWAS' regionalism will form the background against which the economic record of the organisation will be evaluated. The next two sections trace the evolution of ECOWAS into security regionalism and attempt to provide a strong conceptual underpinning.

Historical Background to the Formation of ECOWAS

The creation of ECOWAS can be credited to a multiplicity of factors and actors. This initiative can be traced as far back as 1964 when President Tubman of Liberia spearheaded the creation of a West African free trade zone. Representatives from Cote d'Ivoire, Guinea and Sierra Leone met in Monrovia in August 1964 to discuss the possibility of implementing this proposal. This led to the convening of a West African Summit of free trade zone by the United Nations Economic Commission for Africa (UN ECA) in 1968 which was boycotted by the francophone states (Ojo, 1980). The rivalry between the Anglophone block and Francophone states was a major obstacle that threatened the formation of an inclusive sub-regional grouping. France played on the fear of Nigerian dominance expressed by Francophone states to discourage membership of a sub-region wide grouping including Nigeria. In its place, both France and the dominant Francophone states in the sub-region, Cote d'Ivoire and Senegal pushed for the formation of the *Communaute Economique de l'Afrique Occidentale* (CEAO) with exclusive membership of Francophone states. France's role in discouraging the idea of an all-inclusive West African integration body will be discussed in depth later in this section. Suffice it to say that this negative French influence indirectly galvanised support for the formation of ECOWAS.

General Gowon and President Eyadema of Nigeria and Togo respectively were very instrumental in bridging the gap between the two opposing camps in the sub-region and facilitating the formation of ECOWAS (Francis, 2001). To counter the threat posed by the Francophone CEAO, Togo and Nigeria announced in 1972 the creation of a West African Economic Community (WAEC) with open membership. In a bid to gain the support of smaller Francophone states, Nigeria adopted what Ojo (1980) refers to as 'spraying' diplomacy, the equivalent of America's 'dollar' diplomacy. This involves dishing out lavish grants, interest-free loans and concessionary oil prices. Another factor that shifted the support for integration was the oil crisis following the Yom Kippur War between Israel and its Arab neighbours in 1973. The sudden reduction of Western aid and investment was felt severely by the small West African states. For Nigeria, the sub-region's only oil producer at the time, this crisis was a big blessing as the revenue of the federal government rose from $758 million in 1970 to $2.17 billion in 1973 and 5.8 billion in 1975 (Adibe, 2002). This sudden boost in revenue widened the economic gap between Nigeria and the other states in the sub-region; hence making the idea of integration worthwhile to smaller states and also giving Nigeria the ability and confidence to spend more on the project of establishing ECOWAS. The project of regional integration also benefited enormously from the lobbying power of several groups and individuals. Ojo (1980) cited the support offered by the Nigerian Chamber of Commerce, Industry and Agriculture which culminated in the establishment of a West African Chamber of Commerce, Industry, Mines and Agriculture. An intellectual Think Tank in Nigeria also helped in mobilising support for the project. In addition to leaders like Gowon and Eyadema, individuals like Professor Adebayo Adedeji, then the Nigerian Commissioner for Economic Development, played a dominant role in the establishment of ECOWAS (Adibe, 2002). Following a regional tour of 12 countries by a joint Togolese and Nigerian delegation from July to August 1973, a meeting was convened in Lomé from 10–15 December 1973 to study the draft treaty. A panel of experts and jurists again met in Accra in January 1974 to study the draft and this was followed in January 1975 by a ministerial meeting in Monrovia. The treaty was finally signed by 15 West African states in Lagos on 28 May 1975. Cape Verde joined after independence in 1977 and Mauritania withdrew in 2001. Though the treaty establishing ECOWAS was signed in 1975, the organisation did not start functioning until January 1977 when the Executive Secretary was appointed (Asante, 1986).

Why was Nigeria interested in establishing a sub-regional economic grouping? Nigeria's motivation for the establishment of ECOWAS can be linked to three factors: Security, hegemonic ambitions, and the desire to expand its market. For Nigeria, French and Ivorian support for secessionists during the Civil War of 1967–1970 shifted the domestic debate in favour of integrationists. France reportedly set up a loan scheme with Cote d'Ivoire and Gabon to supply arms to Biafran rebels. French mercenaries were also sent to aid the Biafrans (Adebajo, 2000). French hostility to Nigeria goes back to 1961 when Nigeria severed diplomatic relations with France protesting that country's atomic tests in the Sahara. As the country is literally surrounded by Francophone neighbours, Nigeria's post-civil war foreign policy was geared towards strengthening economic and political ties with its neighbours so as to prevent them supporting any future secessionists. Considering the French role in aiding the Biafrans, Nigeria also concluded that the continued influence of France on its former colonies poses a major threat to its security. Replacing France as the sub-regional power will therefore serve the country's security interest.

Integrationists within Nigeria viewed the establishment of ECOWAS as 'an institutional framework for Nigeria's leadership and the erosion of France's political and economic influence' in the sub-region (Ojo, 1980, 584). Unlike Britain which had relatively weaker ties with its former colonies, the French maintained strong economic, political and military ties with what it regarded as its *pre carre* (backyard). For France, Africa remains a symbol of its great international power. A series of political, economic and military agreements made these former colonies largely dependent on France. With the exception of Guinea, all the Francophone countries in West Africa tied their currency, *Communaute Financiere Africaine* (CFA) to the French Franc. As a result, the French Treasury effectively had control over their economies. Cooperation agreements also gave France priority access to the strategic resources of Francophone countries. French *Cooperants* were assigned to these countries to provide technical assistance to ministries and public institutions. On the military sphere, France signed defence agreements with a number of Francophone West African states and even stationed French troops in Cote d'Ivoire and Senegal. Thus the major obstacle in Nigeria's hegemonic aspirations was France who, according to President Obassanjo, was bent on 'dismembering her and reducing her influence in francophone Africa' (Obasanjo, quoted in Adebajo, 2000, 186). Ibrahim Gambari (1991, 48) puts it bluntly, 'Nigeria considered it necessary to weaken if not break the ties between France and her former colonies in West Africa'. In Nigeria's calculations, a united and strong sub-regional economic grouping will invariably limit France's influence on her former colonies and consolidate Nigeria's status as sub-regional hegemon. Such a grouping will obviously be too difficult for France to manipulate. Whilst serving to diminish France's influence in the sub-region, ECOWAS also represents an expansion of the market for Nigerian goods and services. This reasoning was at the centre of the strong support given to integration by the Nigerian chamber of commerce.

Aims, Objectives and Institutional Framework of ECOWAS

Aims and Objectives

ECOWAS aims to promote economic integration through common market objectives such as trade liberalisation, harmonisation of economic, agricultural and fiscal policies, and free movement of the factors of production, ultimately leading to the establishment of an economic and monetary union. It also aims to 'raise the living standards of its peoples, and to maintain and enhance economic stability, foster relations among member states and contribute to the progress of the African continent' (ECOWAS, 1975).

The 1975 ECOWAS (Lagos) Treaty was replaced in 1993 by the Cotonou Treaty. This revised treaty reflects the changing economic, political and security landscape of the region. It extended cooperation from economic to political and security matters and called for the establishment of a single currency. Marking a significant shift from the provisions of Lagos, Cotonou included Fundamental Principles (Article 4) which call for the 'recognition, promotion and protection of human and peoples' rights' and most remarkably the 'promotion and consolidation of a democratic system of governance in each member state' (ECOWAS, 1993). This is recognition of the link between bad governance and conflict which continue to frustrate sub-regional economic objectives.

Structure and Institutions of the Organisation

In a bid to realise the objectives set above, the 1993 Treaty established a number of institutions to run the activities of the community. In January 2007, the ECOWAS Executive Secretariat was transformed into a Commission with enhanced powers to make it more efficient and capable of meeting the challenges of the twenty-first century. The following are the key institutions of the organisation:

Authority of Heads of States and Government: comprising heads of state and/or government of member states or their representatives, this body constitutes the highest decision making body of the organisation and is headed by a chairman elected on a rotational basis for one year. The Authority meets at least once a year and on extraordinary sessions. It determines the general policy of the community and also appoints the President of the ECOWAS Commission.

Council of Ministers: two ministers from each member state, including the one in charge of ECOWAS Affairs, constitute this council charged with the responsibility of supervising subordinate institutions and making recommendations to the Authority on policy matters. It meets twice a year and makes provision for extra ordinary meetings. The Chairmanship is held by the Minister responsible for ECOWAS Affairs of the member state serving as Chairman of the Authority.

ECOWAS Parliament: this is one of the innovations of the 1993 Treaty aimed at making the organisation more people-centred. Based in Abuja, Nigeria, the parliament convened in May 2002 with 115 MPs representing all the member states except Cote d'Ivoire. Although members have expressed the intention of acquiring legislative powers for the parliament, at present, it only acts on a consultative and advisory capacity.

Community Court of Justice: established in 1999, it takes over the work of the Tribunal and functions as the organisation's legal arm, responsible for interpreting the treaty and settling disputes brought to it by member states.

ECOWAS Commission: previously called the ECOWAS Executive Secretariat, the Commission is based in Abuja, and headed by a President who serves as the organisation's Chief Executive Officer charged with the responsibility of overseeing the day to day running of the community and its institutions. He/she is assisted by a Vice President and seven commissioners, each responsible for a clearly defined sector.

Specialised Aagencies: the following are the current specialised agencies:

- West African Health Organisation (WAHO);
- West African Monetary Agency (WAMA);
- West African Monetary Institute (WAMI);
- ECOWAS Youth & Sports Development Centre (EYSDC);
- ECOWAS Gender Development Centre (EGDC);
- Water Resources Coordination Unit (WRCU);
- ECOWAS Brown Card;
- The West African Power Pool (WAPP);
- The Inter-Governmental Action Group against Money Laundering and Terrorism Financing in West Africa (GIABA);
- West African Regional Health Programme (PRSAO).

Fund for Cooperation, Compensation and Development: it ensures the equal distribution of the benefits and costs of integration. The fund derives its finance from many sources which include contributions from members, external receipts, income from community enterprises and subsidies and contributions from various other sources.

Conceptualising West African Economic Integration

Regional integration initiatives have multiplied over the years and occupied an important place in contemporary international economic and political relations. The European integration experience which started with the formation in 1952 of the European Coal and Steel Community (ECSC) followed in 1957 by the European Economic Community (EEC) served as a model for most development oriented third world countries. The 1960s and 1970s therefore witnessed the proliferation of such groupings in Africa, Asia and Latin America. Third world nations just emerging from colonial rule came to regard regional integration as the answer to their economic problems and a way out of their disadvantaged position in the international political economy (Francis, 2001). By pooling their meagre resources together, these countries hope to promote industrialisation, expand trade and ultimately achieve greater political cohesion.

But despite the proliferation of economic regionalisms in Africa, there has been no corresponding attempt at providing a sound conceptual underpinning. Most of the theories used to explain regionalism in Africa are based on the European model and therefore most often lack applicability. This section will review the limited attempts by scholars to provide a conceptual interpretation of regionalism in the continent in general and West Africa in particular. It is however appropriate to start with a definition of the concept and a review of the classical theories. Regional integration is a political and economic process whereby a group of countries agree to reduce the barriers to trade between each other. El-Agraa (1999) defines it as 'a state of affairs or a process which involves the amalgamation of separate economies into larger free trading regions'. This process is said to have been successful when economies of a region become more closely entwined.

Integration is high on the research agenda of political and economic analysts. Several attempts have been made to develop a conceptual framework that will underpin this process. One of the earliest known theories is *functionalism* having as its main proponent David Mitranny. This theory posits that political divisions are a major source of conflicts between states. Such barriers can however be overcome by gradual cooperation at the economic level which will ultimately lead to political unification (Mitranny, 1996). However this theory was heavily criticised for being too normative and lacking analytical rigour (Mattli, 1999). *Neofunctionalism* refines the conceptual tools of functionalism and attempted to provide rigorous analysis. Propounded by Ernst Haas (1958), this theory assumes that integration is the only mechanism at the disposal of states for the purpose of maximising welfare. It shows how integration evolves over time using concepts like functional spill over, updating of common interests and the dynamics of sub-national and supranational groups. When applied to Africa, Francis (2001) considers this theory to be problematic as it is full of western assumptions which do not necessarily reflect the African reality. For him the African state 'lacks the capacity and institutional viability to lend itself to the integration process as prescribed by neo-functionalists' (2001, 32). This is further complicated by the difficulty in drawing a line between 'low' politics (involving socio-economic and welfare issues) and 'high' politics (security and foreign policy issues). He contends that the reality in Africa has confirmed that politics cannot be dissociated from economics.

The shortcomings of the above theories have led to the emergence of developmental regionalism as an alternative conceptual framework to regionalism in Africa. Regarded mainly as an economic development strategy, regionalism in Africa seeks to tackle underdevelopment in the continent by promoting economic development and improving its standing in the world economy. In a similar vein, Francis defines it as '... concerted efforts of states and non-state actors within a geographical area to enhance the economic efficiency and development of the region as a whole and to improve its position in the world economy' (2001, 32). This theory aims at improving the general welfare of the people. The preamble of the ECOWAS Treaty shares this aim and recognises the '... need to accelerate, foster and encourage the economic and social development of their states in order to improve the living standards of their people ...' (ECOWAS, 1993). By aiming at national and regional development, ECOWAS can therefore be located in this conceptual framework. A key strategy of development regionalism is market integration which espouses liberal economic policies based on capitalistic assumptions and models. But market integration alone cannot solve the economic problems of the sub-region if it is not followed by physical or infrastructural integration.

Evaluating ECOWAS Economic Regionalism

In trying to achieve its market integration objectives outlined above, the ECOWAS treaty provides for intra-community trade liberalisation, industrial and sectoral development, free movement of persons and currency harmonisation. The ECOWAS Trade Liberalisation Scheme came into force in January 1990 with the objective of creating a Customs Union among member states within a 15 year period. Such a union involves the elimination of customs duties and taxes amongst member states and the establishment of a common external tariff (ECOWAS, 2000). However, the efforts of the sub-region to achieve market integration through trade liberalisation have not been successful so far. As of 2000, only eight member states have lifted tariff barriers on unprocessed goods.

The situation is even worst for industrial goods: out of 15 member states, only Benin had honoured the agreements. Consequently, intra regional trade which was supposed to be boosted remained at a very low level increasing from 4 per cent to around 11 per cent over the first two decades of its existence (ECOWAS, 2000). Another attempt to stimulate intra-regional trade and market integration is the proposed monetary harmonisation. The plan was to establish a second monetary zone, the Eco comprising Guinea, The Gambia, Ghana, Nigeria and Sierra Leone. The Eco will circulate simultaneously with the CFA Franc for a specific period prior to the creation of a single currency for West Africa. However, the proposed single monetary union has not materialised. The initial target date of 2003 has been extended several times, first to 2005 and now to 2009. Even the new target date now seems to be unrealistic considering the economic and political conditions on the ground. The decision to postpone the launching was taken following the inability of the countries to satisfy the four convergence criteria for their economies prior to the introduction. These include a restriction on budget deficit to no more than 4 per cent by 2002, reducing inflation to 5 per cent by 2003, a ceiling on central bank financing of budget deficit to 10 per cent of the previous year's revenue and a minimum foreign reserve that would support at least six months of imports by 2003.

Developing the industrial capacity of the sub-region is another major feature of ECOWAS regionalism. However as noted above, ECOWAS has not been successful in boosting industrialisation. To enhance intra-regional trade and attract direct foreign investment, ECOWAS has developed a number of infrastructural projects. This is in realisation that economic integration will be meaningless without physical integration. The organisation has achieved some success in this sphere resulting in the construction of two major trans-West African highways: Trans-West African coastal highway and the Trans-Sahelian highway. Communication continues to be a problem in the sub-region with most calls between member states having to be routed through Paris or London (Francis, 2001). However, the organisation is making steady progress in this sector too. A telecommunications project, INTELCOM is being implemented which will ultimately link West African countries directly to each other (ECOWAS, 2000).

The protocol on visa free travel for ECOWAS citizens remains one of the visible symbols of the existence of ECOWAS amongst community citizens. Under this agreement, community citizens can reside in any ECOWAS state for up to 90 days without entry permit or a visa. In keeping with the provisions of this protocol, visa requirements have been abolished in all member states. However, the intended free movement of persons across borders remains difficult in much of West Africa as evidenced by Nigeria's expulsion of about 3 million ECOWAS citizens in 1985 and the recent xenophobic attacks on ECOWAS citizens in countries like Cote d'Ivoire and the Gambia. Most states still maintain numerous checkpoints and ECOWAS citizens are often subjected to harassment and extortion.

With more than 30 years since its formation, ECOWAS has had little impact on the economic development of the sub-region. Member states, with the exception of Nigeria and Cape Verde, fall within the World Bank's list of Highly Indebted Poor Countries (HIPC) whilst the standard of living is very low. Ten of the organisation's 15 members fall within the Low Human Development Category of the UNDP's Human Development Index Report of 2008. Unemployment rate is very high with a corresponding increase in the number of qualified personnel moving to the West in search of greener pastures. Industrialisation is still at a very low level resulting in insufficient diversification of national economies. This is compounded by the absence of reliable roads, telecommunications and energy infrastructure, bad economic policies in some states and failure to harmonise economic policies. What is responsible for this poor showing by ECOWAS? What has really gone wrong with all the lofty resolutions and protocols passed at Annual ECOWAS summits? External economic factors leading to the economic marginalisation of the continent have already been discussed in the previous chapter. Shaw and Okolo (1994, 7) observe that, 'the proliferation of structural adjustment projects has served to undermine orthodox regionalism even further, with their emphasis on extra-continental externalisation'. But external factors are not enough to explain ECOWAS' troubles. Internal problems and inadequacies do largely account for the organisation's failures. The non-payment of community dues is having a crippling effect on the operations of the organisation. According to the ECOWAS General Secretary, Ibn Chambers, as of August 2002, only five countries have fully paid up with countries like Liberia and Gambia owing 21 and 13 years arrears respectively (Chambers, 2002).

Another major factor impeding the progress of ECOWAS is the Francophone-Anglophone divide. As discussed in earlier sections of this chapter, this rivalry predates the formation of the organisation itself. This has resulted in the proliferation of several rival bodies representing the different linguistic groups. However the organisation that is posing the greatest challenge to ECOWAS is *Union Economique et Monétaire Ouest Africaine* (UEMOA). Founded in 1994, as a successor to CEAO, it is comprised of all Francophone member countries except Guinea which has traditionally been regarded a 'rebel' by 'loyal' Francophone states since opting out of the French Empire in 1958. UEMOA has similar objectives with ECOWAS, which in effect makes it a rival body. Not only is the organisation further polarising an already divided ECOWAS, it is also derailing the process of integration and widening the gulf between Anglophone and Francophone West Africa. Boafo-Arthur interprets this action to mean, 'the Anglophones are being told, we have opted out of ECOWAS; ECOWAS is now for the Anglophones and UEMOA for the Francophone' (2001, 6). The role of extra-regional powers in deepening this rivalry has already been discussed above.

The conflicts gripping the region seriously derailed the aims embodied in the Community's treaty. The Executive Secretary of the UNECA, K.Y. Amoako (1999) perfectly sums up the challenge posed by conflict to the sub-region:

> The critical factor keeping the West Africa sub-region at the bottom of the sustainability ladder is the prevalence of conflict. About 20 percent of Africa's people now live in countries formerly at war or severely disrupted by conflict, and low-intensity conflict is endemic in many others. Various manifestations of conflict and insecurity affect 20 of 47 countries, half of which are members of ECOWAS. It is not surprising, therefore, that of the six countries at the bottom of the sustainability rankings, half are ECOWAS member countries with a history of civil conflict.

These conflicts and economic stagnation led Kaplan (1994, 3) to paint a rather gloomy picture of West Africa:

> West Africa is becoming the symbol of worldwide democratic, environmental and societal stress, in which criminal anarchy emerges as the real 'strategic' danger. Disease, overpopulation, unprovoked crime, scarcity of resources, refugee migrations, the increasing erosion of nation-states and international drug cartels are now most tellingly demonstrated through a West African prism.

Despite raising some of the security concerns facing West Africa, Kaplan's analysis appears to be grossly exaggerated. The peacekeeping initiatives taken by ECOWAS and the relative stability of states like Ghana, Senegal and the Gambia undermines Kaplan's pessimistic analysis. However, the fact remains that ECOWAS has so far failed to meet the economic, social and political expectations of its citizens. Francis blames this on the poor implementation of ECOWAS decisions and the lack of political will and commitment by leaders who 'are often ready to adopt at summit level whatever policies or programmes that enhance their political credibility and prestige' (2001, 35).

Evolution of ECOWAS Security Regionalism

As noted above, the 1975 ECOWAS treaty provided no security role for the sub-regional grouping. This is not unique to ECOWAS, as several other regional organisations have gradually assumed security and foreign policy functions by default. The European Union is a classic case in point. Founded as an economic union, the EU has developed security and foreign policy capacity with the adoption of the Treaty of Maastricht and has been instrumental in devising the Common Foreign and Security Policy. Roper (1998) considers evolution into security regionalism to occur as a result of a military threat or instability. In the West African context, conflict and political instability in several member states made ECOWAS to realise that economic development cannot be achieved in the absence of peace and stability. The need to add a defence protocol to the ECOWAS Treaty became imperative in the 1970s when two ECOWAS states became the victims of external aggression. In November 1970, Guinea experienced an attempted invasion by Portuguese mercenaries whist Benin became the target of another failed mercenary attack in January 1977. Added to these cases of external aggression are the military coups prevalent through West Africa during the 1970s.

It is in this context of external aggression and internal instability that ECOWAS leaders moved to adopt measures that will safeguard the sub-region's security. The organisation's gradual movement into security started in 1978 when ECOWAS adopted the Non-aggression Treaty which called on member states to '... refrain from the threat and use of force or aggression' against each other (ECOWAS, 1978). Critics regard this protocol as merely idealistic as it failed to provide an institutionalised response mechanism in the case of a breach. In recognition of this weakness, West African leaders ratified the Mutual Assistance on Defence (MAD) Protocol at the 1981 Summit in Freetown, Sierra Leone and it came into force in September, 1986. This protocol committed member states to 'give mutual aid and assistance for defence against any armed threat or aggression' directed at a member state and considered them to constitute 'a threat or aggression against the entire community' (ECOWAS, 1981). The protocol spelt out the circumstances requiring action. These include cases of armed conflict between two or more member states after the failure of peaceful means, and in the case of conflict within a state 'engineered and supported from outside' (Art. 4). It created response mechanisms which include a Defence Council, Defence Committee and a sub-regional intervention force: the Allied Armed Forces of the Community (AAFC). However this protocol have been criticised for its lack of effective conflict prevention, management and resolution mechanisms. More over it focused heavily on external threats and did not envisage a role for the regional body in the coups that destabilised the sub-region in the 1970s and 1980s, and the internal conflicts that swept through West Africa in the 1990s. In addition to these limitations, the institutions provided for in this protocol were never established. A possible reason responsible for the non-implementation of this protocol lies in Francophone suspicions of Nigerian hegemonic ambitions. These suspicions were further deepened by the protocol's call for the withdrawal of foreign troops from all member states. With strong military ties with France, most of the Francophone West African states depended on their former colonial power for defence and security. In addition to these security concerns, the presence of a rival Francophone security mechanism adversely affected the chances of success of MAD. The *Accord de Non Aggression et d'Assistance en matière de Défense* (ANAD) was signed by Francophone West African states in 1977 following the border dispute between Mali and Burkina Faso. Unlike MAD, all the institutions of ANAD including its secretariat were made operational by 1981 (Dokken, 2002).

The Liberian crisis, which started in 1989, represents a critical stage in ECOWAS' transition to a security outfit. With no institutions to respond to the conflict, ECOWAS was forced to devise ad hoc security mechanisms for keeping the lid on this conflict. In May 1990, ECOWAS established a Standing Mediation Committee (SMC) charged with the responsibility of finding a peaceful resolution to the conflict. Following weeks of unproductive talks with various faction leaders in July 1990, the SMC took the bold step of establishing and deploying ECOMOG amidst bitter opposition from Taylor and some West African leaders. In neighbouring Sierra Leone, ECOMOG was able to reinstate the ousted President Kabbah and acted as the *de facto* army in the absence of a national army. In 1998, this ad hoc sub-regional peacekeeping force intervened to restore sanity to Guinea Bissau following a revolt in the national army. In December 2002 ECOWAS sent its peacekeeping mission to Cote d'Ivoire and in August 2003, a peacekeeping mission was deployed in Liberia for the second time. Chapter 9 shows how the lessons of ECOWAS interventions in these conflicts have helped it to institutionalise peace and security response mechanisms.

Conceptualising ECOWAS Security Regionalism

The ECOWAS conflict management and peacekeeping activities mentioned above have led to a lively debate aimed at providing it with a strong conceptual underpinning. Max Sesay (1999) describes it as a collective security arrangement. Collective security involves collective defence by a group of geographically proximate states against an external aggressor. Although existing pre-ECOMOG security arrangements within the sub-region supports this analysis, events since the end of the Cold War have made this conceptualisation inapplicable to West Africa. With state collapse and CPEs ravaging large parts of the sub-region, the major sources of threats to West African security are no longer external but internal. ECOWAS/ECOMOG has also been located within the security community debate (Francis, 2001). Pioneered by Karl Deutsch (1957), the theory of security communities was refined and popularised by Emmanuel Alder and Michael Barnet (1998). Deutsch defined a security community as 'a group of people which has become integrated ... there is real assurance that the members of that community will not fight each other physically, but will settle their disputes in some other way' (1957, 5). Adler and Barnet consider mutual trust and collective identity leading to similar orientations, cooperation and policy coordination as benchmarks for a security community. However both Deutsch and Alder and Barnet ignored the impact of internal instability to the evolution of security communities. Another notable oversight is the failure to feature Africa in the debate. However, David Francis considers ECOWAS as an evolving security community since '[T]he institutionalised system of co-operation and increasing socio-psychological transactions are gradually developing dependable expectations of peaceful change in inter-state relations' (2001, 55). But as Francis himself acknowledges, this is a contentious claim as evidenced by the intricate web of cross-border support for insurgencies across the sub-region.

In view of the inadequacies of the above concepts, this work will therefore conceptualise ECOWAS/ECOMOG as representing a security regionalism. Security regionalism is defined as 'security co-operation amongst geographically proximate states, usually acting under the auspices of a regional organisation. Co-operation among these regional states may also include increasing economic interdependence and other issue areas' (Francis, 2001, 53). The expansion of ECOWAS into security regionalism represents what Francis (2001) terms 'pragmatic incrementalism': the recognition that security is an indispensable element for economic regionalism. In the case of ECOWAS, the realisation that economic, social and environmental development cannot be achieved in a climate of widespread conflict and instability forced the sub-regional body to extend into security regionalism. But as the following chapters will show, this expansion has come with its own challenges and opportunities. Chapter 9 reviews the progress of ECOWAS security regionalism and the challenges it still faces.

Conclusion

Founded as an economic integration project, ECOWAS assumed security roles by default rather than by design. The conflagrations threatening to tear the sub-region apart adversely derailed the organisation's economic objectives and necessitated an extension into security regionalism. However, this transition has come with its own challenges and problems. The long-standing Anglophone-Francophone divide became more pronounced and seriously compromised the organisation's effectiveness, both in economic and security terms. These tensions are heightened by the disruptive role of extra-regional actors like France. Nigeria's status as a sub-regional hegemon has also proved contentious. Notwithstanding these hurdles, the organisation can be credited for taking steps to address the dangerous spread of conflicts.

Chapter 4
Duality of ECOMOG Intervention in Liberia: Alternating between Forcible and Non-Forcible Strategies

Introduction

On Christmas Eve 1989, Liberia erupted into a vicious civil war that resulted in the massive abuse of human rights and untold misery for civilians. World attention was however diverted to the ongoing Gulf crisis and major Western powers were becoming less interested in solving African problems. Even the US, which had been a major ally of Doe's despotic regime, was less interested in intervening to stop the carnage. This reflects the changing nature of international politics in which Africa became a marginal actor. It was against this background of a looming humanitarian crisis, lacking proper international attention that forced West African leaders to intervene in Liberia.

This chapter focuses on ECOMOG's forcible and non-forcible humanitarian efforts aimed at ameliorating the suffering of the Liberian people through means such as the creation of a 'safe haven', establishment of a security corridor for the operations of aid agencies, military action to force compliance from the warring factions and implementation of peacebuilding programmes to prevent a relapse into conflict. It therefore seeks an empirical understanding of what actually happens when humanitarian interveners are deployed in complex political emergencies. ECOMOG's twin track approach of forcible and non-forcible strategies had significant humanitarian results. However, this chapter argues that the lack of a coherent policy within ECOWAS towards Liberia undermined ECOMOG's peacemaking and peacebuilding programmes.

The chapter starts with an analysis of the Liberian conflict and provide a background to the deployment of ECOMOG troops and the dynamics of the Liberian conflict. This will help to contextualise ECOMOG's operations and provide the background upon which ECOWAS peacemaking efforts are to be understood and assessed. Next we move on to the debate surrounding ECOMOG's legitimacy and legality, reviewing opposing arguments amongst academics, politicians, diplomats and military personnel and taking a position which will be informed by the conceptual framework in Chapter 1. We will then focus on the establishment and protection of safe heavens. This section will look at the military capacity of the force in protecting vulnerable civilians and the challenges it faced including the sub-regional geopolitics. This will form the basis for an examination of ECOMOG's human rights record. As ECOMOG did not act in a vacuum, its relationship with aid agencies and co-deployment with UN forces will also be studied to reveal the effect they had on humanitarian efforts in the country. The last section will focus on the peacebuilding programmes implemented by ECOMOG which were designed to prevent a relapse into conflict and ask whether such programmes achieved their aims.

'Sowing the Seeds of Terror': The Making of the Liberian Civil War

Though the triggers of the Liberian conflict lay in the decade-long misrule and excesses of the Doe regime, the roots of the conflict can be traced back to the 1820s when freed slaves from America were settled in the country. A combination of ethnic factors, economic, social and political inequalities as well as external influences contributed to the outbreak of the brutal war that ravaged this poor West African country. The 'apartheid' policy of the settler Americo-Liberians sowed the seed of the years of brutal conflict that were to come. Comprising less than 5 per cent of the country's 1.8 million people (Mackinlay and Alao, 1995), the Americo-Liberians dominated all aspects of the country's political, social and economic life and effectively marginalised the indigenous population. Since gaining independence from the American Colonisation Society in 1847, only the settler-dominated True Whig Party ruled the country till 1980. In addition to the True Whig Party, the Masonic Temple and Church provided social and political cohesion for the settler community and ensured their total domination of the indigenous population. Unless they convert to Christianity and adopt the settlers' Western lifestyle, indigenous Liberians were barred from holding public office. This was in line with what the Americo-Liberians considered their 'civilising mission,' meant to assimilate the Aborigines into Western civilisation. Such an ideology was based on the erroneous assumption that the settlers were 'civilised,' whilst the indigenes were 'primitive and backward' and therefore in need of civilisation (Ofuatey-Kodjoe, 1994). The marginalisation of the aboriginals was completed with economic exploitation and the use of slave labour. Allegations of forced labour attracted international attention in 1921 and led to an investigation by the League of Nations (Mackinlay and Alao, 1995). As will be expected, these discriminatory policies had the effect of fomenting the resentment of the local population against the settlers.

William Tubman (president from 1947 to 71) attempted to introduce token reforms. These included the removal of the property qualifications for voting, an increased access to education and an open door policy to foreign investors to exploit the country's natural resources. However, Tubman maintained his tight grip on power through a combination of clientelistic politics and suppression of opponents. These half-hearted reforms created more problems for his regime. His economic policies led to the birth and mobilisation of new social movements among the natives and a period of social upheaval. These groups, including workers, students and soldiers became increasingly aware of the extent of their political and economic marginalisation and the economic disparity between them and the minority Americo-Liberians (Ofuatey-Kodjoe, 1994). William Tolbert (president from 1971 to 80) continued Tubman's integrationist and open door policy. The increased political consciousness created by these piecemeal reforms led to more agitation for increased political participation, access to economic and social opportunities and curbing of corruption, which was endemic in the country. The government's response to these demands was ruthless intimidation and repression. This resulted in a series of protests that served to increase native opposition to the regime. Negative forces of the international market further worsened this state of internal instability. The oil crisis of the 1970s and the slump in iron ore and rubber sales (Liberia's major exports) contributed to massive economic deterioration whilst international aid plummeted from US$80 million in 1975 to a mere US$44 million in 1976. At the same time, external debt rose to an alarming figure of US$168 million in 1976 with inflation hitting a record high of 11.4 per cent (Mackinlay and Alao, 1995). A direct consequence of the high oil prices was a significant increase in the price of rice, the country's staple food. This resulted in the 'Rice Riots' of 1979 which created the atmosphere that precipitated the coup of Master Sergeant Samuel Doe. The coup resulted in widespread brutality and human rights violations. Although the international community condemned the coup for its excesses, the local population welcomed it and many saw it as signalling the end to 'alien rule.'

However the euphoria that greeted the Doe coup did not last long as he merely replaced Americo-Liberian dominance with Khran rule. Even though they were poorly educated and represented only about 4 per cent of the total population, Doe placed his Khran people and their Mandingo allies into all the strategic positions of the land and marginalised the other ethnic groups. Thus what started as a united front soon fragmented. By 1983, Doe had eliminated most of his supporters including his academic allies, Movement for Justice in Africa (MOJA) and all 16 non-commissioned officers, with whom he had staged the coup. Corruption became endemic and the economy virtually collapsed. Doe rigged the 1985 elections and transformed himself into a civilian president. Opposition to his rule was crushed with ruthless brutality. A coup staged by his former friend, Thomas Quiwonkpa in November 1985 was met with unprecedented reprisals and intimidation of his Gio and Mano ethnic groups of Nimba County. Three thousand people, including women and children, were reportedly massacred (Mackinlay and Alao, 1995). This heavy-handed treatment created a strong anti-Doe movement. As a brother-in-law of Quiwonkpa, Charles Taylor, a former official in Doe's government, exploited the resentment of Gios and Manos and recruited the bulk of his forces from this area and used the region as the launching pad for his rebellion in December 1989.

ECOMOG Intervention in Liberia

Through the hegemonic leadership of the Nigerian President General Ibrahim Babangida, ECOWAS in May 1990 established the SMC charged with the responsibility of finding a peaceful resolution to the conflict. It is important to note that the initial SMC mandate reflects ECOWAS traditional approach to inter-state conflict which heavily relies on pacific settlement – an approach completely unsuitable to CPEs. However, following weeks of unproductive talks with various faction leaders in July 1990, SMC took the bold step of establishing and deploying ECOMOG, amidst bitter opposition from Taylor and other West African leaders such as Campaore and Houphet-Boigny. The debate surrounding the legality of ECOMOG and the division it generated within ECOWAS will be discussed later in the chapter. Under the code name *Operation Liberty*, ECOMOG landed in Liberia on 24 August 1990 with the stated mandate of 'keeping the peace, restoring law and order and ensuring that the cease fire is respected' (quoted in Taw and Grant-Thomas, 1999). However this mandate was very ambitious as there was no peace to keep neither was there any cease-fire to observe. This reflects the traditional 'chapter six and half' mandate which is completely unsuitable to the Liberian conflict. The initial ECOMOG force in August 1990 was made up of 4,000 troops with 70 per cent coming from Nigeria while the rest came from Ghana, Guinea, Gambia and Sierra Leone. At its peak in 1994, ECOMOG comprised about 15,000 troops with Nigerians forming more than 70 per cent of the total.

Table 4.2   Composition of ECOMOG, February 1993

Country	No. of troops
Gambia	150
Ghana	1,500
Guinea	600
Mali	6
Nigeria	9,000
Sierra Leone	700

Source: Clement E. Adibe (2002, 121).

On the political and diplomatic front, the SMC convened the All Liberia Conference on 27 August 1990 attended by 17 Liberian political parties and interest groups. The conference noted the absence of a credible government in Monrovia and therefore agreed to establish an Interim Government of National Unity (IGNU) with Dr Amos Sawyer, an academic and long-time opponent of Doe, as its president, to be assisted by Bishop Ronald Diggs. The interim administration was given the task of facilitating national reconciliation and conducting elections. Taylor's NPFL, which boycotted the conference, responded by forming its own National Patriotic Reconstruction Assembly (NPRA), ensuring 90 per cent of Liberian territory was under NPFL control. Even the embattled Doe refused to handover his crumbling administration to the IGNU.

Meanwhile, as participants debated the future of Liberia in the conference, ECOMOG was engaged in fierce fighting with the NPFL. In responding to this attack, ECOMOG compromised its neutrality by aligning with the Independent National Patriotic Front of Liberia (INPFL), a splinter group of the NPFL. These alliances with warring factions were to characterise the military strategy of ECOMOG in the years to come and seriously derail their efforts. A temporary truce negotiated by ECOMOG in early September was shattered when forces of the INPFL exploited the free access it had to ECOMOG HQ by abducting and brutally murdering Doe and his bodyguards. This incident caused serious embarrassment for ECOMOG and led to the replacement of General Quainoo with the Nigerian General Joshua Dogonyaro who was able to establish a 20km security perimeter around Monrovia and force the NPFL to agree a ceasefire that was to last for about two years. An extraordinary summit of ECOWAS was held in Bamako, Mali in late November, in which it was decided to convene a new All Liberia Conference. But when the conference was convened in March 1991, Taylor's NPFL again refused to participate. This marked the beginning of a long and often cumbersome process of peace talks and ceasefire agreements which were hardly respected. In response, ECOMOG's mandate was revised to include peace enforcement as the situation on the ground dictates.

Dynamics of the Liberian Conflict: Escalation and De-escalation

To understand the context within which ECOMOG operated, it will be proper to give an overview of the dynamics of the Liberian conflict. This will also help in understanding ECOMOG's strategy of shifting between peacekeeping and peace enforcement and the challenges faced by the sub-regional force. The Liberian conflict has been characterised by periods of intense fighting and interspersed by periods of relative peace and quiet. A total number of four major battles can be identified in the period between November 1990 and April 1996. The first period, marking the beginning of the war in 1989 lasted till November 1990 when ECOMOG established a security zone around Monrovia. This relative peace was shattered in October 1992 when Taylor's NPFL launched a surprise attack on ECOMOG positions in Monrovia code named 'Operation Octopus'. With the assistance of the Armed Forces of Liberia (AFL) and United Liberian Movement for Democracy (ULIMO) fighters, ECOMOG was able to repulse the invasion and subsequently enlarge the security zone to Robertsfield International Airport, the Firestone Rubber Plantation at Harbel and the port of Buchanan. This round of fighting came to an end with the signing of the Cotonou ceasefire agreement in July 1993. However, the in-fighting within ULIMO which resulted in the splintering of that faction into ULIMO-K and ULIMO-J (followers of Kromah and Johnson respectively) marked the collapse of the cease-fire in late 1993 to 1994. The third major battle started in September 1994 when ULIMO-K and a coalition of the Liberian Peace Council (LPC), AFL, Lofa Defence Force (LDF) and ULIMO-J attacked NPFL positions. The Abuja Accord signed in August 1995 brought a temporary truce. The last major battle erupted in April 1996 when the NPFL and ULIMO-K attempted to arrest Roosevelt Johnson for allegations of murder.

In addition to the constantly changing security situation, the conflict in Liberia was also characterised by the proliferation of factions starting from two and growing to eight. This splintering and proliferation of factions is partly due to the personal tensions and political differences of faction leaders. This can also be linked to the desire of warlords to exploit Liberia's war economy as discussed in Chapters 1 and 2. This selfish political and economic ambition led to the breakaway of Prince Yormie Johnson from the NPFL to form his own INPFL. The emergence of new and breakaway factions can also be linked to the ethnic dimension of the Liberian conflict. Faction leaders have manipulated these differences to recruit and mobilise support for their factions. The splintering of ULIMO into J and K wings (Khran and Mandigoe respectively) represents the most extreme of these cases. There were also reports that bigger factions created sub-factions to act as proxy. The LDF and Bong Defence Force (BDF) linked to the NPFL and ULIMO-K respectively are examples. As will be seen in later sections of this chapter, this dimension of the Liberian conflict seriously derailed ECOWAS/ECOMOG humanitarian and peacemaking efforts.

In response to the fluid and dynamic security situation highlighted above, ECOMOG has been very flexible in shifting between peacekeeping and peace enforcement. This flexibility was a blessing in disguise as it allowed the force to adapt to the ever changing dynamics of the Liberian conflict. In light of the complexities of post-Cold War conflicts, this approach can be seen as a pragmatic response to the volatile and unpredictable nature of CPEs. ECOMOG therefore resorted to force to compel the warring factions to respect the terms of the numerous agreements they sign and violate. Force was also employed to protect the Monrovia 'Safe Zone' and safeguard aid efforts. However, ECOMOG was able to shift to non-forcible humanitarian strategies as and when events on the ground permitted it. These include traditional peacekeeping functions, negotiations with rebel leaders on the ground, confidence building visits to rebel-held territories, humanitarian assistance and peacebuilding programmes. But like many other military missions in volatile environments, this transition has come with its own challenges.

Besides the situation on the ground, the use of force has also to a large extent depended on the personal military and leadership styles of individual Field Commanders. This is partly due to the lack of a clear mandate and effective control of the force by the parent body, ECOWAS. For instance, General Dogonyaro is known for his no nonsense approach, which led to the successful offensive against the NPFL and the establishment of a buffer zone around Monrovia in November 1990. His successor, Rufus Kupolati on the other hand was more diplomatic. In a bid to get the cooperation of the various rebel forces, he initiated confidence visits to rebel strong holds (Da Costa, 1991). General Malu, the last ECOMOG Commander is reputed to combine Dogonyaro's no nonsense military style and Kupolati's diplomatic approach (West Africa, 1997).

Rationale for and Legitimacy of ECOMOG Intervention

Like many other cases of humanitarian intervention, questions surrounding the legality and legitimacy of the ECOMOG intervention have generated heated debate within policy and academic circles. In a damning criticism of ECOMOG intervention, Ofodile (1994) argued that ECOWAS lacked the legal and political basis for intervention. He cited the absence of structures and institutions within ECOWAS for such an intervention, lack of consensus within ECOWAS and UN Security Council Mandate as evidence of its lack of legitimacy. Although his argument appears to be heavily legalistic, Ofodile's analysis deserves some attention as it raises very important and substantive issues. The failure of ECOWAS to develop the security mechanisms provided for by successive security protocols and treaties was highlighted in Chapter 3. It is also a fact that the two main security agreements before 1989 only focused on external threats and did not envisage a role for ECOWAS in civil wars. As argued by Ofodile, the lack of consensus within ECOWAS over intervention in Liberia was also a major blow to the legality of the intervention. As indicated above, the decision to intervene was only taken by a committee of ECOWAS (the SMC) with full sub-regional authorisation coming only after four months (November 1990). However, the lack of consensus within ECOWAS over the intervention is not enough to rob the mission of its legitimacy. Chapter 2 explored the Taylor-Houphouet-Boigny-Campoare and Gadaffi connection. The fact that these countries were strong opponents of the mission was understandable considering the role they played in propping up Taylor and his rebellion. President Campaore, an open supporter of Taylor, was more outspoken in his opposition declaring that the SMC had 'no competence to interfere in a member state's internal conflicts' (President Campaore, quoted in da Costa, 1991). The historical divide between Francophone and Anglophone countries within the sub-region can also help explain the lack of consensus over ECOMOG. As a result of this divide, Cote d'Ivoire as a member of the UN Security Council at the time was very reluctant to have the Liberian conflict on the Council's agenda (Anning, 1994).

From a restrictionist point of view, the lack of a UN Security Council mandate clearly undermined the legality of ECOMOG. However, the fact that the mission received retrospective UN Security Council mandate two years after its intervention suggests that the UN was tacitly in support of its actions. In an address to diplomats in Bajul, President Jawara revealed that he has the backing of UN Secretary-General who wished ECOMOG success and confirmed that the mission would not need Security Council authorisation (da Costa, 1991). The Chairman of the OAU at the time, Yuweri Musuveni also supported the intervention. The fact that the Security Council failed to respond to the unfolding humanitarian emergency in Liberia also undermines Ofodile's argument.

In these circumstances, ECOMOG operations in Liberia can be better justified and understood on humanitarian grounds. This chapter will not revisit the debate on humanitarian intervention, which has already been done in great detail in Chapter 1. Suffice it to note that in the midst of massive human rights abuses and the danger of the conflict engulfing the entire sub-region, ECOWAS cannot afford to wait for UN authorisation. The international neglect towards Liberia has already been noted above and the fact is the UN and the international community were more concerned with the situation in the Gulf. Waiting for a UN Resolution whilst thousands of people continue to die would have been irresponsible on the part of ECOWAS. OAU Secretary-General, Salim Salim also considered the intervention justified 'from the point of view of the sanctity of human life'. He went on to say: 'To argue that there was no legal base for any intervention in Liberia is surprising. Should the countries in West Africa, should Africa just leave the Liberians to fight each other? Will that be more legitimate?' (Salim, interview in *West Africa*, October 1990). Although past humanitarian interveners have been cautious in justifying their actions on humanitarian grounds, ECOWAS had no hesitation in doing that. In its final Communiqué issued in August 1990, the SMC of ECOWAS advanced a humanitarian justification for intervening, which we will quote in length:

> The failure of the warring parties to cease hostilities ... led to the massive destruction of property and the massacre by all the parties of thousands of innocent civilians including foreign nationals, women and children, some of whom had sought sanctuary in churches, hospitals, diplomatic missions and under Red Cross protection contrary to all recognised standards of civilised behaviours. Worse still, there are corpses lying unburied in the cities and towns, which could lead to a serious outbreak of an epidemic. The result of all this is a state of anarchy and the total breakdown of law and order in Liberia. Presently, there is a government in Liberia which cannot govern and contending factions which are holding the entire population as hostage, depriving them of health facilities and other basic necessities of life. (ECOWAS, 1990, *Final Communique of the Standing Mediation Committee on Liberia*, Decision A/DEC.1/8/90)

In reaffirming the ECOWAS position, the Chairman of the organisation, Gambia's Dauda Jawara stated that '… the mission is strictly humanitarian'. He went on to say, 'ECOWAS states cannot stand idly by and watch a member state slide into anarchy' (Dauda Jawara, quoted in da Costa, 1991, 1076). There is ample evidence to justify ECOWAS' humanitarian claim. There were widespread human rights abuses by all warring factions. Among the most despicable of these abuses were the massacre of about 600 Gios and Manos who were seeking refuge at St Peter's Church in Monrovia; the abduction and subsequent killing of about 40 people who had taken refuge at the UN compound in Monrovia; and the reprisal ethnic killings (Human Rights Watch, 1993). The Liberian conflict resulted in unprecedented humanitarian crisis and claimed the lives of an estimated 150,000 civilians and forced 700,000 to flee into neighbouring countries (UN, Sept, 1997). The effect on the security and economy of regional countries was devastating.

However, many critics of the ECOMOG Mission have questioned this humanitarian motive. For E.K. Aning (1994) the real motive behind West African involvement was the fear of the conflict spreading to neighbouring countries. A massive refugee influx into Sierra Leone, Guinea and Cote d'Ivoire, and the danger of small arms proliferation, were becoming causes for concern. Added to these is the inclusion of nationals of other West African states, notably Sierra Leone, Guinea, Ghana, Togo and The Gambia, in the rebel force of Taylor. A military victory by Taylor was seen as the start of a region-wide invasion. This was a fact President Jawara of Gambia acknowledged in an address to diplomats: 'If Charles Taylor, with the support of what I may call mercenaries from the other countries of the sub-region, were to come into power by force, one can imagine the implications it would have for sub-regional stability' (Dauda Jawara quoted in *West Africa*, December 1990, 2894). Francis (1999) therefore reasoned that the major factor responsible for ECOWAS involvement was the desire of leaders to secure their positions against the spreading rebel menace in the sub-region. But the fear of the contagion effects of the Liberian conflict is not necessarily contradictory to ECOWAS' stated humanitarian motive. As discussed in Chapter 1, humanitarian intervention in the post-Cold War era is a response to both the massive human rights abuses within a country's borders, as well as the potential spill over effects on neighbouring countries.

Other critics argue that the ECOMOG intervention was a manifestation of Nigeria's hegemonic ambitions (Adebajo, 2002). Chapter 3 provided a historical background to Nigeria's hegemonic aspirations. Whilst hegemonic aims might have played a role in the decision to intervene, however, humanitarian intervention cannot be completely dissociated from political calculations. This political undertone should however not cloud the important task of saving lives and alleviating the suffering of millions of people. Closely linked with the above are critics who regard the ECOMOG intervention as Nigeria's ploy to support the beleaguered Doe regime (Mortimer, 1996). They point to the fact that President Babangida was a close friend and supporter of Doe.

The Liberian leader even named a major road and a Graduate School of International Relations after him. The Sierra Leonean Leader, Joseph Momoh was a close friend of Banbagida and not in good terms with Charles Taylor, whose appeal for assistance he turned down. Guinea's Lansana Conte was said to be alarmed by the targeting of Mandingoes and Muslims by Taylor's predominantly Mano and Gio fighters. Whilst not dismissing the link between Babangida and Doe, it is worth pointing to the fact that from the beginning of the Liberian Peace Process, Nigeria and the SMC called for the resignation of Doe and the installation of an interim government. We therefore regard the ECOMOG intervention as justified on humanitarian grounds, and considers attempts to de-legitimise the mission and focus solely on restrictionist legalism as ignoring the security and humanitarian catastrophe affecting millions of people in Liberia and beyond.

The Establishment and Protection of Safe Havens

There has been growing interest in the study and analysis of safe havens since the establishment of the security zone to protect the Kurds in Iraq in 1991. This has seen a number of studies on the Kurdish, Bosnian and Rwandan cases. Although the ECOMOG intervention started before all the above cases, it has received little or no attention in the 'safe havens' literature.

Despite the strong humanitarian justification for its intervention in Liberia, the force lacked a clear humanitarian mandate and a coherent humanitarian policy. It therefore took on humanitarian roles by default. Notwithstanding this weakness, ECOMOG was able to establish a *de facto* safe haven in Monrovia and its environs between 1990 and 1997, with the zone coming under attack in 1992 and 1996. As well as protecting the perimeter of the security zone from external NPFL attacks, ECOMOG also took on internal policing roles aimed at maintaining law and order within the zone. This ensured that there was a semblance of security and safety, some basic facilities like water supply, shelter, medical care and education. Another positive outcome of ECOMOG's safe haven was the cessation of reprisal ethnic killings discussed above. In sharp contrast, areas outside ECOMOG control and under factions were considered high risk with high incidence of rape, torture, hunger and insecurity. A study carried out by Outram (1997) shows a vast difference in the quality of life between people living in the ECOMOG zone and those without. As a result, Monrovia attracted so many displaced people searching for the relative stability ECOMOG could provide. With a pre-war population of around 400,000, Monrovia became home to an estimated 1.3 million people by January 1995 (Outram, 1997). In addition to their security functions, ECOMOG troops are also reported to have provided limited amount of humanitarian aid. Although this does not form part of their official mandate, individual units were able to share their rations with the deprived people of Monrovia (Anste, 1997). This act of generosity deserves commendation, especially when one considers the fact that at the height of the war, most UN and aid agencies abandoned Liberians to fend for themselves. However, this has also exposed a fundamental flaw in the conception and planning of the ECOMOG operation. The failure to incorporate humanitarian assistance in a complex emergency such as Liberia's was a serious mistake on the part of ECOWAS. General Iweze, ECOMOG's first Chief of Staff recalled the dilemma they faced with displaced people, 'The refugee situation was reviewed at the planning stages. But surprisingly, in spite of this, the ECOWAS HQ did not treat this issue with the same degree of importance it deserves … Their presence was to pose a problem to us' (quoted in Funmi Olonisakin, 1999, 20). However, in line with the ad hoc nature of the force, ECOMOG was able to respond to these difficulties. At the height of the fighting in Monrovia in 1990, ECOMOG reportedly evacuated civilians in their naval boats to the relative safety of neighbouring countries (*West Africa*, October–November 1990). The multiplicity of roles performed by ECOMOG soldiers prompted *West Africa* Magazine to describe the force as a 'policeman, bodyguard, wet-nurse, social worker and psychiatrist in a city in desperate need of rehabilitation' (*West Africa*, October–November 1990). Even Human Rights Watch, a strong critic of ECOMOG was forced to admit, 'one would be hard-pressed to visit Monrovia without hearing, time and again, "Thank God for ECOMOG"' (Human Rights Watch, 1993, 6). This sentiment is still echoed today in Monrovia, years after the ECOMOG operation.

However, the ECOMOG security zone has had its own failures, weaknesses and excesses. A key failure was its inability to expand its geographical reach beyond the confines of Monrovia, thereby leaving the vast majority of the population under predatory warlords who control up to 90 per cent of the country. Another major weakness of the ECOMOG safe haven was its military instability. On two occasions, in 1992 and 1996, the safe haven came under heavy attack from armed factions which led to heavy loss of life. Whilst ECOMOG could not be dislodged from the city, it however failed in its primary role of safeguarding civilians. Several factors can help explain this weakness, not least the endemic problems of limited resources and logistics, poor conditions of the troops and insufficient intelligence. The force's mandate was not matched by adequate resources and troops. Taking into consideration the weak economies of countries in the sub-region and the international neglect of the operation, this problem was not unexpected. The US gave very limited assistance towards logistics when it contracted the private security company, Pacific Architects and Engineers (PAE). This was in line with the US policy of distancing itself from the undemocratic Nigerian regime which it had decertified for its alleged involvement in the narcotics drugs trade (Howe, 1996). The little support it gave mostly went to other contingents in the force especially the Senegalese and East Africans who joined at later stages. The Special Emergency Fund established by the SMC to solicit funds from donors received few donations. Nigeria therefore shouldered the bulk of the financial burden with some estimates putting it as high as 90 per cent (Adebajo, 2002). The number of troops, which peaked at 15,000, was also relatively small to engage an estimated rebel force of 60,000. As Outram puts it, 'the ECOMOG intervention has been too small to dissuade the factions from mounting attacks on the safe zone' (1997, 201). The force's military capability was also adversely compromised by the lack of consensus within ECOWAS at the political level and the inter-contingent rivalries and coordination problems at the ground level. The sub-section below examines the impact of these differences on the effectiveness of the force. In addition to the above weaknesses, ECOMOG's response to these attacks have brought to the fore a plethora of other issues including the force's human rights record, its association with warring factions, its relationship with the humanitarian aid community and UN observers. As these issues are key to any analysis of ECOMOG humanitarian intervention, they will be addressed in latter sections of this chapter.

The Politics of Sub-regional Humanitarian Intervention: The Francophone Dimension and Inter-force Relations

Chapter 3 provides a historical perspective on the Anglophone-Francophone rivalry within ECOWAS. Disagreements over ECOMOG intervention in Liberia exacerbated these long standing tensions. For the greater part of ECOMOG operations, Francophone states were less cooperative with some even supporting rebel groups against ECOMOG. With the notable exception of Guinea, no Francophone state contributed troops to the initial ECOMOG force. Even Togo and Mali, the two Francophone members of the SMC declined to contribute troops. Senegal, with an enviable record in UN peacekeeping chose instead to contribute troops to the US-led enforcement action against Iraq in 1991 (*West Africa*, October 1990). Taylor therefore persistently pointed to the Nigerian dominance of ECOMOG as an excuse for failing to disarm. In a bid to neutralise this Nigerian dominance and address the apparent anomaly over non participation of Francophone states, the US encouraged Senegal, a key regional ally to contribute a contingent. The offer of $15 million worth of military aid was too attractive for Senegal to decline. Deployment of Senegalese forces started in October 1991. With years of UN peacekeeping experience behind them, the Senegalese were said to have performed exemplary (Mortimer, 1996). However, their commitment to the ECOMOG intervention was tested on 28 May 1992 when six of its troops were killed by NPFL forces in the market town of Vahun. With growing domestic pressure, President Diouf announced the withdrawal of his country's forces from Liberia with effect from January 1993. Hence, the Senegalese presence which was meant to bridge the gap between Francophone and Anglophone states over Liberia ended before it could have any meaningful impact on the conflict.

Differences over ECOMOG policy were not only confined to disagreements between Anglophone and Francophone countries. There were tensions even between Ghana and Nigeria, the major troop contributors. The arbitrary removal of General Quainoo as Force Commander following the brutal murder of Doe considerably strained relations between Ghana and Nigeria. Ghana complained that it was not informed of the decision and only heard about it on the BBC. The Ghanaian press was very loud in calling for the withdrawal of their troops. In response to what it perceived as Nigeria's unilateral action, the Rawlings government attached several conditions on the use of its troops. These tensions reflect the fundamental difference of policy and doctrine between the two main ECOMOG countries. Whilst Nigeria preferred enforcement action, Ghana was more disposed to traditional peacekeeping and peaceful resolution of the conflict. In a letter to the ECOWAS Executive Secretary, the Ghanaian Foreign Minister Obed Asamoah said Ghanaian troops should 'maintain only a defensive posture' and not engage in any offensive fighting (quoted in Adebajo, 2002). This difference in doctrine can partly be attributed to differences in training in the military academies of the various countries. There is also a longstanding rivalry for sub-regional hegemony between these two powers that goes back to the Pan-Africanist days of Kwame Nkrumah.

The differences that manifested at the political and diplomatic level were also evident on the ground. There were glaring instances of inter-contingent tensions and problems with command and control. These problems were made worse by the language divide between the majority Anglophone troops and the Francophone contingent from Guinea. Even before leaving Freetown for Monrovia, tensions between the two main contingents were evident. The Ghanaian battalion commander, for instance, refused to take orders from his Nigerian ECOMOG Chief of Staff. In another instance, Gen. Sani Abacha, then Chief of the Nigerian Army sent a letter to the ECOMOG commander, Gen. Quinoo asking for the return of all Nigerian officers above the rank of colonel because Lamine Magasoumba, the Guinean Deputy Force Commander was only a lieutenant colonel therefore Nigerian officers could not serve under him. The Guinean authorities had to promote him to the rank of Major General before the Nigerians allowed their officers to stay (Adebajo, 2002). On the ground, the Guineans complained that their contingents were given more difficult assignments and see this as a strategy to eliminate the only Franco-phone contingent. The lack of standardised equipment, arms and ammunition and problems of interroptability also affected coordination efforts and compromised the force's effectiveness (Taw and Grant-Thomas, 1999).

The most damaging factor to inter-force relations was the excessive control by home governments over contingents. This resulted in the issuing of different and sometimes conflicting orders. The ECOMOG command has at its head the Force Commander and the commanders of the various contingents serve as his deputies. Ideally the force commander issues operational commands to his deputies to carry out in their respective mission areas. However there were reports that some contingents were withdrawn from their areas of deployment without the permission and knowledge of the Force Commander thus putting the lives of other contingents under considerable risk. Other contingents are also reported to have refused deployment in certain areas without the consent of their home governments (Khobe, 2000). This was possible due to the absence of an effective ECOWAS oversight of the mission. The inability of ECOWAS to control ECOMOG was to a very large extent due to the absence of institutional capacity to direct a peace support operation. As stated in Chapter 3, the institutional mechanisms stipulated by various security treaties were not in place at the time of ECOMOG deployment. This situation was worsened by the lack of prior experience of humanitarian intervention on the part of ECOWAS. Another problem that beset ECOWAS was its inability to fund the operation as agreed. The agreement called for troop contributing countries to fund themselves for the first month after which ECOWAS will take over. As this never happened, it became very difficult for ECOWAS to control a force it can not fund. The absence of an ECOWAS representative on the ground for the greater part of the mission also reduced ECOWAS' political control on ECOMOG. The ECOWAS representative was withdrawn in 1992 citing difficulty of funding. With all these debilitating factors on the way of ECOWAS, it came as no big surprise that troops took orders directly from their home governments, thus relegating the role of the parent body to diplomacy and peacemaking. In the absence of effective ECOWAS control of the force, Nigeria exploited the situation to consolidate her hegemonic position in the sub-region. However, Nigeria's regional dominance has been greatly resented by other sub-regional powers, especially Francophone countries and Ghana, and the regional politics and conflict management and resolution efforts have been seriously shaped by this factor.

Civil-Military Coordination: ECOMOG and the Protection of the Humanitarian Corridor

Following the widespread human rights abuses and breakdown of security in the wake of the NPFL invasion, UN agencies and most NGOs pulled out of Liberia. The few that stayed only operated with skeletal staff. The successful establishment of a safe haven by ECOMOG around Monrovia encouraged aid agencies to return. At this initial stage, there was a good working relationship between NGOs and ECOMOG. Besides securing Monrovia for aid operations, the force also secured Liberia's link with the outside world by safeguarding the Monrovia Freeport and Robertsfield Airport. In addition, ECOMOG provided security convoys to aid agencies venturing out of Monrovia (Scott, 1994).

But this harmonious relationship was to become severely strained after Operation Octopus. This was due to NGO criticism of what they perceived as ECOMOG's heavy handedness in responding to the NPFL attack. The resulting loss of neutrality also made aid agencies to be wary of using ECOMOG escorts into NPFL territory for fear of a backlash. On its own part, ECOMOG accused aid agencies of being sympathetic to the NPFL cause and facilitating their operations.[1] Even the leader of the interim government shares this view when he said:

> Some NGOs and UN-related agencies ... have been too readily prepared to play by the rules set by warring factions in order to reach target groups, and in so doing, have reached an accommodation which has unwittingly assisted in sustaining warring factions and continuing the war. (Amos Sawyer, quoted in Max Sesay, 1996)

There is evidence to substantiate these claims. There are confirmed reports of NGOs 'buying access' into rebel controlled areas by giving food directly to rebel factions (Maresko, 2004). This mistrust led to serious problems with the aid effort. The most notable was the dispute over cross border aid (delivery to NPFL areas across the Cote d'Ivoire border). In May 1993, ECOMOG banned the route as a result of suspicions that aid agencies use relief supplies as a cover to smuggle arms to the NPFL. However some agencies like *Médecins Sans Frontières* (MSF) disregarded the ban and continued to cross the border freely. As a result, ECOMOG jets bombed an MSF convoy in May 1993 that was travelling between Gbanga and Kakata. Many other bombing raids on aid convoys were reported by Human Rights Watch (1993) including the following:

- bombing of the CRS warehouse in Buchanan on 16 November 1992 destroying large quantities of rice and blended food;
- bombing of a CRS truck distributing food outside Buchanan killing 75 to 100 people.

Liberia is not a unique case for poor civil-military relations. The humanitarian aid literature acknowledges this problem and points to issues such as incompatible mandates, lack of training and poor coordination mechanisms as part of the causes. In the case of Liberia, besides the complication caused by ECOMOG's peace enforcement strategy, part of the problem can be found in the lack of humanitarian aid training in the military academies of the respective ECOMOG countries. As noted above, the entire mission was *ad hoc* and only responded to problems as they arise. However, it must be noted here that NGOs also contributed to straining the relationship. Their lack of understanding of the nature of the Liberian civil war and its key actors was very apparent. Whilst not exonerating ECOMOG for its excesses, it must be stated that the persistent and unbalanced criticism of its strategy was not warranted

---

1   Interview with former ECOMOG Officer Monrovia, Liberia, 18 March 2004. This accusation was repeated by several other former ECOMOG officers intervewed.

and was clearly undermining the force's military efforts. On the contrary, the actions of some NGOs amounted to legitimising the status of warlords and sustaining the conflict. Lack of an effective coordination mechanism also had an adverse effect on the relationship. In July 1990, the UN Secretary-General established the United Nations Special Coordinator for Liberia (UNSCOL) tasked with the coordination of aid efforts. At its inception, it succeeded in building a good working relationship between ECOMOG and aid agencies and facilitated NGO access to both government and rebel held areas. But the authority of the UNSCOL Coordinator was eroded with the appointment of a Special Representative of the Secretary-General (SRSG). Aid agencies were angered when the SRSG sided with ECOMOG over the issue of cross-border aid (Scott, 1994). Coordination was also hampered by the absence of a civilian representative of ECOWAS on the ground.

Contradictions in Humanitarian Intervention: ECOMOG and Human Rights Abuses

ECOMOG intervention in Liberia was cast in humanitarian terms and projected as a mission to halt the rampant human rights abuses taking place in Liberia. But despite this altruistic motive, the behaviour of troops on the ground paints a very disturbing picture of ECOMOG as violators of human rights. These violations range from harassment of civilians at check points to indiscriminate bombings. This section highlights the various cases of human right abuses by ECOMOG and examine the explanations given by both ECOMOG and human rights groups concerning these abuses.

The most serious allegations of human rights abuses came in the aftermath of Operation Octopus. Human rights groups have accused ECOMOG of using overwhelming force in response to the NPFL invasion. The most damaging of these accusations is the indiscriminate bombing of non-military targets including civilians, medical facilities and aid agencies. In addition to the cases of ECOMOG bombings of humanitarian aid convoys discussed above, Human Rights Watch (1993) has also documented several incidents involving civilian and medical targets:

- bombing of the Firestone hospital at Harbel in November 1992;
- the attack on Phebe Hospital on 10 March 1993;
- bombing of Commercial Street in Kakata and a market in Gbarnga with reported civilian causalities.

These incidents have prompted accusations of violations of the principles of proportionality and discrimination. In response, ECOMOG commanders argue that the bombing of civilian targets was never intentional but as a result of collateral damage. They also blame Taylor of using civilians as human shields to conceal his military locations. But these excuses are not enough to justify the indiscriminate shelling of civilian targets.

Critics have also accused the force of looting, corruption, and involvement in the exploitation of Liberia's strategic resources (diamonds and timber). In a damning report on ECOMOG's malpractices, Klaas van Walraven (1999) cited instances where the Nigerian contingent helped warring factions to transport their looted goods, in exchange for part of the booty and natural resources of Liberia. In 1995, diplomats uncovered the shady dealings of a Nigerian colonel who traded timber rights for a monthly fee of $500 (Howe, 1997). These malpractices led Liberians to claim that ECOMOG stood for 'Every Car or Movable Object Gone'. ECOMOG soldiers have also been accused of sexual exploitation of vulnerable Liberian women and girls. Reports in Liberia speak of ECOMOG soldiers using their food rations to solicit sex from Liberian women. The legacy of such a malpractice is very evident in Monrovia where an estimated 6000 fatherless children are left behind by departing ECOMOG troops (BBC Africa online, 2005). This foreshadows the sex-for-food scandal that rocked the UN in Sierra Leone and recently Congo DR.

ECOMOG's alliance with various warring factions, notably ULIMO and the AFL, has also come under heavy criticism by human right groups. These factions have been accused of horrific human rights abuses including looting, raping, harassment of civilians and summary execution. These alliances came as a response to continued NPFL attacks on ECOMOG and can be regarded as a pragmatic approach to contain the NPFL. As ECOMOG lack adequate number of troops, resources and knowledge of local terrain, these factions proved very useful in showing the West African forces the Liberian terrain and escape routes of the NPFL. These groups were also reportedly used by ECOMOG to serve as front line of attack with ECOMOG troops at the rear thus reducing causalities of the peacekeepers (Howe, 1997). However, by allying with such groups, ECOMOG exposed itself to accusations of turning a blind eye to their human rights abuses. Besides, it reinforced Taylor's perception of Nigerian bias in the conflict. This apparent lack of neutrality made him view ECOMOG as a party to the conflict; a factor partly responsible for the war's prolongation. To make matters worse, most of the allies in various situations, proved obstacles to the peace process itself. As Howe puts it, 'ECOMOG's cooperation with the factions weakened its desired neutrality. Furthermore, the factions constantly tried to use ECOMOG for their own purposes' (1997, 172).

This apparent complacency in the face of human rights abuses also extends to the top level of ECOWAS decision making process. Human rights issues have not featured prominently in the numerous peace agreements brokered by ECOWAS, and the regional body has not done enough to incorporate human rights in its conflict resolution initiative. To the contrary, there seems to be a pattern of sacrificing human rights on the altar of peace. The Cotonou Accord is a typical example of an agreement offering impunity to war criminals. Article 19 of this agreement grants 'a general amnesty ... to all persons and parties involved in the Liberian civil conflict' (Cotonou Accord, 1993). In addition to the warring factions, this amnesty also covered ECOMOG soldiers accused of the serious crimes outlined above.

But how can we explain this apparent contradiction between the stated humanitarian objectives of the mission and the practice of the troops on the ground? One explanation can be found in the nature of the Liberian conflict and the peace enforcement strategy ECOMOG was forced to resort to. There is clearly a contradiction between peace enforcement and the protection of human rights. Most often, ECOMOG peace enforcement operations are carried out in heavily populated civilian areas and this clearly puts the lives of many innocent civilians under jeopardy. ECOMOG officers also argue that it was very difficult for them to distinguish between rebels and combatants as these fighters do not have recognisable uniforms

But the nature of the conflict alone is not enough to justify ECOMOG's excesses. To help us gain a better understanding of these abuses, it is necessary to distinguish between the human right records of different contingents. Senegalese and Ghanaian troops are said to have performed exemplary whilst Nigerian, Sierra Leonean and Guinean troops were reported to be corrupt, incompetent and undisciplined (Taw and Grant-Thomas, 1997). But why was the record of Nigerians by far more appalling than their Ghanaian and Senegalese counterparts. Many factors can help explain this difference. Firstly, the fact that Nigerians were engaged in most of the enforcement action can be a possible explanation. This situation is similar to Iraq. As the Americans found themselves in the hot spots and therefore mostly engaged in enforcement action, their human rights record is far worse than their British allies who are based in the relatively stable south of the country. However, this is not enough to explain the excesses of Nigerian troops. The human rights record and practices of the home countries of the various contingents is a key factor. Although the militaries of both Nigeria and Ghana were heavily politicised at the time of the intervention, the human rights record of the Nigerian military was by far the more deplorable of the two. Its role in brutally suppressing pro-democracy movements and silencing opposition voices in the country has been well documented (Human Rights Watch, 1999). Besides, the military in Nigeria is often used to brutally quell low intensity conflicts in several localities in the country. For most ordinary civilians, the military has become an icon of brutality and torture and the mere presence of soldiers in a community is enough to send residents packing. To compound the situation, most of these soldiers who are fresh from these deployments are taken over to Liberia for humanitarian and peacekeeping duties. The radical shift from human rights abuser to humanitarian intervener has been very difficult in these circumstances. On the other hand, Ghana has a long history of UN peacekeeping experience behind it. In fact all the Ghanaian soldiers deployed in Liberia had done at least one UN peacekeeping tour in Lebanon (Taw and Grant-Thomas, 1997).

ECOMOG-UNOMIL Co-deployment

Despite the relative success of ECOMOG's peacekeeping-enforcement strategy discussed above, the force's loss of neutrality and credibility and its incapacity to extend beyond the confines of Monrovia meant that it was unable to bring an end to the conflict. Enforcement action only serves as a mechanism for managing conflict and mitigating humanitarian catastrophe. There is therefore need for effective peacemaking, peacekeeping and peacebuilding capabilities to complement enforcement. However, as the above section has clearly shown, ECOMOG was severely constrained by a combination of political, financial, logistical and tactical problems. It is against this background of a force in need of resources and credibility that ECOMOG's cooperation with the UN emerged.

The Cotonou Accord represented a major step in the resolution of the Liberian crisis and set out a new agenda in international peacekeeping. For the first time, the United Nations was to participate in a 'peacekeeping mission already set up by another organisation' (UN, 1993). Signed in July 1993 by the major parties to the conflict (Alhaji Kromah of ULIMO, Charles Taylor of NPFL and Amos Sawyer of the Interim Government), this accord was welcomed by all the factions, diplomats and ordinary citizens as representing the best framework for restoring stability and peace in this war torn country.

Nature of UN-ECOWAS Relationship

Though the Cotonou Accord marked the first formal attempt to include the UN in the Liberian conflict management process, UN involvement dates back to January 1991, when the Security Council President made a statement calling on the conflicting parties to observe the ceasefire. Rhetoric was followed by action in November 1992 with the adoption of Security Council Resolution 788, which imposed an embargo on the importation of arms and ammunition in Liberia, except for use by ECOMOG. The Secretary General was also mandated to appoint a Special Representative to Liberia. A day after the adoption of this resolution, the Secretary General appointed Mr Trevor Livingston Gordon-Somers to serve in this capacity. Based on the findings and report of Mr Gordon-Somers, the Security Council gradually assumed a more proactive role in the Liberian crisis.

Following the signing of the Cotonou Accord, the UN Secretary-General submitted recommendations to the Security Council, which set out the composition and role of the envisaged Observer Force. This mission was to comprise 303 military observers, divided into 41 teams of six observers per team, 25 based at UNOMIL HQ in Monrovia and eight to be based in the four regional headquarters. A number of civilian staff were to provide administrative support to the observers. In making these recommendations, the Secretary-General noted the importance of teamwork between the UN

Force and ECOMOG and assured that 'UNOMIL and ECOMOG would collaborate closely in their operations' (UN, 1993, 4). The Council accepted the Secretary-General's recommendations but called for the widening of the mandate to include post-war reconstruction, with the inclusion of medical, engineering, communications, transportation and electoral components. This reflected the emerging broader peacekeeping concept that characterised the end of the Cold War. Resolution 866 also required UNOMIL to supervise and monitor adherence to ceasefire agreements, observe the election process, coordinate the delivery of humanitarian aid, train ECOMOG engineers in mine clearance, and assist in the demobilisation process. UNOMIL was deployed for an initial period of seven months, subject to extension, and a budget of US$ 42.6 million was approved. A Kenyan, Major General Daniel Opande, was named Force Commander.

Table 4.3   Composition of UNOMIL, January 1997

	Military observers	Medical staff	Total
Bangladesh	7	7	14
China	5	-	5
Czech Republic	2	-	2
Egypt	12	-	12
India	13	-	13
Kenya	11	-	11
Malaysia	2	-	2
Nepal	6	-	6
Pakistan	11	-	11
Uruguay	2	-	2
Total	71	7	78

Source: United Nations (1997), *Twenty-First Progress Report of the Secretary-General on the United Nations Observer Mission in Liberia*, New York: UN Document S/1997/90.

ECOMOG-UNOMIL Co-deployment: Strengths and Weaknesses

From its inception, the success of UNOMIL was closely tied to its collaboration with ECOMOG and the success of the Cotonou Accord. However, like previous agreements, Cotonou soon collapsed shortly after it was initialled. Arguments concerning the membership of the LNTG derailed the establishment of this transitional body whilst in the security sector, disarmament of combatants failed to take off as planned. The expansion of ECOMOG, stipulated in the agreement, never materialised as most African countries failed to honour their pledges of contributing troops to the force. To make matters worse, ECOMOG was drastically downsized as a result of the growing instability in Nigerian domestic politics and growing ECOMOG 'fatigue' gripping Ghana. By June 1994, Nigeria had reduced its troops from 11,000 the previous year to a mere 6,000 whilst Ghana planned a gradual withdrawal of about 50 per cent of its troops (Adibe, 1998). Despite Cotonou's collapse, the UN continued its efforts, aimed at finding a peaceful resolution to the crisis. On the ground, UNOMIL's presence continued to build confidence between warring parties and gave ECOMOG the legitimacy and credibility needed to facilitate the peace process. Consequently, ECOMOG and UNOMIL completed the disarmament and demobilisation process. Meanwhile UN agencies in collaboration with NGOs and donors, extended humanitarian assistance to the entire country. ECOMOG-UNOMIL collaboration also facilitated the election process and a return to constitutional order.

However, despite the mutual gains outlined above, the intended cooperation envisaged by both Cotonou and Security Council Resolution 866 suffered serious setbacks as a result of the parallel command structures maintained by the two organisations. Despite provisions in the Cotonou accord mandating UNOMIL to act in a supervisory capacity over ECOMOG, events on the ground prevented it from properly executing such a role. ECOMOG's actions seriously limited the scope and functions of UN observers and, in practice, reduced them to a position of second fiddle. As Mackinlay and Alao point out:

> Many Liberians saw UNOMIL as subordinated to ECOMOG. For them the signs were visible in everyday events on the street. They saw UNOMIL vehicles stopped and searched at ECOMOG roadblocks. UNOMIL was also required to observe the curfew times and influential Liberians asked – how could UNOMIL be 'verifying' their activities when ECOMOG was free to act, unmonitored, during the hours of darkness (1995, 16).

Adibe summed up the situation when he noted that 'the subordination of regional command structures to global authority was neither attempted nor achieved by UNOMIL' (1998, 83).

But what led to this poor working relationship? Why was the UN unable to command a leading role in this operation, as stipulated by chapter VIII of the UN charter? Several factors account for this failure, not least the flaws in the Cotonou Accord itself. The agreement failed to clearly define the relationship between ECOMOG and UNOMIL and lacked explicit provisions regarding UN supremacy. In fact, the powers to be exercised by the Special Representative of the Secretary General (SRSG) were relatively weak, when compared to other Peacekeeping Operations in the world. Mackinlay and Alao painted a vivid picture when they observe that:

Mr. Gordon Somers held a much less powerful executive position which reflected the unique constituency of UNOMIL and its relationship with the other factions in the peace process. Unlike his predecessors, in the event of UNOMIL's role being challenged or his officers becoming exposed to danger, he would have to rely on the military support of ECOMOG, a force palpably not under his control or even within his aegis of influence. At the crucial point of interface with the ECOMOG Field Commander, Gordon Somers precedence was unclear; however it was certain that the ECOMOG Commander held final authority over his forces. (1995, 16)

The late arrival of the UN in the Liberian crisis was a key factor that generated ill feeling amongst ECOMOG troops, who argued that 'UNOMIL was deployed after they had done the 'dirty job' of shedding their blood for Liberians' (Olonisakin, 1996, 41). The vast disparity in the working conditions between ECOMOG and UNOMIL also served to sour their relationship. Whilst UNOMIL soldiers were well paid and equipped, their ECOMOG counterparts received poor allowances, paid irregularly. This partly explains the low moral amongst ECOMOG troops and their animosity towards UNOMIL. These poor conditions of service also account for the unprofessional behaviour of some ECOMOG soldiers and officers discussed above. This ill-feeling was further worsened by UNOMIL public education programme with handbills and radio broadcasts saying the rebels should 'trust the UN', implying that ECOMOG could not be trusted (Africa Confidential, 2004).

Logistical constraints within ECOMOG also contributed to straining the relationship. Annan was right when he pointed out that 'the success of this innovative model of peacekeeping, and the ability of UNOMIL to carry out its mandate, rested on the assumption that ECOMOG would be provided with the resources needed to perform the wide-ranging tasks entrusted to it by the Liberian parties' (UN, 1997, 7). But as mentioned earlier, ECOMOG received little support from the international community. In a further blow to ECOMOG, the US, due to alleged rackets by Nigerian officers vetoed the use of the UN Trust fund for Liberia to help ECOMOG purchase badly needed fuel (Africa Confidential, 1994). As a result, troop strength remained low, despite pledges by other African countries to provide reinforcement. ECOMOG could, therefore, not ensure effective disarmament and demobilisation as stipulated by Cotonou, neither could it provide UNOMIL with the security it needed. There were many instances when UNOMIL observers were deployed in areas not covered by ECOMOG. It came as no surprise, therefore, when UN observers were kidnapped by a warring faction in lower Lofa County in the summer of 1994 (Olonisakin, 1996). This incident also reveals a clear sign of lack of effective coordination and consultation between the two. ECOMOG officials complained that UNOMIL officials failed to consult them prior to deployment in the area. In a similar vein, ECOMOG officials also complained about the failure of the SRSG, Gordon-Somers to brief them ahead of negotiations with the NPFL and ULIMO (Africa Confidential, 1994).

Internal problems within ECOWAS and ECOMOG further served to complicate UN-ECOMOG co-deployment and adversely affected the working relationship between the two forces. These problems have already been discussed above. The most crucial factor has been the apparent lack of accountability of ECOMOG to its parent body, ECOWAS. Political directives from ECOWAS were often lacking on the ground and partly account for ECOMOG's excesses and treatment of UNOMIL. Some critics have argued that by collaborating with ECOWAS, the UN has legitimised Nigerian dominance in the region and also turned a blind eye to ECOMOG's lack of neutrality and abuse of international law and code of conduct for peacekeeping (Adibe, 1998).

Linking Peacemaking to Humanitarian Intervention: ECOWAS and the Liberian Peace Process

ECOWAS/ECOMOG dual strategy of military sticks and political carrots led to a series of peace agreements starting from Bamako in 1990 to Abuja in 1996 – a total of 14. As the number of peace agreements suggests, the Liberian peace process has been characterised by repeated failures and intransigence by warring parties. This section examines the various agreements and the obstacles and challenges they faced.

Following the failure of the Nigerian-led peace efforts at the beginning of the conflict and the deepening Anglophone-Francophone divide, leadership of the peace process was transferred to Cote d'Ivoire. This resulted in the establishment of a predominantly Francophone Committee of Five to work alongside the Anglophone dominant SMC. Under the chairmanship of Cote d'Ivoire's Houphouet-Boigny, the Committee organised four meetings culminating in the signing of the Yamoussoukro Agreement. This Accord has similar features with many other agreements that followed. There are provisions for the formation of an interim government which will work with ECOMOG and the warring factions in implementing a DDR programme. Elections of a civilian government and the training of a new Liberian army were also integral parts of successive agreements. Yamoussoukro soon collapsed as the NPFL refused to honour the terms of the accord. The emergence of ULIMO further complicated the process and operation octopus finally killed any hopes of reviving the agreement.

Following the collapse of Yamoussoukro and the problems of ECOMOG discussed above, the international community became more involved in facilitating the Liberian peace process. This brought about the UN brokered Geneva Agreement and the Cotonou Accord. Its 19 articles cover issues ranging from ceasefire, disarmament and demobilisation to elections, repatriation of refugees and the relationship between ECOMOG and a UN Observer Force. It marks a dramatic shift from the Yamoussoukro agreements. In the first place, in order to build the NPFL's confidence, ULIMO became a signatory to the accord, thus removing the former's excuse for refusing to disarm. In a bid to limit Nigerian dominance of ECOMOG, provision was made for the inclusion of forces from East African countries and the establishment of UNOMIL. Whilst ECOMOG was charged with the primary task of implementing the agreement, UNOMIL was given a supervisory role. ECOMOG's influence was greatly diminished by the constant mention in the accord of the phrase 'under the monitoring and verification of the United Nations Observers'. ECOMOG's enforcement powers were also severely curtailed. Unlike past arrangements wherein ECOMOG could resort to enforcement as soon as it receives orders from ECOWAS or the Nigerian government, it can now only do so after the failure of a long and complicated process.

The accord attached prime importance to disarmament and regarded it as 'the ultimate objective of the ceasefire' (Art. 6). ECOMOG was given the task of collecting and storing all weapons and warlike materials, to be 'monitored and verified by the United Nations Observers' (Art. 6.1). Factions were required to submit a list of all weapons to ECOMOG. Non-combatants were also required to 'report and surrender' weapons to ECOMOG, which would be returned to their owners after 'registration, licensing and certification by the governing authority after elections' (Art. 6[5]). ECOMOG was empowered to use force in disarming combatants that refused to willingly disarm and also search for lost and hidden weapons. However, the accord was silent on how disarmament could be ensured. The framers of the agreement envisaged a best-case scenario and depended on the factions' 'intent and willingness to disarm' (Art. 6).

IGNU was to be replaced by the inclusive Liberia National Transitional Government (LNTG), which comprised legislative, executive and judiciary organs. The parties agreed a formula for the sharing of positions. This body was mandated to 'hold and supervise general and presidential elections in accordance with the ECOWAS peace plan' (Art. 14[2]). However, Cotonou soon collapsed despite the high hopes and aspirations embodied in the agreement. A common theme running through all the agreements up to this point is the over reliance on civilians and the exclusion of warlords in the interim governments. The next phase of the peace process tried to remedy this problem and accommodated the warlords within the framework of the Transitional Administration. Another notable change is the shift from Francophone led peace process to the Anglophone. This appears to be a clear sign of dissatisfaction with the Francophone strategy of appeasing Taylor. Joint ECOWAS-UN efforts resulted in the signing of the Akosombo Agreement of 1994, by which faction leaders reaffirmed most elements of Cotonou and agreed to declare a cease-fire. Like previous agreements, Akosombo soon collapsed. The Abuja agreement of August 1995 was able to resolve the sensitive question of membership of the LNTG. However, despite the pomp and fanfare surrounding the installation of the LNTG, the collective presidency was soon plunged into an intractable power struggle over the distribution of government posts. Intra-factional fighting between two factions of ULIMO also posed a major threat to the survival of the peace process. The final blow to the Abuja Agreement came in April 1996 when full-scale war erupted in Monrovia, triggered by an attempt to dismiss and arrest Roosevelt Johnson of ULIMO-J, following murder allegations against him. This new round of hostilities led to another massive exodus of refugees and created an enormous humanitarian catastrophe. Following the cessation of hostilities, ECOWAS, in concert with the UN, convened a meeting of all Liberian factions in Accra in August 1996 to salvage what was left of the Abuja agreement. The parties agreed to a timetable which started with disarmament and demobilisation by 31 January 1997 and culminated in the conduction of general elections in May 1997 and the establishment of a government by 15 June (ECOWAS, 1996). The tragic events of April 1996 convinced faction leaders that the only way out of Liberia's political problems was a negotiated settlement. This rethinking was vital in the progress that was to follow in the peace process.

Why did it take 14 peace agreements and seven years for ECOWAS to achieve its objective of bringing peace to Liberia? A number of factors can be identified ranging from lack of understanding of the nature of warlord politics on the part of ECOWAS to the proliferation of factions and intransigence of warlords. There have been several references through out this chapter relating to ECOWAS' apparent lack of a coherent approach to the Liberian peace process. The Anglophone-Francophone rivalry and the Accra-Abuja tensions seriously undermined the success of peace talks. Warlords like Taylor were very quick to capitalise on this weakness and succeeded in playing around with the organisation. The fact that some ECOWAS countries were also supporting various warring groups further paralysed the organisation's position as a neutral third party intervener. The late intervention of the UN and the international community also delayed the resolution of the conflict. As ECOWAS/ECOMOG neutrality was already compromised, an earlier UN involvement would have provided the credibility, neutrality and resources needed to facilitate the peace process.

Another key obstacle to the resolution of the Liberian conflict was the lack of understanding on the part of ECOWAS of the nature of the Liberian warlords and their motivation for war. This is demonstrated in several agreements which heavily relied on the good will and commitment of the warring parties. The understanding that most of these warlords were more interested in personal power and wealth came at a very late stage in the process. This warlord politics of self interest and winner-take-all mentality brought about intransigence on the part of faction leaders. In due course, it also led to the proliferation and splintering of factions along ethnic and personal lines. The proliferation of factions adversely affected the peace process as it presented third party interveners with many groups to placate – a process that is not always easy.

ECOWAS/ECOMOG and Post-War Peacebuilding in Liberia

In Chapter 1 we argued that post-Cold War humanitarian intervention has expanded from its nascent task of halting human rights abuses to incorporating elements of peacebuilding and state formation aimed at preventing a relapse into conflict. This section looks at three main post-war programmes implemented by ECOMOG during the period 1990-97 with the assistance of the UN and aid agencies. These are DDR, election assistance and security sector reform.

Disarmament, Demobilisation and Reintegration (DDR) of Ex-Combatants

DDR programmes have become main components of successful peace processes in complex political emergencies. Not only must such programmes ensure complete disarmament of ex-combatants, they must also be able to cater for the economic, social and psychological reintegration of these ex-fighters. As mentioned above, a key component of Liberian peace accords since Yamoussoukro (October 1991) is the provision for a DDR programme. Cotonou laid out the most comprehensive framework for this programme. However, successive DDR programmes failed to take off the ground due to the unwillingness of faction leaders and the proliferation of factions. The emergence of ULIMO in late 1991 coupled with Taylor's attempt to overrun Monrovia in October 1992 wrecked the Yamoussoukro disarmament exercise. Again in August 1994 inter-faction fighting led to the collapse of another round of disarmament. The April 1996 fighting in Monrovia brought an abrupt end to yet another frustrating venture. Not until after the signing of Abuja II that a relatively successful DDR programme kick off in Liberia. Despite the weaknesses of Abuja II discussed above, the accord was able to force compliance from warring factions by threatening a series of sanctions and even the establishment of a war crimes tribunal to prosecute perpetrators of human rights abuses. The accord also shifted responsibility for the success of the DDR programme to faction leaders.

Comprehensive DDR started on 11 November 1996 and lasted till February 1997. ECOMOG was responsible for the disarmament of an estimated 60,000 ex-combatants. This process was verified and supervised by UNOMIL. A National Disarmament and Demobilisation Committee was set up to coordinate the entire programme. The process involves ex-combatants handing in their weapons to ECOMOG at 18 designated collection points in return for benefits and a reintegration card. Between November 1996 and February 1997 ECOMOG collected an estimated 10,000 weapons and 1.24 million pieces of ammunition (UN, 1997). The actual number of disarmed ex-combatants fell drastically from the initial 60,000 estimate to a mere 20,332. The number of weapons disarmed also did not coincide with initial estimates. This fuelled suspicions that some factions may have simply moved their fighters and weapons across borders for safekeeping in the event of any resumption of hostility. Taylor was believed to have moved some of his combatants and weapons to his RUF allies in South Eastern Sierra Leone, ULIMO-K to Guinea and ULIMO-J, LDF, and LPC to the Liberia-Cote d'Ivoire border (Anning, 2000). Some factions even hid some weapons in Monrovia as evidenced by the ECOMOG discovery of a large cache of arms in Alhaji Kromah's residence (West Africa, 1997). There were also reports that faction commanders were controlling the DDR programme by determining the number of ex-fighters to disarm. Some ex-combatants were even ordered to hand in weapons to their commanders, thus disqualifying them from receiving the reintegration benefits due them (Creative Associates, 1997). This can be attributed to the lack of a proper information and sensitisation campaign as envisaged by the Abuja accord. Instead, ECOMOG and UNOMIL relied on local commanders to sensitise their fighters. Most often these commanders gave misleading information to the fighters either by discouraging them from disarming or raising their expectations. These unrealistic expectations led to a series of disturbances at disarmament points as ex-combatants failed to receive what they have been promised. It also seriously undermined the demobilisation and reintegration phases of the programme.

The disarmament itself was riddled with many problems not least ECOMOG's perennial logistical constraints. The poor infrastructure in Liberia further worsened the situation. Inadequate communication and transport facilities made it very difficult to access assembly points thus delaying the programme. The inconsistency surrounding the eligibility criteria for disarmament caused confusion not only among ex-combatants but also amongst the various agencies responsible for programme implementation. These criteria changed frequently, starting with a serviceable weapon, to any weapon, 100 rounds of ammunition and ended with any individual that came forward (Creative Associates, 1997). There were credible reports of civilians buying ammunition in the open market in order to be disarmed and get part of the benefits of DDR. One can understand the difficulty ECOMOG and UNOMIL encountered in this aspect. It is very difficult to distinguish irregular forces from civilians. Even the various faction leaders do not have a clear account of the people under their control.

The weapons-buy-back scheme introduced to induce compliance was another source of controversy. Ex-combatants complained that incentives were not attractive enough. However, most civilians were reportedly not happy for what they consider a payment for the massive human rights abuses committed by these ex-combatants. This scheme has continued to generate heated debate among academics, practitioners and policy makers. According to the World Bank:

weapons-buy-back programmes have had limited medium-term impact in reducing the number of weapons circulating in countries which have (1) porous borders with countries with active weapon markets; (2) lack of capacity to enforce regulations on the open carrying and criminal use of weapons; (3) apolitical, economic or security climate which enhances the security and economic value of owning and using a weapon. (1993, para. 173)

Whilst not dismissing the above reasoning, it is necessary to point to the fact that these types of conflicts are fuelled and sustained by economic agendas. Telling a fighter to abandon his/her predatory lifestyle without providing an alternative means of livelihood is bound to be a failure in the long term.

Despite the problems outlined above, the disarmament exercise in Liberia can be considered a qualified success as it achieved its main objective of restoring security to the entire country, although temporary. Following the completion of disarmament, no major incident was reported. This in turn boosted the confidence of civilians and led to the resumption of normal life. Aid agencies were able to access hitherto inaccessible parts of the country. Hundreds of thousands of refugees and Internally Displaced Persons returned to their communities and business activities resumed.

The next key phase of the programme is demobilisation which aims to demilitarise a faction by dismantling the military command and control apparatus and neutralise its military capacity. In Liberia, the plan called for the registration, encampment, interview, counselling, medical screening and transportation of ex-combatants to their chosen destinations across the country. However, most of these were not accomplished. For instance, no encampment took place thereby failing to undertake rehabilitation and education programmes. Besides Harper, no transportation of ex-fighters to their destinations took place (Creative Associates, 1997). The result was that the envisaged physical separation of forces was never achieved and the command and control chain remained intact in most cases. The decision by many ex-combatants to remain in their area of operation was due to a variety of factors including fear of returning home and confronting victims of their atrocities. Living in groups in their former operational areas increases their sense of security. The major problem however was lack of sustained international attention to the Liberian conflict. This problem also adversely affected the reintegration process.

No sustained efforts were taken to reintegrate ex-combatants into society. Implementers of the programme focused much attention on the disarmament and demobilisation phases of the programme. After offering them a bag of rice and US$60, ex-combatants were left to fend for themselves. There were very limited opportunities for economic reintegration of these former fighters, which would have revived their livelihood and provided a suitable alternative to life with the gun. ECOWAS did not play an active role in the reintegration process. This can partly be linked to the weak economic status of sub-regional countries and the heavy toll of financing ECOMOG operations. Whilst publicly pledging support to Liberia's post-war economic recovery, in private 'many felt that Liberia should better look to Western Europe and NGOs for any enduring relief' (Alao, Mackinlay and Olonisakin, 1999, 113). But was such support forthcoming? Among other issues, Chapter 7 will focus on the failures of international support to Liberia's post-war reintegration strategy and how it contributed to a relapse into conflict.

ECOMOG and the Liberian Elections

The election process benefited immensely from the relationship between ECOMOG and UNOMIL. Whilst ECOMOG maintained a climate of security conducive to holding elections, UNOMIL assisted with the provision of logistical, transportation and communication facilities. UNOMIL also trained and deployed 200 electoral observers and its countrywide public information campaign succeeded in educating voters (UN, 1997). Mr Taylor won a decisive victory with over 75 per cent of the votes cast. This overwhelmingly victory can be attributed to fear. The majority of the Liberian people believed that electing Taylor would put an end to the conflict. They expressed this by the slogan 'He killed my papa, he killed my mama, but I will vote for him' (Walraven, 1999, 67). The dramatic shift of Nigerian support towards Taylor also played a part in securing him the presidency. After years of thwarting Taylor's presidential ambitions, Nigeria under Abacha suddenly shifted support and made an alliance with him. Like the Liberian people, Nigeria came to the conclusion that peace in Liberia was solely dependent on the will of one man and his war machine. This amounted to appeasement of the strongest warlord and as Chapter 7 argues, this policy adversely undermined the Liberian peace process. Some analysts believe that Nigeria was becoming weary of the protracted intervention in Liberia and was seeking an exit strategy. Other critics argue that Abacha, whose dictatorial regime was widely condemned, was hungry for success at any cost, to deflect local and international criticism. This led to allegations by Ellen Johnson-Sirleaf, Kromah and Boley that ECOMOG soldiers rigged the elections in favour of Taylor. Although there were confirmed reports that ECOMOG soldiers compromised voter secrecy by assisting illiterate voters (Adebajo, 2002), such malpractices do not amount to vote rigging.

Security Sector Reform

Under the terms of the Abuja II Agreement of 1996, ECOMOG was to remain in Liberia for the purpose of restructuring the armed forces. It was hoped that such an army would be inclusive of the various factions and ethnic groups. However, the accord's failure to provide for the restructuring of the Liberian army before elections was exploited by Taylor. After seven years of dealing with the Liberian warlords, ECOMOG/ECOWAS should have been in a vantage position to understand their mentality. However, this oversight appears to be a deliberate ploy to appease the strongest warlord, Taylor due to the rapprochement with Abacha mentioned above.

Just after a year in his presidency, Taylor cited concerns over Liberian sovereignty and asked ECOMOG to leave. This paved the way for him to fill the security forces with his former NPFL fighters in gratitude for their efforts during the war. Rather than strengthening the constitutional army, Taylor created several militia groups and paramilitary bodies whose primary loyalty was not to the state but to him. Such groups include the feared Anti-Terrorist Unit (ATU), the Special Security Service (SSS) and the Special Operations Division (SOD). To avoid the possibility of collaboration in a plot, Taylor kept each of these units separate. In addition to these paramilitary outfits are militia groups under the control of Taylor loyalists and logging companies. As Chapter 7 reveals, the failure to restructure the armed forces of Liberia seriously undermined ECOWAS/ECOMOG efforts as it marginalised a large section of opposing ex-combatants for whom there were no real re-integration prospects.

Conclusion

Putting the ECOMOG operations into context, this chapter has tried to demonstrate the difficulties faced by the sub-regional body and the peculiar circumstances within which they operated. The fact that ECOWAS was willing to intervene in a crisis lacking international attention represents a commitment by African countries to take a lead role in the resolution of their conflicts. However, the above analysis of ECOMOG's humanitarian intervention in Liberia reveals a mixed result of failures and successes. On the question of legitimacy, the force's legal status is questionable from a restrictionist's point of view. However as the above analysis indicates, there is overwhelming evidence to legitimise ECOMOG's intervention from the emerging expanded conceptualisation of humanitarian intervention. Central authority had collapsed in Liberia and there was widespread massacre of innocent civilians and indiscriminate human rights abuses. The threat to sub-regional security was becoming all too real as rumours of involvement of other West African dissidents within Taylor's force persist. These fears were confirmed when the RUF invaded Sierra Leone in 1991. On the ground, the force's flexibility enabled it to respond and adapt to the ever changing fluid security situation in Liberia. The force can also be credited for establishing and safeguarding the Monrovia safe haven, protecting a humanitarian space for the operations of aid agencies and even providing emergency relief for victims of the conflict. However, ECOMOG has also been rocked with numerous allegations of human rights abuses and related excesses. The failure to prevent two major attacks on the safe haven resulting in thousands of deaths also undermined ECOMOG's credibility. This failure has been linked to a number of problems ranging from lack of logistics and resources to the incoherent policy towards ECOMOG by ECOWAS member states.

ECOMOG's peacemaking and peacebuilding efforts have also been flawed due to the lack of consensus at the political level. The UN-ECOWAS collaboration which was meant to improve the situation also ran into a number of difficulties including poor working relationship between the two forces on the ground. The inability of ECOWAS peacemakers to understand the mentality of the Liberian warlords also led to a number of failed peace processes. The international indifference and lack of support to ECOMOG's peacebuilding efforts can also be partly blamed for the failure of the peacebuilding programme. That notwithstanding, the force can be credited for attempting to integrate peacemaking and peacebuilding to the humanitarian objective of saving lives. And by providing for an Interim Government in Liberia, ECOWAS was mindful of Liberian Sovereignty.

Chapter 5
ECOMOG in Sierra Leone: Restoration of Democracy and Humanitarian Intervention

Introduction

This chapter focuses on ECOMOG's humanitarian intervention in Sierra Leone from 1997 to 2000. It will locate the operations of the force within the expanded post-Cold War conceptualisation of humanitarian intervention as discussed in Chapter 1. ECOMOG's role in Sierra Leone evolved from peace enforcer to combatant and finally peacekeeper. Similar to the situation in Liberia, the force's flexibility enabled it to respond to the ever changing and fluid security situation in Sierra Leone. However, this chapter argues that ECOMOG's flexibility of mandate and robust military response to the AFRC/RUF's atrocities were not matched with an effective humanitarian policy, a coherent political plan and a well thought-out post-war peacebuilding and exit strategy. These failures severely limited its success. The chapter begins with an analysis of the Sierra Leone civil war and looks at ECOMOG's role in the restoration of democracy and the debate and controversies it sparked. It will then assess the force's role in protecting safe havens. This section will also focus on contentious issues surrounding the mission such as its poor human rights record, its relationship with NGOs and civil society and its alleged link with the exploitation of strategic resources. The next section will focus on ECOMOG's co-deployment with the UN with a bid to identifying the strengths and gaps of this relationship. An analysis of the peacemaking efforts of the parent body, ECOWAS, will form the basis for an assessment of the political foundations of the peace process in Sierra Leone. This will be linked with the post-war programmes implemented by the sub-regional body to prevent a relapse into conflict.

State Decay and Clientelism: 'Footpaths to Destruction in Sierra Leone'

On 23 March 1991, Sierra Leone descended into violent conflict when rebels of the Revolutionary Untied Front (RUF) attacked the Southern town of Bomaru near the Liberian border. Due to years of neglect and politicisation, the national army was ill prepared to deal with the insurgents whose guerrilla style of fighting saw them take over key towns and by 1995 were launching daring attacks near the capital, Freetown. An initial ECOWAS plan to create a buffer zone between Liberia and Sierra Leone was never implemented due to problems of funding and logistics (Francis, 2002). For over a decade, the conflict became notorious for its extreme levels of violence and disregard for international humanitarian law perpetuated by all parties including the RUF, national army, civil defence forces and regional and international peacekeepers. This was manifested by the deliberate targeting of civilians by armed factions resulting in the deaths of an estimated 50,000 civilians and a further 100,000 mutilated (UNIFEM, 2007). Several conflict analysts and international relations scholars have come up with contending views in their quest to provide a sound and accurate explanation of the underlying factors responsible for the unprecedented scale of brutality and violence that gripped Sierra Leone. However, as highlighted in Chapter 2, such analyses have labelled African conflicts in broad categories such as 'ethnic wars' and 'resource based wars' and disregarded the underlying political, economic, social and international factors that sow the seeds of bitter conflict. The Sierra Leone conflict itself has often been labelled a war over diamonds. Ian Smillie et al. for example regard diamonds as '*The Heart of the Matter*', arguing that they are the root cause of the country's civil war. They dismissed analysis of the conflict linked to state failure and patrimonialism on the basis that '… similar problems elsewhere have not led to years of brutality by forces devoid of ideology, political support and ethnic identity' (2000, 3). Successive Sierra Leone governments have also analysed the conflict in a similar vein. For example, Ibrahim Kamara, Sierra Leone's Permanent Representative to The United Nations opined that 'the root cause of the conflict is and remains diamonds, diamonds and diamonds' (quoted in Keen, 2005, 50). This simplistic analysis of the Sierra Leone conflict have fed into international responses and deflected attention to the fundamental political and socio-economic causes of the war thereby protracting the processes of conflict management, resolution and peacebuilding. Whilst diamonds played a key role in financing the activities of the RUF and other warring factions, they cannot be regarded as the *root cause* of the war. The background to the formation of the RUF supports this view. Abdullah (1997) traced the beginning of the RUF to exiled former students of Fourah Bay College (FBC) with genuine socio-political and economic grievances against the ruling APC elites. Besides, greed and resources did not form a major part of the rebellion during the initial stages of the war. In fact the RUF spent the first four years of the war in the agricultural districts of Pujehun and Kailahun in South-eastern Sierra Leone. Greed and opportunism cannot therefore adequately explain why war erupted in March 1991. This requires an in-depth and far reaching study of Sierra Leone's history which goes as far back as the colonial period and the post-independence era.

Like most sub-Saharan African countries, Sierra Leone was subjected to colonial rule for over a century. The capital Freetown was founded as a settlement for freed slaves in 1787 and became a British Crown Colony in 1808. In 1896, a protectorate was declared over the interior. The British colonial masters deliberately created two separate polities in what is supposed to be the same country. Whilst the colony was ruled directly by the Governor and unelected legislative and executive councils, the protectorate was administered through a system of indirect rule which relies on the cooperation of local paramount chiefs. As these chiefs held their positions at the pleasure of their colonial masters, little regard was given to meeting the needs of their people. The strong colonial support for chiefs also eroded the traditional mechanisms of checks and balances. Most Paramount Chiefs also benefited financially by diverting money meant for chiefdom development into personal use. The powers and economic opportunities bestowed upon chiefs by the colonial administration brought intense competition among rival ruling families for the post. Through their divide and rule policy, the colonialists manipulated these rivalries to their advantage. Central government interference in chieftaincy matters continued into the post-colonial period as chiefs became part of the neo-patrimonial and clientelistic politics that dominated post-independence Sierra Leone. The APC for instance arbitrarily deposed chiefs who were not in support of their regime and imposed unpopular choices in their place (Keen, 2005).

Separate legal systems were also maintained whereby the colony was subjected to the English legal system and the protectorate was under customary law which was effectively open to abuse by local chiefs. Draconian sentences were levied on young people ranging from heavy fines to banishment, causing deep resentment among youths in rural areas. These abuses continued into the post-independence period and the RUF was able to capitalise on such grievances to recruit many rural youths. It therefore came as no surprise that chiefs were singled out by the RUF for humiliation and brutality.

The dual system of governance also led to uneven levels of development between the colony and protectorate. It resulted in the over-centralisation of resources and amenities in Freetown at the detriment of the protectorate and its inhabitants. For instance, whilst Freetown could boast of relatively good educational, health and social services, the protectorate lagged far behind. In keeping with the underlying economic motives of the colonialists, the few infrastructural projects implemented in the protectorate were geared towards facilitating the exploitation of the region's raw materials. Consequently, young men were lured from rural areas lacking in amenities to Freetown and a few other urban centres. Those that chose to stay in the rural areas became more alienated. It was not surprising that the bulk of the RUF fighters came from this deprived section of society.

The British also failed to build a democratic political culture in Sierra Leone. As mentioned above, the colony was ruled through unelected legislative and executive councils whilst the protectorate was subjected to the personal rule of chiefs. In Sierra Leone, pluralist politics and universal adult suffrage were only introduced about a decade before independence. This legacy of authoritarianism laid the foundations of neo-patrimonialism and clientelistic politics that undermined the economic and political development of post-colonial Sierra Leone and sowed the seeds of state failure and violent conflict.

The country gained its independence on 27 April 1961 under a parliamentary democracy with Sir Milton Margai as the first Prime Minister. This assessment by Thomas Patrick Melady, a former US diplomat sums up the general mood of optimism surrounding the new state:

> Sierra Leone can emerge as a showcase of West Africa, progressive in its politics and forward-looking in its policies … Building on a solid agricultural base, the economy has profited from diamond deposits and growing interest in its promising industries, which range from fish to oil. Sierra Leone is more than a symbol of freedom; it is an embodiment of the aspirations of Africa. (Quoted in Pham, 2004)

However, the euphoria that greeted independence was short-lived as successive post-colonial regimes failed to deliver on their promises of economic development and political emancipation for the masses. In post-colonial Sierra Leone, the politics of patrimonialism led to growing tendencies towards authoritarian rule. The slide to authoritarian rule started during the regime of Sir Albert Margai who became Prime Minister following the death of his brother in 1964. He attempted unsuccessfully to introduce one party rule and passed draconian laws to suppress and intimidate the opposition. For example, the 1965 Public Order Act effectively criminalised 'libel' and was used to silence any critic of his regime. He also asked Paramount Chiefs not to encourage the APC in their chiefdoms. Besides intimidating his opponents, Sir Albert was also accused of ethnicising the country by dominating the government, civil service and army with his Mende tribesmen. For example, during his reign, the number of Mende officers in the army rose to 52 per cent as compared to 26 per cent during Sir Milton's premiership (Keen, 2005). Upon losing the 1967 elections to the opposition APC, it was widely believed that he conspired with Brigadier David Lansana to prevent the swearing-in of Siaka Stevens as Prime Minister. This marked the beginning of the politicisation of the military that would later lead to a series of coups and widespread unprofessionalism in the military.

Patrimonialism became entrenched in the political system from 1968 onwards when Siaka Stevens took over power. He effectively turned politics in Sierra Leone into an affair for and on behalf of supporters of the ruling All Peoples' Congress (APC) party. The state was virtually privatised within a patrimonial network of unscrupulous Lebanese Businessmen and close associates of the ruling circle. For example, the Afro-Lebanese, Jamil Sahid Mohamed became the President's closest business associate and had a very strong influence on state policy. Complete concentration of power on Siaka and his APC party was achieved with the adoption of the one party system in 1978. It is worth noting here that Siaka Stevens and his APC party were among the strongest opponents of one party rule when Albert Margai had earlier attempted to introduce it. However this did not stop them from making a dramatic U-turn when it suits them. As would be expected, one party rule resulted in the total concentration of power in the hands of the President and his closest allies. Opposition was branded as unpatriotic and brutally suppressed. The APC formed the Special Security Division (SSD) to act as primary regime protectors. Made up of strong supporters of the regime, the SSD were given superior training by Cuban and Chinese advisers and used by the regime to brutally suppress any opposition or dissenting voice. Their brutality earned them the nickname 'Siaka Stevens' Dogs'. The SSD often teamed up with youths popularly known as 'APC Thugs' to unleash unspeakable acts of violence on opponents of the regime. For instance, extreme violence was used to suppress the Student demonstrations of 1977. The press was also heavily censored and in 1981, the offices of the only independent newspaper in the country, *The Tablet*, were blown up by thugs and security forces (Keen, 2005). State sponsored violence became more intense during election time. In fact the SLPP had to withdraw from the 1973 elections due to the high level of violence that preceded them. Even after the adoption of one party rule in 1978, violence continued to mare elections.

To complement his heavy handed tactics against opponents, Stevens skilfully used clientelism as a 'carrot' to supporters. This guaranteed the support and loyalty of key institutions like the army and police on whose loyalty the APC relied for survival. State collapse and conflict became inevitable due to massive corruption and mismanagement of public funds. William Reno (1998) coined the term 'shadow state' to explain the relationship which existed between corruption and politics in Sierra Leone. Public services and corporations withered in the midst of neglect and massive corruption. In his autobiography, *What Life Has Taught Me*, Stevens himself gives a revealing explanation for this level of corruption, which we will quote in length:

> As far as an African is concerned, once he is elevated to a position of authority he is expected to support a horde of hangers-on .... He must hand out largesse, educate not only his own children but those of family members .... It is all part and parcel of his new position. Money slips through his fingers like quicksilver and he can never have enough of it to satisfy his dependents. When it can be had so easily, when all that is required of him is his influence in tipping the scales in the award of a contract or manoeuvring some other proposition in favour of the donor, the temptation is enormous and it seems foolish to him to refuse such an offer. Fresh in his memory, too, is the hardship he suffered on the way up the ladder, the years of poverty and near starvation he endured and the longed-for education he could never afford .... With plenty of money in the Bank at least his own children would be spared such a deprivation. (1984, 163)

But despite this massive officially sanctioned corruption, Stevens' tight grip on power and intimidation of dissidents prevented a credible challenge to his authority. However, the stage for rapid descent into civil war was set when he handpicked his army chief, Joseph Momoh as his successor. Momoh's apparent weak and inept leadership increased the incidence of corruption to alarming levels. With dwindling resources, the state was incapable of fulfilling even some of its most basic tasks like paying workers and running hospitals and schools (Reno, 1999). The consequence for the masses was a state of declining social services, dilapidated infrastructure, weak and collapsing economy and widespread poverty.

Around the 1980s and 1990s, patrimonial-clientelistic politics in Sierra Leone and indeed across Africa suffered a major crisis of legitimacy. In the case of Sierra Leone, the economy was experiencing a rapid decline by the late 1970s. The country's Gross Domestic Product (GDP) fell from US$1.1 billion in 1980 to US$857 million in 1990. In 1995 it had a debt burden of US$1.2 billion (Kandeh, 1999). The increasing 'informalisation' of the state and weakening of state institutions subsequently led to state failure and collapse. The political and economic discontent generated by this collapse sowed the seeds of the country's decade-long civil war. The ensuing economic hardship drifted thousands of unemployed and disgruntled youths to the diamond-producing region of Kono where they became socialised in a climate of violence, drugs and crime (Pratt, 1999). With endemic poverty and growing unemployment, most of the country's youths became easy prey for disgruntled politicians keen on furthering their political ambitions. The RUF was therefore able to recruit the bulk of their fighters amongst these disillusioned youths; in fact onetime RUF Field Commander, Sam 'Maskita' Bockarie was one of such youths.

Growing student activism and disenchantment with the APC provided the triggers of the conflict. Student radicalism heightened in the mid-1980s resulting from government's suppression of their demonstrations and the exposure to new ideas, mostly those of Colonel Qadafi as expressed in his *Green Book*. In the absence of opportunities and avenues for organised forms of democratic opposition and dissent, violence becomes the only means to seek redress.

Politicisation of the Military in Sierra Leone: The AFRC Coup

Military rule is not a new phenomenon in Sierra Leone and indeed the entire West African sub-region. Between 1967 and 1968 alone, the country had three different military juntas. The politicisation and indiscipline of the military in Sierra Leone can be traced to a multiplicity of factors bordering around patrimonial politics and neglect. The discussion in Chapter 2 clearly shows how the fight for regime survival through patrimonial politics and clientelism has led to widespread politicisation of the military across Africa. In this sense, Sierra Leone is not a unique case. A spate of military coups in the 1960s and 1970s increased President Stevens' suspicion of the force. To counter this growing threat, successive governments have sought to incorporate the top members of the military into the patrimonial politics of the state whilst weakening the institution in a bid to ensure regime survival. To maintain a tight grip on the force, a system of preferential appointments and promotions was put in place whereby only known supporters of the government were given top officer posts. MPs were also given recruitment quotas and the head of the military was made a Member of Parliament. In fact Stevens' successor, J.S. Momoh was head of the military at the time he was hand picked. In a bid to neutralise the majority of the force, Stevens severely weakened the army by downsizing it to 2000 troops and also drastically reducing its budget (Ero, 2000). In its place, the APC formed the Special Security Division (SSD) to act as primary regime protectors. Made up of strong supporters of the regime, the SSD were given superior training by Cuban and Chinese advisers. The effect was the total marginalisation of the military. In response to the RUF threat, Momoh hastily recruited civilians without following established criteria and principles. Dramatically increasing the size of the army to 6,150, most of those recruited were taken from the streets and poorly educated (Ero, 2000). This resulted in a force of inadequately trained and undisciplined soldiers who were incapable of mounting a credible defence against the RUF. In fact the activities of these poorly paid and unmotivated soldiers fuelled the war and earned them the pejorative 'sobels' (soldiers by day and rebels by night).

Growing dissatisfaction in the force over conditions of service and the civilian government's handling of the war led to another military coup in April 1992, which ousted the 24-year old APC government and installed the National Provisional Ruling Council (NPRC) headed by Captain Valentine Strasser. The NPRC junta continued the mass recruitment initiated by Momoh. But despite its pledge, the military government was unable to put an end to the conflict and in January 1996, a palace coup replaced Strasser with his number two man, Brigadier Maada Bio. Responding to both internal and external pressure, the junta organised parliamentary and presidential elections in February 1996 that ushered in the Sierra Leone Peoples Party (SLPP) led by President Ahmed Tejan Kabbah.

The new government's mistrust of the army was apparent. In a secret memo from Solomon Berewa, then Justice Minister, to President Kabbah, he questioned the loyalty of the Chief of Defence Staff and warned against his total control of the military. He went on to recommend the complete restructuring of the armed forces (quoted in Musah, 2000, 93). Kabbah and his SLPP government heeded the advice and transformed the Kamajors into an effective fighting force to rival the national army. The policy of downsizing the army and reducing their influence on national politics also did not go down well with the military. The stage was set for a bitter rivalry between the Kamajors and the military which led to a series of skirmishes between the two in the East and South of the country. After several attempted coups, the government was toppled 14 months later by a coalition of soldiers and the rebel RUF who formed the Armed Forces Revolutionary Council (AFRC) in May 1997 headed by Major Johnny Paul Koromah. In justifying the coup, Koromah said,

Whilst the Armed Forces of the Republic provided for under the Constitution were being starved of logistics and supplies, the SLPP tribal hunter militia, the Kamajors, received logistics and supplies far beyond their immediate needs. This was enough indication of the preference for the private army over our Armed Forces, foreshadowing the ultimate replacement of the Constitutional Defence Force by Mr Kabbah's hunters.[1]

This policy of marginalising the army in favour of the CDF is reminiscent of the APC reliance on the SSD. This also forms part of a calculated attempt to create a military balance to counter weigh the army. However, any sympathy for the AFRC position soon dissipated due to the massive human rights abuses that followed the coup and the determination by the Sierra Leone civil society to defend the fledging democracy they have passionately campaigned for.

ECOMOG and the Restoration of Democracy in Sierra Leone

The coup was widely condemned both at home and abroad. ECOWAS led the international condemnation of the junta in Freetown and the OAU at its 33rd summit in Harare, Zimbabwe also passed a resolution supporting the ECOWAS initiative. In supporting the ECOWAS position, OAU Secretary-General said: 'It is lamentable that some soldiers who have no mandate to rule at all should decide to challenge the legitimate position of the people. It is a setback for Africa's transition to democracy ... This development will not be welcome in Africa' (quoted in Francis, 1999, 149). UN Secretary-General also joined in the chorus of calls for the junta to relinquish power: 'Africa can no longer tolerate and accept as *faits accompli*, coups against elected governments, and the illegal seizure of power by military cliques.'[2] Not to be outdone, the Commonwealth also released statements condemning the *putsch* and called for the unconditional restoration of the Kabbah government.[3]

Hundreds of ECOMOG troops stationed in Liberia were moved to bolster the skeletal ECOMOG force based in Freetown's Lungi Airport. A number of Nigerian and Guinean troops were also based in Sierra Leone as part of Defence Agreements between both countries. Meanwhile behind the scenes, there were frantic diplomatic efforts led by the Nigerian and UK High Commissioners to

---

1   Letter from AFRC Chairman Major Johnny Paul Koromah to ECOWAS Chairman Sani Abacha, August 1997, available online at www.sierra-leone.org, accessed on 18 March 2005

2   UN Secretary-General's Address to the Annual Assembly of Heads of State and Government of the Organisation of African Unity, Harare, 2 June 1997. New York: UN Document SG/SM/6245 AFR/9.

3   Sierra Leone Web, available online at www.sierra-leone.org accessed on 19 March 2005.

secure a peaceful restoration of democracy. Following the breakdown of these talks, Nigerian naval vessels stationed off the Freetown coast began shelling the capital on the morning of 2 June 1997. This ended in humiliation for the Nigerian forces as the combined troops of the RUF and AFRC, known as 'The People's Army', were able to forestall the Nigerian attack and took about 300 Nigerian troops hostage (Sierra Leone Web, 1997). The Ghanaians joined other francophone countries in opposing what they perceive as Nigeria's unilateralist action. In a bid to deflect such criticism, the Nigerian Foreign Minister, Tom Ikimi engaged on a tour across West Africa soliciting support for the Nigerian initiative. During a meeting of West African ministers in Conakry on 26 June 1997, ECOWAS issued a statement calling for 'the early reinstatement of the legitimate government of President Ahmed Tejan Kabbah, the return of peace and security and the resolution of the issues of refugees and displaced persons' (ECOWAS, 1997a). Later in August, ECOWAS foreign ministers formally mandated ECOMOG to 'monitor the ceasefire, enforce sanctions and embargo and secure the peace in Sierra Leone' (ECOWAS, 1997b). This new force became known as ECOMOG II. To achieve their stated objective of restoring democracy in the country, the ministers adopted a three-pronged strategy namely 'dialogue, imposition of sanctions and the enforcement of an embargo and the use of force'. An implementation Committee of Four composed of Nigeria, Ghana, Guinea and Cote d'Ivoire was formed to oversee the process. This was later increased to five to include Liberia, a neighbour that was heavily involved in the Sierra Leonean quagmire. For analytical purposes, we will now take a closer look at the three approaches bringing out their successes and failures.

Negotiations and Dialogue

The dialogue process following the AFRC coup is a tale of frustrated efforts and intransigence on the part of the coup makers. The process started with meetings between ECOWAS and the AFRC junta on 17–18 July and again on 29–30 July 1997. The latter talks collapsed when the AFRC Chairman, Johnny Paul Koromah announced a four-year timetable for the return of democracy and new elections (Koroma, 1997b). The most comprehensive agreement between ECOWAS and the Freetown junta came in October 1997 when both parties agreed on the Conakry Accord. Conakry provides for the following:

- the reinstatement of the legitimate government of President Tejan Kabbah within a period of six months;
- the immediate cessation of hostilities;
- cooperation of the junta with ECOMOG in order to peacefully enforce the sanctions;
- disarmament, demobilisation and reintegration of combatants;
- the provision of humanitarian assistance;
- return of refugees and displaced persons;

- immunities and guarantees to the leaders of the 25 May 1997 coup d'etat;
- modalities for broadening the power base in Sierra Leone.

As in Liberia, the framers of this accord envisaged a best case scenario that did not reflect the junta's intransigence. By allowing the Junta to remain in power until April 1998, Conakry legitimised an illegal regime and set the stage for the mutineers to try and consolidate their hold on power. The junta regarded the ECOWAS six-month plan as an opportunity to regroup, rearm and consolidate their position. Soon after the signing of the accord, the junta's unwillingness to abide by the terms of the agreement was apparent. Contrary to the provisions of Conakry, the AFRC renege on its promises to disarm by insisting on three pre-conditions: (1) the unconditional release of Foday Sankoh; (2) the withdrawal of Nigerian troops from ECOMOG; and (3) the exemption of the AFRC troops from DDR (Koroma, 1997c). There were also credible reports of importation of arms and ammunition across the Liberian border (UN, 1998). To make matters worse, there were frequent attempts by combined AFRC/RUF forces to dislodge ECOMOG troops from their bases at Jui and Lungi. This intransigence seems to have been boosted by undercover support from some West African states mostly Liberia and Burkina Faso. The apparent disagreement on ECOWAS strategy by key states like Nigeria and Ghana also sent the wrong message to the coupists.

Imposition of Sanctions and the Enforcement of the Embargo

The breakdown of the 29–30 July Abidjan Talks exposed the nature of the AFRC regime to ECOWAS Foreign Ministers. In keeping with their three-point plan, ECOWAS member states meeting in Abuja on 28–29 August imposed sanctions on the AFRC. These include 'a general and total embargo on all supplies of petroleum products, arms and military equipment to Sierra Leone' except for the use of ECOMOG (ECOWAS, 1997b). In addition to preventing the importation or exportation of essential commodities, members of the junta were also handed a travel ban. Permission was however granted for the importation of humanitarian goods but only with the approval of ECOMOG. ECOWAS called on member states to respect and help enforce the sanctions and also asked the UN Security Council to make the embargo universal and mandatory. By adopting Security Council Resolution 1132, the UN imposed universal and mandatory sanctions and an embargo on the junta. A special committee comprising of neutral states such as Kenya, Sweden and Costa Rica was set up to oversee the implementation of sanctions. On the ground, ECOMOG was mandated to monitor and enforce the sanctions. It did this through regular naval patrols off the shores of Freetown and reconnaissance flights of Nigerian Alpha Jets.

How effective were the sanctions? According to Oudraat, sanctions 'are intended to deter parties from engaging in certain types of behaviour or to compel parties to undo or reverse certain political or military acts' (2001, 325). The effectiveness of sanctions can therefore be measured in observable behavioural change. In Sierra Leone, did they achieve their objective of dissuading the AFRC from holding onto power and facilitating a peaceful resolution of the conflict? Notwithstanding the lack of modern patrol and reconnaissance equipment, ECOMOG did a remarkable job in enforcing the blockade. After initial lapses that led to breaches of the embargo by few vessels and aircraft using an old airstrip in Magburaka, Northern Sierra Leone, ECOMOG was able to prevent would-be sanction busters from entering the Freetown port. The air patrols also succeeded in intercepting arms supplies from Monrovia. However, the heavy-handed approach adopted by ECOMOG made the sanctions counter-productive. Human rights groups complained that ECOMOG shelled vessels carrying rice, the country's staple food (Amnesty International, 1998). The result was a serious humanitarian crisis. This played very well into the hands of the junta who portrayed ECOMOG and the ousted regime as enemies of the state. This can be understood within the context of the emerging debate on smart sanctions. How can the international community ensure that sanctions hit the target and not punish innocent civilians? Many commentators have questioned the efficacy and morality of sanctions on the grounds that they have unintended social and humanitarian effects (Pape, 1997). Various cases of so-called smart sanctions have revealed how leaders, the primary targets, have been able to circumvent the sanctions at the expense of innocent civilians. The examples of the 'Oil for Food' scandal in Iraq and the sanctions on Zimbabwe are indicative of this point. In Sierra Leone, it was clear that ordinary citizens borne the impact of the sanctions, this is a fact acknowledged by Sam 'Maskita' Bockarie in an interview to the BBC in which he boasted that 'as long as we have our natural resources, like our diamonds and gold, I can tell you that sanctions will affect our poor innocent civilians, but not us as the AFRC'. The fact that there were governments in the region prepared to burst the sanctions also reduced the intended impact. Credible reports show the gun running network involving Burkina Faso and Liberia. The travel ban on members of the junta was also reportedly flouted as AFRC/ RUF elements moved freely in Liberia (UN, 1998). Despite the best efforts of ECOMOG, the sanctions failed in their attempt to facilitate a peaceful restoration of democracy.

The Use of Force

Following months of unproductive talks and intransigence by the Freetown junta, it became clear that force is the only language that the AFRC understands. Responding to an AFRC attack on its Jui Garrison in early February 1998, ECOMOG troops mounted *Operation Sand Storm* that lasted barely a week and succeeded in ousting the junta from Freetown. ECOMOG has dubbed this move as a 'defensive-offensive' operation. However the speed and effectiveness with which the operation was carried out suggests it was pre-planned. In fact during peace talks with Junta representatives, Nigeria's Foreign Minister, Ikimi was reported to have told the AFRC that they should either step down or be flushed out of Freetown (Adebajo, 2002).

The rapid success of ECOMOG can be attributed to a number of factors including the massive civilian opposition to the coup. Nearly all sectors of society were dormant as civil society adopted a policy of civil disobedience. Civilians and loyal soldiers within the AFRC also acted as spies and passed on sensitive intelligence to ECOMOG. As discussed in latter sections of this chapter, the Civil Defence Force especially the Kamajors also played a key role in facilitating ECOMOG victory as they contributed their strength in numbers and knowledge of local terrain to the intervention force. The role of the clandestine pro-Kabbah Radio Democracy should also not go unnoticed as it took the upper hand in the air war between the ousted government and the coup makers. It considerably demoralised the rag tag 'people's army' and sustained civil opposition to the coup. Perhaps the most decisive factor for the ECOMOG success was the indiscipline and unprofessionalism of the AFRC fighters. There was clearly a breakdown of command structures between the RUF and SLA. Preoccupation with looting and human rights abuses deflected their attention from fighting.

A month later, Kabbah was reinstated amidst pomp and celebration. But beneath these scenes of jubilation lie very contentious issues surrounding the entire use of force: legitimacy of the action and the alleged role of a UK-based Private Military Company, Sandline International. We will now examine how these issues impacted on the mission and their implications for future humanitarian intervention.

Legitimacy and Positions of Member States

The ECOMOG forcible intervention in Sierra Leone reignited heated debate about the legitimacy of the use of force for humanitarian or good governance purposes. The ECOWAS pro-democracy intervention in Sierra Leone heralded a new phase in Africa's international relations and a significant shift from the OAU's sacrosanct principle of 'non-intervention' in the domestic affairs of member states. For the very first time, coup prone West Africa had taken steps to restore democracy. One might wonder about the real motives that lay behind the ECOWAS decision to restore democratic rule in Sierra Leone, considering the fact that most of the region's leaders came to power through military coups. In fact the champion of the ECOWAS cause, Sani Abacha was an epitome of dictatorship. Critics accuse Nigeria of exploiting the Sierra Leonean situation to its advantage. They note the irony involved in Abacha's military Junta, known for its deplorable human rights record, using force to oust another military Junta (Conciliation Resources, 1997). Other critics regard the intervention as a calculated attempt by Abacha to deflect international criticism towards his regime and win international credibility (Human Rights Watch, 1997). It must be noted here, however, that ECOWAS, especially Nigeria, was very concerned that instability in Sierra Leone would eventually spill over to Liberia and shatter that country's fragile peace (Francis, 2001).

Other opponents of the ECOMOG intervention question the authority of an outside power to use force in restoring democracy. In his book, *Democracy by Force?*, the former ECOWAS Executive Secretary Abass Bundu attacked the ECOMOG intervention and posits that the regional force had no legitimacy in interfering in the internal affairs of another country because 'there had been neither consultation with other ECOWAS leaders nor any vestige of evidence of an ECOWAS decision in favour of military intervention' (Bundu, 2002). Bundu's position however contradicts his strong support for the ECOMOG intervention in Liberia when he was ECOWAS Executive Secretary. This sudden change can be attributed to his strong opposition of the Kabbah government against whom he contested and lost the 1996 elections. The junta, through their spokesman, Allieu Kamara, was also strongly opposed to what they perceive as a 'violation of the sovereignty and territorial integrity of Sierra Leone'.[4] But as Francis argues, this does not constitute a violation of sovereignty as the junta 'lacked any semblance of internal and external claim to sovereignty' (Francis, 1999, 153). In fact the ousted president was still recognised as the legitimate leader of the country as evidenced by his attendance of the ECOWAS, OAU and Commonwealth summits. Domestically, the widespread civil disobedience that crippled the country is evidence of the junta's lack of internal legitimacy.

The use of force was also condemned by other ECOWAS member states who regarded the action as unilateralist on the part of Nigeria. Blaise Campoare was very blunt in his criticism, 'The agreements between the states of West Africa do not authorise military intervention to restore a regime or organize a countercoup' (Sierra Leone web, 1998). Most other francophone states and Ghana opposed the action and preferred a peaceful resolution of the impasse. The fact that the eventual intervention was not mandated by ECOWAS angered many countries in the sub-region. Others also argue that ECOMOG should have waited for the date stipulated in the Conakry Accord for the handover to Kabbah. However based on the intransigence of the AFRC outlined above, the possibility of a peaceful restoration of democracy seemed remote. It was clear from the actions of the Junta that they were using negotiations to buy time and opportunity to strengthen their hold on power. Although the intervention was not formally approved by ECOWAS, it can be argued that force was part of the three-pronged approach approved by ECOWAS in June 1997. International

---

4   Due to his repeated use of this phrase, Kamara was nicknamed 'Territorial Integrity'.

support for ECOMOG intervention was also widespread. Perhaps it is within the remits of humanitarian intervention that the ECOMOG intervention can best be understood. Following the AFRC/RUF take over, there was widespread abuse of human rights against innocent civilians including incidents of rape, torture and killings of perceived Kabbah sympathisers. There was total break down of law and order and the rule of law was replaced by 'rule of the gun'. As argued in Chapter 1, there is an emerging consensus in post-Cold War international order that regard intervention in complex political emergencies as an acceptable breach of international law.

ECOMOG, Kamajors and the Sandline Connection

British Press reports in March of mercenary involvement in the ousting of the military junta sparked a major row for the Blair government and ignited hot debate on the use of private military companies in peacekeeping and peace enforcement. In what was dubbed 'the arms for Africa affair', the British government was accused of covertly supporting Sandline in shipping arms to Sierra Leone in contravention of UN Sanctions (Africa Confidential, 1998a). Whilst in exile in Guinea, President Kabbah was reported to have held discussions with representatives of a London based Private Military Company, Sandline International in the presence of Nigerian military representatives and UK High Commissioner to Sierra Leone, Peter Penfold. The deal involves a Vancouver-based businessman Rakesh Saxena financing the Sandline Operation with US$10 million in return for mining concessions. Sandline shipped an estimated 35 tons of Bulgarian weapons for the use of the pro-Kabbah Kamajor militia and provided logistics and intelligence support to ECOMOG. It is important to note however that the said weapons only arrived after the restoration of Kabbah.

The Legg Inquiry set up by the Foreign Secretary attributed the problem to overworked officials and faulty office procedures. But despite the inquiry's conclusion that the government had no hand in the matter, it is clear that senior government officials covertly supported the Sandline deal. It seriously damaged Prime Minister Tony Blair's 'ethical foreign policy' claim. Declared following New Labour's landslide 1997 election victory, it aims to 'make the protection and promotion of human rights a central part of our foreign policy' (1997 Manifesto of the Labour Party, cited in Witchell, 1998). This includes banning the sale of arms to repressive regimes around the world. On its part, Sandline argued that it did not break the sanctions as ECOMOG was exempted from the sanctions imposed on the junta. Speaking on behalf of the government, Minister of Information, Julius Spencer pointed to the unpopularity and brutality of the junta and the minimal role played by Sandline (Africa Confidential, 1998a). ECOMOG Officers also share this view and regard the whole Sandline affair as blown out of proportion by the Western press. Whilst they privately acknowledge the logistical and technical support received from Sandline, they however maintain their involvement was not as decisive as the British media suggests. This leads some officers to suggest that the Sandline Affair was a calculated ploy by the west to rob ECOMOG and indeed Nigeria of the credit it deserves. This is a view also shared by Africa Confidential (1998a) when it opines that the Sandline Affair was orchestrated by the US to deny Nigeria the credit for restoring democracy in Sierra Leone.

Whilst these suggestions may be true or not, one thing is certain, the fact that a mercenary company cooperated with a peacekeeping/enforcement mission is bound to raise a lot of debate. Brooks (2000) represents a growing school of thought calling for the legitimisation and use of Private Military Companies (PMCs) in peacekeeping. Using Angola and Sierra Leone as examples, he argues that PMCs are cost effective and capable of providing stability and security and 'end violent wars, provide effective peacekeeping and peace enforcement, and force warring parties to the negotiating table' (141). Consequently, PMCs are increasingly been employed by big powers to do the 'dirty job' for them. For instance the US hired a PMC for the OSCE Observer Mission in Kosovo in 1998–1999 in place of its own officers (Jakobsen, 2001). From Liberia to Sierra Leone, the US used PAE to provide logistical support to ECOMOG. Even the UN is reported to have used mercenaries for protecting their staff and enhancing the enforcement of sanctions (Jakobsen, 2001). Mercenary companies have often acted as foreign policy instruments of Western states, and as Francis argues, 'in their guise of providing security for collapsing but mineral-rich developing states, only accentuate their international exploitation (2001, 187). Williams (2001) consider this an abdication of the international community's responsibility to help resolve third world conflicts. He regards 'any positive humanitarian and political outcomes they may have helped secure have been brief and incidental to their primary goal of profiting from the country's civil war' (145).

The involvement of mercenaries has been a key feature of the Sierra Leone conflict and involves groups such as Gurkha Security Guards Ltd, Executive Outcomes and Sandline International. The fact that all of these groups have been linked with mining concessions confirms the exploitative motives of PMCs. The focus on Sandline should however not overshadow the contribution of the Kamajors in the restoration of democracy. With little more than hunting guns and a deep belief in mystical powers, these traditional hunters played a remarkable role in ensuring that the country is ungovernable under the junta. Vast territories in the south east were effectively under their control leaving the junta with only areas in the North and the capital, Freetown. The Kamajors were also reported to have played a major role in the ousting of the junta from Freetown (Francis, 1999). As people who know the terrain and guerrilla tactics of the RUF/AFRC, they proved to be a major compliment to ECOMOG. But this relationship is not without its problems. Many ECOMOG officers complain about the excesses of the Kamajors and the fact that they disrupt their strategic plans (Adeshina, 2002). Human Rights groups have also accused ECOMOG of turning a blind eye to the human rights abuses committed by the Kamajors. The relationship however survived on the basis that both parties were mutually indispensable to each other: the Kamajors because they needed ECOMOG heavy fire power and ECOMOG because they require the local knowledge and strength of numbers of the Kamajors.

The Establishment and Protection of Safe Havens

In the aftermath of the restoration of constitutional order in Sierra Leone, ECOMOG acted as the *de facto* army since the national army was disbanded by the restored Kabbah administration. This is a decision which foreshadows the US attempt to disband the Iraqi national army and the consequences of such a misjudgement are still evident in that country. In Sierra Leone, the disbanded members of the army fled to the bush together with their RUF colleagues and waged a campaign of mayhem and brutality in the countryside, declaring barbaric operations such as 'operation spare no soul', 'operation no living thing' 'operation cut hand' etc. ECOMOG was forced to deploy in major towns and cities across the country to protect civilians from AFRC/RUF violence. In these difficult circumstances, ECOMOG was able to provide military deterrence to the RUF and use robust action to bring a semblance of security and stability to the traumatised civilians. This achievement earned them the respect and admiration of Sierra Leoneans which is evident to this day.

Just like they did in Liberia, the troops facilitated the resumption of normal services in their areas of deployment like schools and hospitals. The force also assisted the government in re-establishing its authority across the country although local authorities complained that ECOMOG Officers most often usurp this authority as they became by default the judges and police officers of their respective areas of deployment. Adeshina (2002) acknowledged this fact but attributes it to the lack of civilian personnel serving with the mission. Besides their role in restoring essential services, the troops have also been credited for evacuating 'to safety and medical facilities some of the hundreds of victims of amputations and other injuries' (Amnesty International, 1998, 13). For the many starving and hungry people within their areas of deployment, ECOMOG troops were reported to have shared their rations and even assisted with the reconstruction of key infrastructure like roads, schools and bridges (Adeshina, 2002). It must be noted here that most of these activities were undertaken solely by the discretion of troops on the ground and do not form part of any planned ECOWAS/ECOMOG response. The failure to learn from the mistakes of Liberia is very glaring in this respect and cast a big shadow of doubt on the ability and commitment of the sub-regional body to learn from its mistakes. Incorporating humanitarian assistance in a mission operating in a complex emergency is a vital requirement for success. The ECOMOG Force Commander,

Timothy Shelpidi therefore recommended the 'need to consider this aspect in the computation of logistics requirements of the peacekeeping force' (West Africa, 1998, 606). The problem remains a deep lack of resources and commitment on the part of ECOWAS. In addition to the lack of a humanitarian strategy, the force also faced a number of difficulties and failures that evoke memories of Liberia. Key amongst these problems are the failure to secure the safe havens from AFRC/RUF attacks, the poor human rights record and their alleged link with the exploitation of mineral resources. We will now take a closer look at these setbacks and draw the lessons to be learned from them.

The attempt to protect safe havens was plagued by several political and military problems. On the political front, the mission suffered from the lack of adequate international and sub-regional support, financing, commitment and strategy. As was the case in Liberia, major powers like the US and UK were reluctant to support a mission headed by Nigeria, a country they perceive as undemocratic and upon which they have imposed sanctions. Finance was a serious setback as the pledges made to ECOMOG in numerous UN and ECOWAS meetings were not forthcoming. Within the sub-region, the old rivalries that plagued the Liberian mission resurfaced. The Francophones, this time joined by Ghana and Liberia were for the most part bitterly opposed to Nigeria's unilateralist behaviour. The newly elected President of Liberia, Charles Taylor even banned ECOMOG jets from taking off from Monrovia's Robert field for bombing raids on RUF locations.

On the military front, ECOMOG was severely handicapped by differences in strategy amongst troop contributing countries. It was Liberia all over again. Whilst Nigeria continued with its tough military strategy, the Ghanaians maintained their diplomatic and non-enforcement policy. This also affected the military operations as it led to poor command and control. Already affected by language differences, national control of contingents exacerbated the problem. As in Liberia, troops received instructions from their home governments; most often these directives contradicted orders on the ground. It came as no surprise therefore that Ghanaians and Guineans were reluctant to engage in any offensive action, leaving most of the fighting to be done by Nigerians (Adeshina, 2002).

ECOMOG's deployment across the entire country was a big departure from Liberia where they only managed to secure Monrovia and its environs. However, this countrywide deployment plan did not match the available numbers and logistics of the force. The force lacked adequate sea and airlift capabilities in addition to vital air-to-ground support like ground helicopters (UNDPKO, 2003). As of March 1998, the total troop strength stood at 12,000. Troop pledges by some ECOWAS countries like Niger, Gambia and Cote d'Ivoire were never honoured. As a result, the force was seriously over stretched thereby limiting their effectiveness (UN, Aug. 1998). At one point, ECOMOG deployment in the provincial headquarter town of Makeni did not exceed 20 troops (Adeshina, 2002)! This can be attributed to an underestimation on the part of ECOMOG military planners of the strength and capacity of the enemy. After the return of Kabbah, ECOMOG officers constantly referred to the AFRC/RUF as 'remnants' that will soon be flushed out. This also exposed the lack of understanding of the guerrilla tactics employed by the RUF. In several instances, ECOMOG troops have been caught off guard by infiltrating RUF rebel forces. One such incident occurred in Kabala on 27 July 1998 when few armed RUF combatants approached an ECOMOG base with white flags asking to be disarmed. In the process, a massive force of RUF fighters overran the town and ECOMOG base killing several troops (UN, Aug. 1998).

This military instability led to the overrunning of several towns starting from Kono district in December 1998 and eventually to the daring AFRC/RUF assault on Freetown in January 1999. The massive loss of life and unspeakable human rights abuses evoke memories of ECOMOG failures in Monrovia and seriously undermined the force's claim to safeguarding civilians. The inability to secure Freetown can be linked to a number of factors amongst them internal squabbles between the ECOMOG high command and the Nigerian Head of the reconstituted Sierra Leone Army, Gen. Maxwell Khobe (Africa Confidential, January 1999). Although Gen. Khobe had more experience of the Sierra Leone situation, he was often overruled by his senior colleagues in ECOMOG. These confused lines of communication adversely affected the response to the AFRC/RUF assault. To compound the situation, Khobe was also hit with the problem of loyalty of the approximately 3,000 SLA troops under his command. There were reports that some of these troops changed sides – a fact Khobe acknowledged in an address in Lungi. This problem was so serious in Makeni that ECOMOG had to withdraw (Africa Confidential, Jan. 1999). There was also clearly a failure of intelligence and surveillance. Whilst ECOMOG press officers were busy reassuring Sierra Leoneans of their security, the rebels were easily bypassing poorly-manned ECOMOG checkpoints and infiltrating the city with arms and ammunition (Adeshina, 2002). The support given to the AFRC/RUF by the Taylor and Campaore governments also proved decisive and reports of Ukrainian mercenaries within the ranks of the rebel forces further boosted their capacity (UN March, 1999). In response to this humiliation, ECOMOG launched a counter-offensive code-named 'Death before Dishonour'. Within three weeks, the force was able to recapture the whole of Freetown but most parts of the interior remained under rebel control. Besides the humiliation suffered, ECOMOG also came under fire for its deplorable human rights record and its complicity in exploiting the country's minerals.

ECOMOG and Human Rights

The issue of human rights abuses has featured prominently in all ECOMOG operations. But despite the experience gained in Liberia, not much seems to have been done to improve the force's human right record or set in place a system of accountability for excesses. In Sierra Leone, human rights groups and civilians have accused ECOMOG of committing serious violations of human rights (Amnesty International, 1998). These include shelling of civilian targets by ECOMOG alpha jets, summary torture and execution of suspected RUF combatants and their sympathisers and the harassment of civilians at check points. The force was also criticised for its inability or unwillingness to stop the reprisal killings of rebels and their sympathisers by civilians after the restoration of democracy in February 1998. The most serious allegations came in the wake of the January 1999 RUF attack on Freetown when dozens of suspected rebels or collaborators were summarily executed by a notorious Capt. Evil Spirit on the Congo Cross Bridge in Western Freetown. Even the UN which has been very reluctant to oppose ECOMOG was forced to report that 'certain ECOMOG personnel do not consistently ensure full respect for provisions of international humanitarian law, such as those regarding the protection of non-combatants in combat situations ...' (UN March 1999). Perhaps the most embarrassing account of ECOMOG abuses came in the form of a CNN documentary, *Cry Freetown*, filmed by Sierra Leonean journalist Sorious Samura. Although supporters of ECOMOG and the Kabbah government complained that the film is one sided, that should not deflect attention to the excesses of the force. In response to the persistent reports of excesses, the ECOMOG Force Commander established a Civil-Military Relations Committee tasked with investigating allegations of human rights abuses by ECOMOG and CDF and recommending appropriate action to the authorities. The committee included the National Commission for Democracy and Human Rights (NCDHR), the Bar Association, the Police, media, civil society, government and UNOMSIL as observers. But despite this laudable move, human rights abuses continued with reports of escapees from rebel controlled areas intimidated and even executed as alleged rebel collaborators (UN, June 1999).

As usual, ECOMOG officers were quick to defend their excesses as unavoidable due to the nature of the conflict they were engaged in as the lines between combatants and civilians were very blurred. They cited especially the RUF tactics of using civilians as human shield as a factor responsible for the heavy civilian casualties. But peacekeepers or humanitarian interveners in any type of conflict have a primary responsibility of protecting and safeguarding the human rights of civilians. There is hardly any convincing excuse for failing to do just that. The fact that ECOWAS was unprepared to bring the perpetrators into account further undermined the human right credentials of the force. As will be shown below, the organisation also continued its policy of promoting unjust peace by pushing for a blanket amnesty for all perpetrators of human right abuses.

Civil-Military Relations

In addition to securing major towns and cities across the country, ECOMOG also protected major roads linking Freetown and the provinces (Richards, 2003). This allowed vital aid supplies to reach suffering people. However, reminiscent of the situation in Liberia, relations between ECOMOG and NGOs were very tense and full of mistrust. The problems revolve around issues of access and security, mandate, management of information and coordination. NGOs complained that ECOMOG and the Kabbah government restricted their access to needy populations behind rebel lines citing fears of helping the enemy. At one point, the Red Cross was banned from operating in the country. During the period of junta rule, ECOMOG also came under heavy attack for what the aid agencies regarded as calculated attempts to prevent them from operating in the country. Although exemptions were made in the sanctions for humanitarian operations, ECOMOG was accused of deliberately bombing vessels carrying aid supplies. NGOs that operated within Sierra Leone during junta rule were branded by ECOMOG and Kabbah supporters as junta collaborators and subsequently had a tough time with authorities. ECOMOG reportedly harassed national staff of INGOs operating under junta rule accusing them of collaborating with the rebels (UN, March 1999).

Aid agencies also complained that enough security was not provided for them by ECOMOG. They cited frequent ambushes and attacks on aid convoys as demonstrating the risky situation they were operating in. This links up with another allegation that ECOMOG, UNOMSIL and the government deliberately withheld sensitive security information from aid agencies. It is claimed that at the eve of the AFRC/RUF assault on the city, ECOMOG and government officials were still reassuring the public and aid agencies that the situation was under control. In other instances, ECOMOG was said to have declared areas safe when they were still under rebel control. Civilians and aid workers who returned to such areas became the victims of rebel atrocities. These allegations show a lack of effective Coordination mechanism. The absence of an ECOWAS political representative on the ground, similar to the situation in Liberia, clearly hampered coordination with NGOs.

ECOMOG, Nigeria and Diamonds: Linking Strategic Minerals and Humanitarian Intervention

Most of the recent reports and studies on strategic resources in conflicts have focused on insurgent groups with little or no attention on peacekeepers. In Sierra Leone, as was the case in Liberia, ECOMOG troops have been accused of involvement in exploiting the country's diamonds. In a leaked report on the situation in Sierra Leone, the former UNAMSIL Commander, Gen. Jetly first brought this issue to international attention. The report implicated key

Nigerian ECOMOG officers with complicity in exploiting the war economy, claiming that 'the Nigerian army was interested in staying in Sierra Leone due to the massive benefits they were getting from the illegal diamond mining' (Jetley, 2000). Whilst this claim might have been exaggerated, there is ample evidence to support allegations that the Nigerian army was involved in diamond mining in Sierra Leone. Many eyewitnesses of the RUF attack on the Kono district, in December 1998, seem to suggest that ECOMOG forces were caught off guard due to their concentration on diamond mining. In his memoirs, the former Nigerian Commander of the 24th Brigade responsible for Kono district acknowledged this fact:

> Most of the personnel of units deployed at Kono district except those located at Njaima Nimikoro were deeply involved in illegal mining of diamond. Our boys forgot our main mission in Sierra Leone and opted for material gains due to the influence of the SLA soldiers. The allure of having a few gem stones in their pockets was too tempting to resist especially as the only gratification to take back to Nigeria was a paltry $150 as opposed to $900 they often collect while on UN operations. This unprofessional attitude reduced their will to fight tremendously. (Adeshina, 2002, 143)

Africa Confidential (January 1999) was blunter when it claimed that

> the involvement of some Nigerian officers in diamond-mining operations in the east did not just distract them from peace-keeping and frustrate their troops...but also caused major security breaches. Several clandestine RUF militants, male and female, offered their services to the Nigerian officers in their diamond-mining operations as a means of gathering information about ECOMOG troop deployment.

However, it would be hard to substantiate claims of ECOMOG complicity with the RUF in the diamond trade, due to the sensitive nature of this trade. Most of the evidence seems to confirm that this was not a formal policy but a decision taken by a few corrupt officers. As recent examples have indicated, this situation is not unique to ECOMOG. UN peacekeepers in the DRC have also come under attack for involvement in exploiting the illegal war economy. But this involvement in exploiting the illegal war economy risks eroding the credibility of the force and distracts the troops from their task of safeguarding lives.

UNOMSIL/UNAMSIL-ECOMOG Co-deployment

The failure of ECOMOG to militarily defeat the RUF necessitated collaboration with the UN. But were the lessons learned in Liberia of any help to this case? Did the Sierra Leone co-deployment mark a significant step in refining this *ad hoc* UN-ECOWAS relationship? This section seeks to engage with these questions.

The collaboration between ECOWAS and the UN will be critically analysed to determine whether or not the lessons learned in Liberia were applied and to identify strengths and gaps in the relationship.

UN involvement in the crisis dates back to November 1994 when, upon the request of the National Provisional Ruling Council (NPRC) military government, the UN Secretary-General dispatched Mr Felix Mosha, a member of the Department of Political Affairs, to explore dialogue possibilities between the RUF and the government of Sierra Leone. Following this, the UN which was until then silent over the crisis, developed an interest in facilitating a negotiated settlement. A Special Envoy, in the person of Mr Berhanu Dinka, was appointed in February 1995 to facilitate the negotiation process. The UN was instrumental in supporting the democratisation process and facilitating the transition from military to civilian rule in February 1996. Following the restoration of the Kabbah government in March 1998, the UN Secretary-General proposed to the Security Council that a UN Observer Force be deployed alongside ECOMOG to complement the work of the latter. In justifying his proposal, Kofi Annan noted that 'a more visible United Nations' presence could serve to bolster the confidence of the Government and people of Sierra Leone in the commitment to their cause of the international community and encourage more substantial donor support for disarmament, demobilisation, and longer-term rehabilitation and development' (UN, March 1998, 11). By adopting Resolution 1181 of June 1998, the Security Council accepted the Secretary-General's recommendations and established UNOMSIL for an initial period of six months, subject to extension. The initial authorised strength comprised 70 military observers, a 15-person medical unit, 5 civilian staff, 50 international civilian personnel and 48 locally recruited staff. This number was increased in August 1999 to 210 military observers, 35 medical personnel, 107 international civilian personnel and 69 locally-recruited staff.

UNOMSIL's mandate included the monitoring of disarmament, demobilisation and re-integration of ex-combatants, documenting human right abuses and assisting the government's post-war peacebuilding efforts in such areas as restructuring of the country's civilian police and armed forces. As was the case with UNOMIL in Liberia, UNOMSIL's mandate included the monitoring of ECOMOG in the execution of its security tasks. As the force was basically made of unarmed observers, ECOMOG was to ensure its security. Such a relationship called for close coordination and cooperation between the two forces. Yet such collaboration was severely strained as the section below shows.

'Politics of Co-deployment'

The unhealthy working relationship experienced in Liberia between ECOMOG and the UN resurfaced again in Sierra Leone, this time with very dire consequences. This stems from the huge disparity in working conditions of

Table 5.1   Composition of UNOMSIL, September 1998

Country	Military observers	Medical staff	Total
China	3	–	3
Egypt	2	–	2
India	6	15	21
Kenya	4	–	4
Kyrgystan	1	–	1
New Zealand	2	–	2
Pakistan	5	–	
Russian Federation	7	–	7
United Kingdom	7	–	7
Zambia	4	–	4
Total	41	15	56

Source: United Nations (October 1998), *Second Progress Report of the Secretary-General on the United Nations Observer Mission in Sierra Leone*, New York: UN Document S/1998/960.

ECOMOG and UN observers. Whilst ECOMOG soldiers, who suffer heavy casualties, go for months without pay, their UN colleagues drive around in flashy cars and live in expensive houses. This certainly did not go down well with ECOMOG soldiers who describe the UN observers as 'holiday makers enjoying their dollars'. The local media joined ECOMOG in calling UNOMSIL 'beach-keepers' (Cocker, 2003). This situation was compounded by the lack of a proper mechanism for liaison and coordination between the two forces. The UN itself acknowledged this problems and cited 'differences concerning the relative status of military officers, assignment of specific tasks, ways of conducting military operations, all gave rise to unhealthy comparisons and were a source of tension' (UNDPKO, 2003, 29).

Following months of bitter wrangling between the Nigerian-led ECOMOG and UNAMSIL, the Indian Force Commander wrote a damning report of the relationship between the two forces which we will quote in length:

> The accord called for deployment of a peacekeeping force comprising ECOMOG and UNOMSIL to oversee the peace process. This was interpreted by the Nigerians ... that ECOMOG would form a major part of the UN Peacekeeping Force and that this Force would be headed by the ECOMOG Force Commander Maj. Gen. Kpamber. However when Gen. Kpamber went to UN HQ New York, he was very disappointed to learn that he was not going to be the Force Commander of UNAMSIL and that Nigeria would have three battalions as part of UNAMSIL, out of this they had to concede one battalion to the Guineans. The Nigerians therefore felt that they were

not getting a fair deal in the peace process in Sierra Leone despite the sacrifices they had made to pave the way for the peace process. This to a very large extent is the genesis of the present crisis. It is my opinion that the ECOMOG Force Commander along with the SRSG and DCF have worked hard to sabotage the peace process and show Indians in general and me in particular in a poor light. (Jetley, 2000)

Gen. Jetley's allegations sparked a war of words with the Nigerian government. The Nigerian Army Chief, Gen. Malu responded angrily by saying Jetley was 'trying to justify his ineptitude, inaction and inefficiency in the leadership of a multinational force' (quoted in BBC Africa online, September 2000). Nigeria and ECOWAS called for his replacement. The UN gave in to this demand and appointed a Kenyan, Lt General Daniel Opande as the new Force Commander. India responded by withdrawing its contingent from UNAMSIL. The UN was criticised for failing to support Gen. Jetley in his dispute with Nigeria. But as Francis said, this was part of a 'realist political ploy not to antagonise the Nigerian leadership, given the country's dominant role in ECOMOG' (Francis, 2001, 171). This is not unique to Sierra Leone though. In Liberia, the UN was very reluctant to criticise ECOMOG for their excesses and treatment of UNOMIL. The reason for this is not difficult to find: the UN and major powers do not want to commit themselves too deeply in African crises and therefore are always willing to accommodate the role of a regional hegemon. In closely collaborating with the Nigerian-led ECOMOG, critics have accused the UN for turning a blind eye to ECOMOG's human right abuses and legitimising the undemocratic regime of Sani Abacha.

Transition from ECOMOG to UNAMSIL

Article XIII of the Lomé Accord called for the revision of ECOMOG's mandate from peace enforcement to a neutral peacekeeping force and provided for its phased withdrawal and its replacement with an enlarged United Nations force. The Security Council, by its Resolution 1270, authorised the establishment of UNAMSIL with initial troop strength of 6,000, to assist the parties in the implementation of the Lomé Accord. This resolution was passed on the assumption that ECOMOG will remain in the country to provide much needed security until the situation is stable enough. But the burden of maintaining ECOMOG in the face of mounting international neglect was proving unbearable for Nigeria and its regional allies. Speaking at the UN General Assembly in September 1999, President Obasanjo noted that 'Nigeria's continual burden in Sierra Leone was unacceptably draining Nigeria financially' and called upon the UN to assume its responsibility of maintaining peace and security (Obasanjo, 1999). This is a point echoed by Algeria's representative at the Security Council when he stated that 'many appeals by ECOWAS for significant international logistics and financial assistance for ECOMOG went unanswered' (quoted in Williams, 2001, 152). Finally in December 1999, citing the unbearable financial cost and international apathy to ECOMOG, Nigeria informed the UN of its decision to completely pull out of ECOMOG. Ghana and Guinea did likewise. Although Nigeria had been sending signals to withdraw from ECOMOG, the final decision caught UN officials by surprise and clearly sent shock waves throughout UN HQ in New York. In addressing this imminent security vacuum, Resolution 1289 of February 2000 revised UNAMSIL's mandate to include Chapter VII powers of enforcement and expanded the military component to a strength of 11,000, in effect making it the largest UN peacekeeping force in the world.

Despite considerable experience in managing take over of peacekeeping responsibilities in places such as Yugoslavia, Haiti, and Central Africa, the UN was ill-prepared to handle the ECOMOG withdrawal. The handover itself was not properly planned and there were clear signs of lack of coordination and confusion. In some areas of the country, ECOMOG did not even handover to an incoming UNAMSIL contingent (UNDPKO, 2003). In a rush to fill the security gap created by this haphazard withdrawal, UNAMSIL had to deploy troops 'without adequate preparation and training for the conflict environment' (UNDPKO, 2003, 30). The 're-hatting' of some ECOMOG troops also added to the confusion. It was envisaged that these troops will bring with them the considerable experience they have gained in ECOMOG over the years. However, in addition to the logistical constraints they faced, these troops were also not fully aware of their new mandate and rules of engagement. The command and control problems experienced in ECOMOG were also carried over into UNAMSIL. For instance, the BBC reported an allegation made by a senior Indian officer who accused the Nigerians of failing to carry out an order by the Indian force commander, Gen. Jetley to deploy troops to the front line town of Masiaka. A senior Nigerian Officer confirmed this allegation but defended the decision and accused the Indians of taking a back seat and making his men do all the dangerous jobs (BBC Africa online, 2000).

It did not come as a big surprise therefore, after ECOMOG's withdrawal on 2 May 2000, UNAMSIL faced humiliation from the RUF. Under a well-orchestrated plan, RUF combatants attacked UN peacekeepers stationed at the Makeni Disarmament Centre, following the voluntary disarmament of ten of its members. The Makeni incident sparked a wave of RUF attacks on UN peacekeepers deployed all over the country and resulted in the kidnapping of more than 500 *blue helmets* and the killing of four soldiers. UNAMSIL was only saved from total collapse and humiliation with the timely intervention of British paratroopers and Special Forces, who helped to forestall the RUF advance on the city and stabilised the situation.

The Sierra Leone case can be added to a string of UN humiliations in internal conflicts in Somalia, Bosnia-Herzegovina and Rwanda. As discussed in Chapter 1, most of these failures can be linked to the UN's inability to develop appropriate response mechanisms to the complexities and challenges posed by complex political emergencies. Previous experiences in Bosnia and Rwanda highlighted the dangers inherent in sending poorly trained and ill-equipped troops, acting under a weak mandate, into a volatile conflict situation. But as past experiences have shown, the UN hardly learns from these lessons. The Security Council mission dispatched in October 2000 to investigate the factors responsible for the May incident noted that 'different contingents had different perceptions of the mandate and tasks of UNAMSIL. To some extent, this stems from national perceptions, but may also be linked to a lack of precision in the elements of the mandate itself' (Security Council, 2000, 3). Francis reinforced this point when he noted that, 'the largely ill-equipped, un-coordinated and poorly armed UN peacekeepers were powerless and lacked the robust mandate needed to respond to RUF aggression' (Francis, 2001, 169). The ease with which Zambian contingents were overpowered by disorganised elements of the RUF speaks a lot about the force's capability. This reinforced the point made by several commentators who stressed the need for the active participation of the major powers if UN peacekeeping is to achieve its stated objectives. However, like most other operations, the big powers were very reluctant to commit their troops to the Sierra Leone operation. America was still reeling from the Somalia fiasco. And, as part of British official policy, the UK hardly commits its troops to UN command, which it considers weak and inefficient, opting instead for unilateral operations, as evidenced by the Sierra Leone case. That 2,500 British troops serving under 'Operation Palliser' were able to effectively check RUF advance and stabilise the fluid security situation, which a 11,000-strong UN force was incapable of doing, speaks clearly of the need for big power involvement in peace support operations. But the problems that beset the beleaguered UN operation in Sierra Leone go beyond internal UNAMSIL inadequacies and inefficiency and encompass the serious threats posed by the complex politics of co-deployment with ECOMOG and all the regional rivalries and coordination problems that go with it.

In Search of Peace: ECOWAS/ECOMOG and the Sierra Leone Peace Process

Momentum for the peace process in Sierra Leone was kept alive by the combined efforts of both domestic and international actors. At home, the peace process was facilitated by civil society groups such as the Inter-religious Council, the Civil Society Movement, Campaign for Good Governance and the government's National Commission for Democracy and Human Rights. At the international level, the process has been boosted by the involvement of the UN and the British-led International Contact Group on Sierra Leone. However, it is the role of the regional body, ECOWAS that stood out prominently. This is in line with its policy of using diplomatic carrots and military sticks to elicit compliance from the warring factions. The Sierra Leone peace process itself is a story of failed and often frustrated attempts that resulted in several flawed agreements. Between 1996 and 2000, four major agreements were signed namely Abidjan

(November 1996), Conakry (October 1997), Lomé (July 1999) and Abuja (November 2000). As the Conakry Accord has already been discussed above, this section will look at the other agreements and determine how they enhanced or undermined peace efforts.

Despite the involvement of ECOWAS member states like Cote d'Ivoire, the Abidjan Accord is the only agreement not to have been negotiated under the auspices of ECOWAS. That notwithstanding, it forms the basis of successive peace agreements. Signed in November 1996 under the chairmanship of the Ivorian President, Konan Bedie the agreement calls for the cessation of hostilities, a DDR programme, withdrawal of the Private Military Company, Executive Outcomes and an amnesty for the rebels. However, it was clear from the actions of both parties that they were not committed to the agreement. The RUF was said to have signed due to the considerable military pressure they were subjected to in the months following Abidjan. The combined Kamajor/EO forces were able to destroy the RUF HQ at Camp Zogoda. Francis therefore concludes that the RUF signed the agreement in order 'to buy time … to rearm' (Francis, 2000, 360). On its part, encouraged by the successes of the Kamajor/EO offensive, the government sought a complete military victory. It is said to have been behind the arrest of Sankoh in Nigeria under trumped up charges of gun running and also supported a RUF dissident group led by Philip Palmer to challenge Sankoh's leadership (Musah and Fayemi, 2000). At the end, the 25 May military coup derailed all that has been achieved in Abidjan.

With the return of Kabbah in 1998, the government in Freetown and its international backers all went for the military option. Political initiatives to end the conflict took a back seat. As pointed out above, the rebels were regarded as 'remnants' to be flushed out soon. ECOWAS assumed that restoration of democracy and legal state sovereignty will guarantee peace and security. Steps to promote reconciliation were neglected as evidenced by Kabbah's execution of 24 coup plotters. As a result, the call for AFRC/RUF fighters to surrender fell on deaf ears as they feared retribution by government and the civil populace.

Calls for a negotiated settlement only surfaced in the aftermath of the 6 January 1999 AFRC/RUF attack on Freetown. ECOWAS, in collaboration with the UN, the OAU, the Commonwealth and Sierra Leone's Western backers, the United Kingdom and the US, initiated a series of diplomatic efforts aimed at opening up dialogue with the AFRC/RUF rebels. Negotiations between the government and rebels commenced in May 1999 and resulted in the signing of the Lomé Accord on 7 July. Even before the agreement was signed, the government position was increasingly weakened by Nigeria's announcement of an imminent withdrawal from ECOMOG. This premature announcement also bolstered the RUF's confidence of a military victory and considerably strengthened their intransigence. It came as no surprise therefore that Lomé called for the broadening of the government's power base to include rebels in a power-sharing deal and a blanket amnesty to all perpetrators of the decade-long civil war. The RUF leader was rewarded with the chairmanship of the

Board of the Commission for the Management of Strategic Resources with vice-presidential status. This controversial appointment served to legitimise Sankoh and ceded to his control the diamonds that had financed his campaign. The RUF was transformed into a political party with four ministerial and four deputy ministerial positions.

The UN, ECOWAS and Sierra Leone's Western backers became the subjects of widespread criticism for facilitating an unfair peace deal. The agreement was criticised for rewarding the rebels' political violence with a power-sharing deal (Francis, 2000). The blanket amnesty sparked domestic and international outrage for the impunity accorded to war crime perpetrators. By failing to address the issue of justice, the Lomé Accord set the stage for the obstacles that the peace process was to later face. Francis sums up the situation thus

> After years of de-legitimising the RUF and branding Sankoh a war criminal, London and Washington pressured the Kabbah regime to do business with him as a 'legitimate' political actor. The Lomé agreement is a product of a hastily negotiated peace settlement, preoccupied with short-term objectives and glossing over issues of justice .... (Francis, 2000, 364)

Eager to make up for their blunder, The UN soon issued a disclaimer to the blanket amnesty provision. The British and American governments also tried to deflect international criticism by claiming that the deal was solely negotiated by the Kabbah government. Peter Hain, the British Minister for Africa, made the point for his government, 'it is a myth that Britain and the US foisted the Lomé peace agreement on the people of Sierra Leone; on the contrary, it was negotiated by President Kabbah ... and supported by the various African organisations involved' (quoted in Francis, 2001, 168). Despite claims to the contrary, there is overwhelming evidence to support the allegation that the deal was forced on the beleaguered Kabbah government. With the return of democratic rule in Nigeria, and public opinion increasingly questioning the wisdom of Nigeria's protracted and costly involvement in West Africa's conflicts, the Obasanjo government was keen to seek an exit strategy, no matter the consequences (Saliu, 2000). The US envoy to Africa, Rev. Jesse Jackson played a direct role in pressurising Kabbah to agree a cease-fire and subsequently the peace deal. But as Francis (2000) rightly noted, these would have been the same governments to claim credibility had the deal been successful.

The events of May 2000 revealed the uncommitted nature of the RUF to a negotiated settlement. It also revealed the problems inherent in the Lomé accord. However, a combination of military and political pressures succeeded in returning the RUF to the negotiating table. On the military front, an enlarged and revamped UNAMSIL, a restructured government army and highly visible UK-Military presence provided a credible military deterrence to the RUF. On the political front, the RUF also suffered several reverses. The capture and incarceration of the RUF leader, Foday Sankoh dealt a heavy blow to the organisation and put the leadership of the force in disarray. The RUF connection with Charles Taylor was also severely strained after targeted sanctions were imposed on his government. These set of events formed the backdrop for a renewed peace initiative spearheaded by ECOWAS and the International Contact Group on Sierra Leone. In a determined bid to reach a settlement, several ECOWAS leaders took the unusual and highly risky step of visiting the RUF stronghold in Kono. These concerted efforts led to the signing of the Abuja Ceasefire Agreement of 10 November 2000 and the Abuja Ceasefire Review Agreement of 2 May 2001(Abuja II). Both agreements are offshoots of Lomé and reaffirm the parties' commitment to the peace process.

ECOWAS/ECOMOG and Post-War Peacebuilding in Sierra Leone

Disarmament, Demobilisation and Reintegration of Ex-combatants

As was the case in Liberia, successive Peace Agreements from Abidjan to Abuja have placed DDR at the centre of the transition from civil war to sustainable peace in Sierra Leone. But like the peace process, DDR has faced serious challenges and several setbacks. The programme itself collapsed on several occasions as the peace process in the country was plunged into crisis. As a result, DDR in Sierra Leone went through three phases, each with its own challenges and dynamics:

- Phase I: From the restoration of Kabbah in 1998 to the Signing of the Lomé Accord (July 1999);
- Phase II: July 1999 to May 2000;
- Phase III: May 2001 to January 2002.

As this chapter is dealing with ECOMOG's role in the Sierra Leone peace process, we will specifically focus on Phases I and II as they cover the period of ECOMOG deployment in the country. Chapter 8 will however attempt an overall assessment of the programme including the role of international actors and donor agencies.

Overall responsibility for the coordination of the programme was vested in the National Commission for Disarmament, Demobilisation and Re-integration (NCDDR) established in July 1998. ECOMOG was tasked with disarming an estimated 45,000 ex-combatants. Its responsibilities included provision of security at DDR sites, guarding weapons and ammunition and disarming of combatants, to be monitored by UN Observers. The first phase of the programme was a big failure as only 2,973 combatants came forward to be disarmed (UN, December 1998). As action against the AFRC/RUF was still ongoing, the CDF and re-inducted former SLA soldiers could not be disarmed. On the part of the AFRC/RUF, there was a high level of fear and mistrust of ECOMOG. After having fought against ECOMOG for more than a year, RUF/AFRC combatants harboured a deep feeling of animosity and mistrust towards them. Some fighters fear that DDR was just a ploy by ECOMOG and the Kabbah administration to bring them to justice for the massive human rights abuses they committed. These difficulties with the DDR programme did not come as a big surprise though, considering the circumstances under which ECOMOG operated. Both ECOMOG and UNOMSIL were expected to keep a 'peace' that did not exist. Following the removal of the junta by ECOMOG in February 1998 and subsequent ECOMOG action throughout the country, the Abidjan and Conakry agreements were rendered dead and invalid. ECOMOG, therefore, became more of an enforcement than a peacekeeping force. This was a continuation of its policy of constantly shifting from peacekeeping to enforcement. The neutrality and impartiality expected of a peacekeeping force was all but missing, as ECOMOG became, in effect, a party to the conflict. As the security situation near Freetown deteriorated, the few disarmed rebels camped in Lungi were moved to the Freetown Pademba Road Prisons. This action further undermined confidence building and confirmed the rebels' suspicion that DDR was a ploy to get rid of them. The 6 January 1999 attack on Freetown virtually killed off all hopes for a successful DDR as even the few disarmed combatants joined forces with their rebel colleagues.

The Lomé Agreement has the most comprehensive provisions for DDR. It tried to calm the fears of the AFRC/RUF by calling for a revised ECOMOG mandate and a strengthened UN presence. But soon after it was signed, the problems were apparent. The Accord called for DDR to start within six weeks, (a date that was clearly unrealistic) but it did not kick off until 20 October. When it was finally launched, 15 December was set as the deadline for the completion of the disarmament phase. However by April 2000, only 18,000 combatants have been disarmed. The weapons surrendered are also reported to be of very low quality whilst the number of disarmed ex-combatants did not tally with weapons submitted (UN, March 2000). A key factor responsible for this slow pace of disarmament was Foday Sankoh and the RUF's lack of commitment to the peace process. The success of any DDR programme hinges on the cooperation of the warring factions and such compliance was noticeably missing from the RUF. Despite frequent meetings involving the warring parties, UN, ECOMOG and donor agencies, Sankoh and his RUF rebels had different plans. The lack of an effective information dissemination strategy also worked in Sankoh's favour and limited the success of the programme. Ex-combatants are often reluctant to give up their guns (symbols of authority and means of livelihood) unless they have a clear idea of the benefits to be achieved. The absence of an effective information dissemination system therefore meant the ex-combatants were unaware of the provisions of the programme. This void was unfortunately filled by Foday Sankoh and his RUF commanders who exploited the ignorance of the fighters to further their ambitions. During one of his 'sensitisation tours' with the ECOMOG Commander, Sankoh was reported to have told his fighters in the local language not to disarm.

Logistical constraints also severely disrupted the DDR programme. Logistical problems as basic as the preparation of Identification Cards delayed the discharge of ex-combatants from demobilisation camps (UN, January 2004). This delay resulted in the overcrowding of camps and unrest at Port Loko and Lungi Camps. The demobilisation phase also failed to severe the link between ex-combatants and their commanders. Efforts to relocate ex-combatants to their areas of origin were hampered by the ongoing violations of the Lomé Accord as well as fear of reprisal from the civilian population. Linked to this was the lack of an effective reintegration package which would have helped to refocus ex-combatants into desirable and productive activities. But despite numerous lessons learned and repeated calls by UNSG Kofi Annan, international support for the reintegration phase was remarkably low key. The undesired effect was the rearmament of hundreds of disarmed combatants at the outbreak of the May 2000 crisis.

Security Sector Reform under ECOMOG

The sections above have described the unprofessionalism of the Sierra Leone Army and its role in fuelling conflict in the country. Upon assuming power in 1996, the Kabbah administration made army reform a top priority. But as stated above, the deep mistrust of the army and over reliance on the CDF partly led to the AFRC coup. After the restoration of democracy in March 1998, army reform again became part of Kabbah's agenda. ECOWAS, as well as other international actors like the UN and UK also encouraged this plan as a way of building local security capability. There was considerable debate about the possibility of implementing the 'Costa Rican option' whereby the country will have no army but instead depend on a strong and larger police force (Ero, 2000). This option failed to gain public support due to the nature of multiple security threats facing Sierra Leone. In a country still struggling to free itself from internal war within a sub-region characterised by failing and highly unstable states, the need for a highly efficient and mobile force cannot be overemphasised. However as the army has become severely tainted by the events of the past decade, the government attempted a clean break with the past by disbanding the entire force. In retrospect, this was a big miscalculation as the commanders of the defeated army exploited this action to drive home their accusation that the government wanted to supplant the army with its Kamajor militia.

The initial government plan was to have a small army of 5,000 to 8,000 recruited on the basis of equal representation from the country's 12 districts. This army was also expected to include ex-combatants of the RUF, AFRC and Kamajors. ECOMOG/ECOWAS were expected to play a crucial role in the reform process. The ECOMOG Task Force Commander was therefore seconded to serve as Chief of Staff of a skeletal army made up of surrendered AFRC troops and new recruits. The Nigerian government, as the biggest troop contributor, offered to train 250 Officer Cadets. These new troops were deployed alongside ECOMOG contingents. But this reform process was fraught with problems. In the wake of January 6 AFRC/RUF attack on Freetown, a large section of re-inducted former soldiers joined their colleagues to wreak havoc on the very civilians they were supposed to protect. The enormity of the task at hand was again demonstrated during the May 2000 crisis. Despite the gains they were making against the RUF, the army soon disintegrated into factional fighting between new recruits and former AFRC soldiers in Lunsar. Some commentators have also questioned Nigeria's credentials in training the new Sierra Leone army citing the poor record of the Nigerian army as 'years of interference in political life and human rights violations have eroded internationally accepted models' (Ero, 2000). At the end, the Nigerian/ECOMOG role in reforming the army failed to achieve the desired effect of a well trained and disciplined army due to the abrupt withdrawal of the force. Amongst others, Chapter 8 looks at how effective the UN, British and Commonwealth have been in continuing the work started by ECOMOG/ECOWAS.

Conclusion

In response to the question of ECOMOG's legitimacy, this chapter has argued that ECOMOG operations can be justified on humanitarian grounds. There is overwhelming evidence to support this position as the above analysis reveals. Firstly, the scale of human suffering and anarchy constitutes a legitimate humanitarian cause. Secondly, the junta and its supporters' claim of territorial sovereignty was overstated as they lack both internal and external legitimacy or claim to sovereignty. And finally, the international community's continued recognition of the Kabbah government and the subsequent approval of the ECOMOG intervention, including a UN resolution in support of the action, is indicative of international acceptance. The unusual support given to the action by the OAU opened up a new phase in Africa's international relations and provided an opportunity for the regional body to play a constructive role in Africa's increasing civil wars. The force was successful in restoring democracy to the country. In a region notorious for military coups and insurrection, this is a remarkable achievement. However, this outstanding military success was clouded in controversy surrounding the involvement of mercenaries. The mercenary question poses a major threat to the future of peacekeeping.

ECOMOG's robust military response to the RUF threat managed to restore a semblance of security. But the over-reliance on military options at the expense of a coherent political strategy meant the security enjoyed by Sierra Leoneans was short-lived. This, coupled with the perennial logistical and financial constraints of the force, led to the collapse of the safe havens. Besides failing in their primary objective of safe guarding civilians, these attacks also revealed ECOMOG's failure to learn from the mistakes of Liberia. Human rights abuses and allegations of complicity in exploiting mineral resources continued to taint the record of the force whilst relations with NGOs, UN and civil society groups are still fractured. The lack of a well planned and coordinated exit strategy also undermined the peace making and peacebuilding efforts of ECOWAS. This led to the unjust and flawed Lomé accord which in turn set the stage for the dramatic events of May 2000. At the end, ECOMOG/ECOWAS failed in its long term aim of building an effective security apparatus capable of maintaining an environment of peace and stability. But in the midst of these failures and excesses, ECOMOG deserves commendation for venturing into a forgotten crisis and drawing the world's attention to the plight of Sierra Leoneans.

Chapter 6

Peacekeeping without Nigeria: ECOWAS Intervention in Guinea Bissau and Cote d'Ivoire

Introduction

This chapter traces the background to the conflicts in Guinea Bissau and Cote d'Ivoire, the role of ECOWAS and the wider international community in facilitating peacemaking and peacekeeping processes and examine the opportunities and challenges facing these countries as they seek to consolidate peace. Whilst previous peacekeeping missions have been deployed in Anglophone countries, these operations represent the first time ECOWAS is venturing into Francophone (Cote d'Ivoire) and Lusophone (Guinea Bissau) countries. The absence of Nigeria, a country that has dominated peacekeeping missions in Liberia and Sierra Leone also sets these missions apart as is the fact that both conflicts were triggered by army mutinies. These characteristics of the ECOWAS interventions in Guinea Bissau and Cote d'Ivoire add a new dimension to the analysis of sub-regional peacemaking and peacekeeping efforts and provide a fresh perspective to the Anglophone-Francophone rivalry and Nigeria's role in West African security.

Background to the Conflict in Guinea Bissau

Although the trigger of the war can be located in the rivalry between President Joao Bernardo 'Nino' Vieira and his army chief, General Ansumane Mane, the root of the conflict can be traced back to the 24-year misrule of the *Partido Africano da Independencia da Guine e Cabo Verde* (African Party for the Independence of Guinea and Cape Verde – PAIGC). A former Portuguese colony, Guinea Bissau waged a bloody liberation struggle under its charismatic leader – Amilcar Cabral in the 1970s. A liberation army of 6000 succeeded in forcing the withdrawal of 30,000 Portuguese troops and independence was declared in September 1974. As in other newly independent African countries, the PAIGC inherited a country that was ill-prepared to govern itself with an illiteracy rate of 95 per cent and a weak economy (Adebajo, 2002). However, once in power, the high expectations of the masses never materialised as the party became engulfed in massive corruption, dictatorship and repressive rule. The army staged a coup in November 1980 that brought in 'Nino' Vieira. The new administration continued the same repressive policies of its predecessor. Power was concentrated in the presidency and security forces were used to suppress opponents. For instance, during his first six years in power, he uncovered three 'coups'. Most of the people accused in these plots were opposition figures. Due to pressure from Guinea Bissau's external allies mainly France and Portugal, Vieira allowed gradual liberalisation of the political system. He introduced multiparty rule in 1990 and conducted elections in July 1994. However, these reforms were mere tokens meant to legitimise his tight grip on power. His autocratic and repressive leadership style led to widespread discontent amongst the people and even the military, which had been his major support base. The army's grievances included issues such as delays in the payment of salaries, political interference in the management of the military and the forced demobilisation of veterans of the liberation struggle (Ferreira, 2004).

The trigger for the conflict came in January 1998 when Vieira suspended his army chief, Ansumane Mane, accusing him of supplying arms to the MFDC rebels in neighbouring Senegal. Following his sacking and attempted arrest, Mane staged a coup on 7 June 1998 that led to fierce fighting in Bissau. The fighting resulted in hundreds of deaths in Bissau, the stagnation of its weak economy and massive destruction of the country's infrastructure. Most of the army deserted to Mane and managed to seize about three-fourths of the country including its international airport. Vieira therefore recruited young people from his Pepel ethnic group to constitute a Militia called the *Arguentas*. To further shore up his fragile government, Senegal and Guinea deployed 2000 and 400 troops respectively in Bissau. Like Nigeria in Liberia and Sierra Leone, ECOWAS approval for the Senegal and Guinean intervention only came a month later in July 1998 when they met to sanction the operation.

The Politics of Peacemaking: ECOWAS and CPLP in Guinea Bissau

ECOWAS foreign and defence ministers met on 3 July 1998 to discuss the Guinea Bissau conflict at the request of the besieged President Vieira. The ministers condemned the coup, reaffirmed their support for the legitimate Vieira government and sanctioned the intervention forces from Senegal and Guinea. The ministers also recommended the extension of ECOMOG's duties to cover Guinea Bissau. To find a peaceful resolution to the conflict, a committee of seven was constituted made up of Burkina Faso, Cote d'Ivoire, Ghana, Guinea, Senegal, Gambia and Nigeria. It was later expanded to nine with the addition of Togo and Cape Verde. Meanwhile, the *Comunidade dos Paises de Lingua Portuguesa* (Community of Portuguese-speaking Countries – CPLP) consisting of Brazil, Portugal, Cape Verde, Sao Tome and Principe, Mozambique and Angola also took an active part in the resolution of the conflict. It facilitated the signing of a Memorandum of Understanding between Bissau's conflicting parties on a Portuguese frigate, the *Corte-Real* on 26 July 1998. The agreement's key point is the withdrawal of the Senegalese and Guinean contingents and their replacement with troops from lusophone countries. This CPLP peace initiative did not go down well with ECOWAS and its members who saw it as an attempt by an outside body to interfere in its backyard. However, with continued fighting in and around Bissau and deteriorating humanitarian conditions, both the CPLP and ECOWAS joined forces to broker a cease-fire in Praia, Cape Verde on 26 August 1998. This agreement lasted barely two months before heavy shelling erupted in Bissau and surrounding towns.

Following months of failed peace accords and cease-fire agreements, the parties signed a comprehensive peace accord in Abuja in November 1998 facilitated by ECOWAS and the CPLP. The agreement called for a power sharing deal between the government and the mutineers, a national unity government to oversee elections, the withdrawal of foreign troop and their replacement with ECOMOG forces. As part of the implementation of the Abuja Accord, Francisco Fadul was appointed Prime Minister in December 1998 and ministries were allocated to representatives of Vieira and Mane in January 1999. In the same month, Senegalese and Guinean troops started a gradual withdrawal of Bissau but stopped short of complete withdrawal to prevent a security vacuum that will be exploited by Mane's forces. The peace process hit a crisis of confidence with all the parties suspicious of the others' intentions. Mane called for the inclusion of troops from CPLP countries in the proposed ECOMOG force for fear that France and Senegal would manipulate the Francophone countries of the force. The Prime Minister-Elect, Fadul refused to take office until the complete withdrawal of Senegalese and Guinean forces. Vieira accused Portugal of supporting his rival, Mane. In the midst of this climate of deep mistrust, heavy fighting erupted again on 31 January 1999 with dire consequences for the city's civilian population. With the intervention of Togo's Foreign Minister, Kokou Koffigoh, Vieira and Mane signed a cease-fire agreement on 3 February 1999. This eventually led to the inauguration of the government of national unity on 20 February.

ECOMOG III and Peacekeeping in Guinea Bissau

In planning for the ECOMOG mission in Guinea Bissau, ECOWAS dispatched the ECOMOG Force Commander in Sierra Leone, Nigerian General Timothy Shelpidi to carry out a needs assessment in Bissau. In his report, he recommended the deployment of a 5000-strong force to oversee the implementation of the peace agreement with initial 2000 troops to replace the departing Senegalese and Guinean troops. However, due to financial and logistical constraints, ECOWAS reduced the numbers to 1450 with the initial force number of 600 (Adebajo, 2002). The first ECOMOG troop deployment took place between 26 December 1998 and 2 January 1999 when Togo dispatched 110 troops. This deployment however led to controversy as the ECOMOG Force Commander in Sierra Leone, Shelpidi, complained that the troops were deployed in Bissau without his knowledge. Having done the needs assessment, Shelpidi assumed that the force would be under his command. But on a visit to Togolese troops in Bissau in December 1999, he was told by their Commander, Colonel Gnakoude Berema that the force was under Togolese and not Nigerian command. This incident is indicative of the uncoordinated and ad hoc nature of ECOMOG deployment.

After a brief delay in deploying other contingents due to the usual logistical and financial constraints, ECOMOG III started operations in February 1999 with 712 troops. Contributing countries included Benin, Gambia, Niger and Togo. The troops successfully reopened the country's international airport and secured its seaport. ECOMOG also facilitated the disarmament process and was able to recover some heavy and light weapons (Adebajo, 2002). ECOMOG's effectiveness was however seriously hampered by poor logistics and low numbers. The force was said to have very few vehicles which frequently broke down. The lack of radios and communication equipment also meant the force could not patrol at night. The low numbers prevented them from venturing out of Bissau and deploying along the Senegalese border as envisaged by the Abuja Accord. General Mane exploited these weaknesses to stage a coup in May 1999 that succeeded in routing the demoralised forces of Vieira. ECOMOG troops became bystanders and unable to enforce the terms of the peace accord they were tasked to implement. ECOWAS foreign ministers meeting in Lomé on 24 and 25 May condemned Mani's coup and decided to withdraw the force in June. By adhering to traditional peacekeeping duties, ECOMOG in Guinea Bissau became a dismal failure and mere spectators to the conflict. This underlines the argument that peacekeeping troops in complex political emergencies require a robust strategy to force compliance from warring parties. Another factor responsible for ECOMOG's humiliating withdrawal is the absence of Nigeria, a country that has provided the bulk of personnel and resources towards the ECOMOG missions in Liberia and Sierra Leone. All the contributing countries to the mission in Guinea Bissau are relatively smaller countries that are financially and militarily incapable of maintaining a long drawn out campaign in a foreign country. Although many states in the sub-region are worried about Nigeria's domination, the debacle in Guinea Bissau is a clear indication that the sub-region needs a hegemon like Nigeria who should constructively use its military and financial might to support West African peace and security efforts.

Peacebuilding in Guinea Bissau

Following the signing of the Abuja Accord, the UN Security Council established a small political mission – the UN Peacebuilding Support Office in Guinea Bissau (UNOGBIS) tasked with the implementation of the Abuja Accord and consolidation of the fragile peace. However, the peacebuilding process in Guinea Bissau suffered from lack of international financial support. Donors at the Geneva Round Table Conference for Guinea Bissau held in May 1999 pledged $220 million but only $6 million was actually given to the country before the General elections in 1999 (Ferreira, 2004). This lack of funds seriously undermined the transitional government's effort to implement peacebuilding programmes.

In late 1999, elections were organised and Kumba Yala of the *Partido da Renovacao Social* (Social Renewal Party – PRS) was elected President. But as experiences elsewhere have shown, the mere holding of democratic elections is not a guarantee of good governance and by extension, peace and stability. Soon after the inauguration of the new government in February 2000, tensions between the leaders of the military junta and the government threatened to unravel the fragile peace process. Following an unsuccessful military coup, the former head of the military junta, Ansumane Mane was assassinated. Disagreements and poor working relationship between the ruling party and its coalition partner, *RGB-Movimento Bafata* (RGB-MB) also added to the climate of uncertainty and instability overshadowing the peace process. President Yala's constant reshuffling of cabinet ministers and his erratic style of governance led to the withdrawal of the RFB-MB party from the coalition government in January 2001 thus plunging the country into political turmoil. Besides the frequent friction with the legislature, Kumba Yala's relationship with the judiciary and press was also problematic. Contrary to the country's constitution, President Yala dismissed senior judges of the Supreme Court. He closed down radio and TV stations that were critical of his rule. In November 2002, he dissolved the national assembly thereby plunging the country into political paralysis. These actions led to widespread social discontent as evidenced by the frequent riots, strikes and unsuccessful military coups. With waning public support, the president turned to his ethnic group, the Balanta for legitimacy. Most appointments for public posts went to Balantas leading to observers calling it '*balantasation*' of Guinea Bissau (Ferreira, 2004). Following the frequent postponement of legislative elections, the military capitalised on the prevailing political instability and economic hardship to wage a successful coup in September 2003. The transitional government conducted legislative elections in March 2004 and Presidential elections in 2005 which returned the pre-war ruling party, the PAIGC and leader, Nino Vieira.

However, despite the remarkable progress in maintaining the fragile peace, the country faces major challenges. The security sector reform programme is lagging behind. The security sector in Guinea Bissau is characterised by its large size, inverted hierarchical pyramid (i.e. more high-ranking officers than junior ranks), politicisation and lack of capacity (Observatoirie de l'Afrique, 2008). With help from the UK Security Sector Advisory Team, the government was able to prepare a SSR Strategy Document in October 2006 which was presented to donors in Geneva in November 2006. However, despite pledges of support, SSR continues to suffer from lack of resources. Consequently, the security forces are poorly trained and equipped and incapable of policing the country's borders. This has led to problems of cross border crime, drug trafficking and terrorism. The country risks becoming a narco-state as cocaine traffickers from Latin America transit through Bissau on their way to Europe. Revenue from the trade has corrupted military officers and government functionaries. This ugly development threatens to unravel the fragile peace, undermine the ongoing democratisation process and further weaken the state's limited capacity to deliver economic and social amenities. In recognition of this threat, the UN Peacebuilding Commission added Guinea Bissau to its agenda in December 2007. However, the international community and Guinea Bissau's external partners need to prioritise security sector reform and coordinate their programmes.

Cote d'Ivoire: From 'Oasis' of Peace to a Divided Nation

Cote d'Ivoire descended into conflict in September 2002 when 800 soldiers, who were about to be demobilised from the Ivorian Armed forces, mutinied in the Commercial capital of Abidjan (Malan, 2004). The attacks quickly spread to the northern cities of Korhogo and Bouaké with very devastating consequences. Just in the first few days of violence, an estimated 400 people were killed including the country's first military leader, Robert Guei. The Ivorian army, known to be ill-equipped and unprepared for battle, quickly mobilised and succeeded in flushing the rebels from Abidjan but failed in their bid to take the northern half of the country. The country became effectively divided into two – the northern half controlled by *Mouvement Patriotique de Côte d'Ivoire* (MPCI) rebels and the south by the government. French troops already based in the country as part of bilateral ties maintained a buffer zone between the belligerents. In November 2003, two new groups emerged in the west of the country calling themselves the *Mouvement Populaire du Grand Quest* (MPIGO) and the *Mouvement pour la Justice et la Paix* (MJP) claiming to avenge the killing of General Guei. However, both groups, made up of former RUF fighters from Sierra Leone and Liberian government soldiers are believed to be proxies of Liberian President Taylor. Unlike their northern counterparts, MPIGO and MJP became notorious for vandalism, pillage and terror.

The conflict itself is a manifestation of the deep rooted grievances held by people from the north over what they perceive as political marginalisation by the south. Since independence in 1960, the country's government, civil service, commercial sector and academia have been dominated by Southerners. At independence, the Ivorian government made it a policy to encourage immigration from neighbouring states to boost its booming agriculture sector. Consequently, the population grew dramatically from 3 million in 1960 to 17 million in 2002 (Malan, 2004). Of this figure, 3 million were from Burkina Faso, 2 million from

Mali, between half a million to 1 million from Ghana and over 250,000 from Guinea. Besides, there were thousands of refugees from Liberia. However, when world market prices for cocoa and coffee fell drastically in the 1980s, the huge number of immigrants began to be seen as a burden by many Ivorians. Subsequent Ivorian politicians have exploited this anti-immigrant sentiment to gain political support. In his desperate bid to cling on to power, President Bedie institutionalised the political concept of *Ivoirite* which distinguishes between 'mixed' and 'pure' Ivorians. A controversial law was passed that stipulates that presidential candidates must be born in Cote d'Ivoire to parents who were themselves born in the country. This law was aimed at disqualifying the main opposition leader, the former Prime Minister, Alanssan Quattara. The law stoked up ethnic tensions and infuriated the millions of non-native residents and the majority of Ivorians living in the North who support Quattara. The tensions also took on a religious dimension as the majority of northerners are Muslims and Christianity is dominant in the South. The concept of Ivoirite also had implications for land ownership as only 'pure' Ivorians can own land. This led to skirmishes in many localities (WANEP, 2002).

In the midst of this political turmoil, the army staged a coup in December 1999 that ousted the unpopular Bedie and the former army chief, Robert Guei was named Head of State. Using Bedie's law, Guei again banned Quattara from contesting elections he conducted in October 2000. He attempted to rig the elections but was forced to flee by massive demonstrations. Long time opposition leader, Gbagbo became president by a wide margin. However, his attempt to demobilise 800 members of the Ivorian Armed Forces was the catalyst that led to the outbreak of the civil war in Cote d'Ivoire.

ECOWAS and International Peacemaking Efforts in Cote d'Ivoire

ECOWAS was very swift to condemn the mutiny in Cote d'Ivoire and offer its support to the democratically elected President Gbagbo. An extraordinary summit of ECOWAS Heads of State and Government was convened in Accra, Ghana on 29 September 2002. The summit named the Heads of States and Government of Ghana, Guinea Bissau, Mali, Niger, Nigeria and Togo to constitute a High Level Contact Group to negotiate a peaceful end to the conflict. The group began its peacemaking efforts by meeting with President Gbagbo and leaders of the MPCI in early October. However, these early efforts were frustrated by the government's refusal to sign a cease-fire agreement on the grounds that it would legitimise the partition of the country. The Senegalese Foreign Minister together with the UN Secretary-General's Special Representative for West Africa and the ECOWAS Executive Secretary spearheaded another effort that culminated in the signing of the cease-fire on 17 October 2002. The agreement calls for the return of normal services in all the occupied territories and for the two parties to maintain their positions. President

Gbagbo requested French forces already based in the country to monitor the ceasefire and maintain a buffer zone between both forces.

ECOWAS designated the Togolese President, Eyadema, to facilitate the peace process. The talks began on 24 October 2002 and a first agreement reached on 31 October. Under this agreement, both parties reaffirmed their commitment to the ceasefire, respect human rights and preserve the territorial integrity of the country. However, the talks stalled over the rebels' insistence that President Gbagbo should resign and the constitution be revised and fresh elections held. The government on the other hand insisted that the rebels should disarm and honour their commitment to the preservation of the country's territorial integrity. Despite this setback, Eyadema was able to secure a cease-fire agreement with the western based rebel groups, MPIGO and MJP who were not parties to the earlier ceasefire agreement.

A fresh initiative was spearheaded by the French Foreign Minister, Dominique de Villepin, when he visited the country in early January 2003 and invited all the conflicting parties to peace talks in France. The talks were held in *Linas-Marcoussis*, outside Paris from 15–24 January 2003. The agreement provided for a government of national unity and a new prime minister with extensive powers, the conduct of free and fair elections and the amendment of the constitution to address the problem of identity and citizenship. In March 2003, a second summit was hosted in Accra which put together the government of national unity and appointed a new prime minister, Seydou Diarra. However, both parties never adhered to the terms of the peace process and in March 2004, the *Forces Nouvelles* (FN – a coalition of the three main rebel groups) and opposition parties worked out of government in protest at the killing of 120 of their supporters. Gbagbo subsequently sacked three opposition ministers including the rebel leader, Soro. The Accra III agreement signed in July 2004 resulted in the return of the rebel and opposition ministers to the transitional government. However, like previous agreements, Accra III soon stalled amidst rising political tensions and failure to implement key provisions of the agreement like DDR.

Following the problems with the Linas-Marcoussis and Accra III agreements, South African President Thabo Mbeki led mediation efforts to end the conflict. This led to the signing of the Pretoria Agreement and the appointment of Konan Banny as Prime Minister. The FN soon expressed their disapproval of the agreement in August 2005 and the country remained in a state of war, what Ivorians call no-war-no-peace situation. Upon the expiration of President Gbagbo's term of office in October 2005, the UN passed a resolution establishing a transitional government whilst Gbagbo remained President. Following the recommendation of ECOWAS and the decision of the African Union Peace and Security Council, the UN Security Council passed Resolution 1721 in November 2006 extending by one year the term of the transitional government. Most notably, it strengthened the powers of the Prime Minister by giving him '… all the necessary powers, and all appropriate financial, material and human resources, as well as full and unfettered authority … [and] … the necessary authority over the Defence and Security Forces of Côte d'Ivoire'. The widening of the powers of the PM did not go down well with the President who decided to hold direct talks instead with the rebel leader, Guillaume Soro. Gbagbo saw direct talks with the rebels as a strategy to maintain control of the peace process and prevent succumbing to the dictates of the international community. The talks, hosted by Burkina Faso culminated in the signing of the Ouagadougou Peace Accord in March 2007. Key provisions of the agreement include the establishment of a new transitional government, registration of undocumented residents, disarmament and demobilisation of ex-combatants, reunification of the FN and the Ivorian defence forces and the holding of elections. The head of the FN, Soro was made PM. A timeline of 10 months was agreed for the implementation of the accord. However, considering the challenges facing the peace process in Cote d'Ivoire, that deadline was very ambitious and unrealistic. Although observers have commended the agreement as representing the best chance for peace in the country, the exclusion of civil society and other political parties in the direct talks is a major flaw of Ouagadougou.

The ECOWAS Mission in Cote d'Ivoire (ECOMICI)

On 26 October 2002, the ECOWAS Defence and Security Commission submitted a proposal for the deployment of the ECOWAS Mission in Cote d'Ivoire (ECOMICI) to the organisation's Mediation and Security Council. This was in response to the Ivorian government's request for an ECOWAS peacekeeping force. The force was approved by ECOWAS and mandated to 'monitor the cessation of hostilities; facilitate the return of normal public administrative services and the free movement of goods and services; contribute to the implementation of the peace agreement; and guarantee the safety of the insurgents, observers and humanitarian staff' (Malan, 2004). Total troop strength of 2,386 was approved. A Nigerian, Raph Uwechue was appointed the Special Representative of the Executive Secretary whilst a Senegalese, Brigadier General Papa Khalil Fall was named Force Commander.

However, deployment of the force was delayed due to lack of planning capacity at the ECOWAS secretariat and the perennial problem of logistics. The office of the Deputy Executive Secretary for Political Affairs, Defence and Security which was responsible for peacekeeping only had two staff. ECOWAS countries, the UNDPKO and the US European Command had to second some of their officers to help with mission planning. On the issue of logistics, the lack of a standing ECOWAS logistics base meant the mission had to wait until there were sufficient offers of support from Western countries. Memoranda of Understanding were signed between the various troop contributing countries and a Western partner to assist with logistics and communication equipments. The UK supported Ghana; Belgium assisted Benin whilst France channelled its support to Senegal, Togo and Niger. The US provided support towards strategic transportation within the mission area and two-thirds of the force's food requirements (Faye, 2004). ECOMICI finally deployed on 29 March 2003. The force comprised of 1,300 troops from Ghana, Benin, Niger, Senegal and Togo. It was deployed alongside French forces serving under *Operation Licorne* and the UN Mission in Cote d'Ivoire (MINUCI), a political mission. From the outset, the number of troops was too low for the enormous task at hand. Some of the countries that had promised troops failed to honour their pledges. The mission was therefore not able to deploy to designated areas. However, the presence of French troops greatly complimented the task of ECOMICI. Although the support the mission received from Western countries enhanced its logistical capacity, it inadvertently led to a lack of integration in equipment and communication.

Despite the above difficulties, ECOWAS deserves commendation for the quick response to the Ivorian conflict. Unlike past interventions, the organisation was also able to get the agreement of all its members for the mission before it was deployed. There were very clear rules of engagement and troops on the ground were very well trained. However, although there was donor support, such help was very slow in coming. This underlines the need for ECOWAS to maintain a logistical support base which will be used for rapid deployment whilst awaiting donor support.

Building the Peace in Cote d'Ivoire

Unlike Sierra Leone and Liberia which were effectively collapsed states needing massive international support, Cote d'Ivoire still has a functioning, albeit divided state. Nevertheless, the challenges facing the country are enormous. These include implementation of the DDR programme, reform of the security sector, addressing the identity and citizenship question and holding free and fair elections. However, like the peace process itself, implementation of peacebuilding programmes has been hampered by lack of political will by the faction leaders. The Ouagadougou agreement provided a new lease of life to the peace process. This has resulted in the dismantling of the 'zone of confidence' – the buffer zone dividing the country between the rebel controlled north and the areas under government control. Although the country is now technically 'united', the re-establishment of government authority in rebel controlled areas is moving at a slow pace due to problems of infrastructure and finance. Many civil servants redeployed to the north had to return to Abidjan citing poor working conditions and infrastructure. In April 2008, the UN reported that the committee responsible for the extension of state authority reported a funding shortfall of $20 million (UN, April 2008). The vacuum created has been filled by rebel commanders who continue to control local structures and collect revenue for themselves.

DDR has been a key component of successive Ivorian peace agreements from Linas-Marcoussis to Ouagadougou. The Ouagadougou agreement stipulates 22 December 2007 as the commencement date for the cantonment of the two armed forces. Whilst the Ivorian government forces were able to encamp 12,000 of its soldiers by January 2008, the FN only had 109 ex-fighters in cantonment sites as of April 2008 (UN, April 2008). The lack of progress on the part of the FN is partly due to logistical and financial constraints. Only 65 per cent of the $420 million required to complete the DDR and elections have been received as of June 2008. International donors have been reluctant to offer funding due to doubts about the programme's capacity and structure. This has led to growing unrest amongst ex-rebels who rioted in Boake in June 2008 over failure to pay their reinsertion benefits. The civic programme which is designed to reintegrate estimated 20,000 ex-fighters and 20,000 youths at risk is also facing difficulties of funding and is yet to commence. The disarmament of militias has also stalled due to disagreements between the government and militia leaders over the payment of stipends and reintegration benefits. Like the DDR programme, the reform of the security sector is also progressing at a slow pace. The third supplementary agreement to the Ouagadougou Peace Agreement stipulated 15 December 2007 as the deadline for developing a framework for the organisation, composition and functioning of the new Ivorian security forces. The deadline was not met and in January 2008, the President established a working group to develop the framework. Disagreements over the number of FN soldiers to be integrated into the force and their ranks threaten to undermine efforts to reunify the two forces.

The question of identity and citizenship remains a thorny issue in resolving the Ivorian conflict. As part of the Ouagadougou agreement, the government and FN agreed to set up mobile courts to conduct public hearings and issue duplicate birth certificates to Ivorians who are 18 or above and whose births were never registered. One hundred and eleven teams were deployed through out the country to carry out the exercise which was successfully completed in April 2008. A French company, SAGEM were contracted to work with the National Statistics Office and to issue identity documents and voter cards. Although the identification process has gone well in most of the country, there are concerns that many Ivorians in the west of the country have not been able to access the mobile courts due to fear of militias (UN, April 2008).

Under the terms of the third supplementary agreement to the Ouagadougou Peace Accord, elections were scheduled to take place in June 2008. The conduct of free and fair elections is dependent on the timely and successful implementation of the other provisions of the accord discussed above. However, considering the delays and problems facing those programmes, the June date became unfeasible. Elections have now been rescheduled for November 2008 and even that date is looking increasingly unlikely at the time of writing this book. As elections have been at the centre of the Ivorian conflict, the success of the peace process will to a very large extent depend on the conduct of free, fair and inclusive elections. Continued delay poses a major threat to the consolidation of peace.

Conclusion

The conduct and outcome of the ECOWAS missions in Guinea Bissau and Cote d'Ivoire have far reaching implications for West African security. Besides being the first ECOWAS missions to be deployed in non-Anglophone countries, they are the only operations where Nigerian troops were not involved. Consequently, the Guinea Bissau mission ended in dismal failure when the troops were reduced to mere spectators after one of the parties to the conflict decided to break the terms of the peace accord. In Cote d'Ivoire, had it not been for the presence of French troops, ECOMICI would have been a big failure considering the missions low troop numbers. Two lessons can be learned from these experiences. Firstly, ECOWAS has still not overcome the rivalry between francophone and Anglophone countries. This rivalry has been a crucial factor that shaped the organisation's economic, political and security decisions and was clearly manifested in earlier ECOMOG operations. Although classified as Lusophone, Guinea Bissau has tend to lean more towards francophone states as evidenced by her desire to join the CFA Franc zone. In both Guinea Bissau and Cote d'Ivoire, Anglophone states were less involved in the peacekeeping operations. This inaction, according to analysts, was Nigeria and Anglophone way of saying 'this is a matter for the francophone states; let them be in charge and know how it feels to be undermining sub-regional peace efforts.' This stresses the importance of building a sub-regional security mechanism that transcends linguistic and cultural affiliations if the high sounding aims and objectives embodied in the security protocols of ECOWAS are to yield any fruit

The second lesson to be learned from the ECOWAS peacekeeping operations in Guinea Bissau and Cote d'Ivoire is the pivotal role played by Nigeria in West African security. With more than half of West Africa's population and 75 per cent of its GNP, Nigeria is without doubt the sub-regional hegemon. However, her dominance has always been greatly resented by other sub-regional powers especially Francophone countries who are worried with 'the spectre of a bulldozing hegemon' (Ero, 2001, 15). Yet, experiences in both countries have underlined Nigeria's indispensable position in West African security. Nigeria provided more than 75 per cent of the troops and money to carry out the missions in Liberia and Sierra Leone and when it failed to intervene in Guinea Bissau, the ECOWAS force in that country became a dismal failure. In Cote d'Ivoire, it was only saved by French forces deployed alongside. This hegemonic position therefore requires Nigeria to constructively use its economic and political strength to diffuse tensions and build a sub-regional consensus. Analysts call for Nigeria's actions to be 'responsible, accountable and transparent' (Ero, 2001, 15) and encourage her to resort to multilateral action through the building of alliances both within and outside the region (Adebajo, 2000). With the new democratic dispensation in the country, it is hoped that Nigeria will be better placed to meet the challenges and responsibilities that come with sub-regional leadership.

Although there are ongoing efforts to consolidate the fragile peace in Cote d'Ivoire and Guinea Bissau, both countries continue to face formidable challenges. SSR and DDR continue to pose the most immediate danger to the stability of both countries. As both conflicts were sparked by military mutinies, the need to prioritise SSR cannot be overemphasised. In Cote d'Ivoire, the SSR and DDR programmes are experiencing serious delays and disruptions owing to lack of sustained donor support and disagreements over the structure of security forces. Despite the dismantling of the 'zone of confidence' the country remains practically divided and continued delays to address SSR, DDR and extension of government authority risk unravelling the gains achieved so far under Ouagadougou. Guinea Bissau faces even more daunting challenges that threaten the very survival of the sate itself. The incapacity of the security forces and the widespread corruption has created a safe haven for drug traffickers.

Chapter 7

Elusive Peace or Flawed Strategy: The LURD-MODEL Rebellion and Relapse into War in Liberia

Introduction

The resurgence of fighting few years after ECOMOG troops withdrew from Liberia raises serious questions about the success of the force. What are the factors responsible for this relapse into fighting in Liberia? Was it due to a flawed post-war peacebuilding strategy taken by both the government and international community or purely one of those cases of intractable conflicts? This chapter seeks to identify the causes of Liberia's relapse into conflict and assess the performance of the second ECOWAS peacekeeping force in Liberia. What lessons did the ECOWAS Mission in Liberia (ECOMIL) learned from its predecessor, ECOMOG? The chapter argues that the failure of the Liberian peace process was inevitable due to flawed peacebuilding strategies, lack of international support and the repressive policies of former president Taylor.

A Flawed Strategy?

The failure of the 1997 Liberian Peace Process can be attributed to both inadequate peacebuilding strategies and Taylor's authoritarian and corrupt leadership style. Chapter 4 highlights the failures of the DDR and SSR programmes in Liberia. The limited opportunities for economic reintegration of former fighters further served to undermine the peace process. Such opportunities would have revived the livelihood of thousands of young combatants and provided them with a suitable alternative to life with the gun. This was partly due to lack of international support to the Taylor government. International aid to Liberia was suspended due to the country's inability to pay its international debt of US$3 billion. On the insistence of Britain, the EU suspended a package of development aid worth £35 million to Liberia in June 2000 (BBC Africa, June 2000). And after Liberian soldiers pursuing Roosevelt Johnson fired into the US Embassy in Monrovia, US-Liberia relations, already severely strained, suffered a further setback. The UN sanctions imposed on Liberia for supporting the RUF worsened an already hopeless situation. But it was the inconsistency of the international community's policy towards Liberia that carried the bulk of the criticisms. Whilst some sections of the international community including the US, Britain and the UN Security Council were openly in favour of containing Taylor, others adopted a less tough stance and made efforts to engage him. This later group included the UN Peacebuilding Office in Liberia (UNOL), some members of ECOWAS and the EU until 2001. Critics have accused the UN office in Liberia of failing to act tough on issues of human rights and good governance. On the contrary, this office legitimised most policies of the Taylor government (Human Rights Watch, 2002). The support for Taylor by some ECOWAS member states does not come as a surprise as most of these states have been behind Taylor since the early days of the Liberian conflict. Attempts to impose UN sanctions on Taylor's regime were openly opposed by some of these states forcing the UN to postpone implementation. The effect of these contradictory policies was to make Taylor even bolder in defying international calls for political and security reforms.

However, the major factors are, firstly, the desire of Taylor to create a 'Greater Liberia' encompassing the entire Mano River Union (MRU) and, secondly, his repressive and corrupt internal policies. The Liberian case provides an empirical evidence of how the zero sum character of these conflicts can seriously hamper the prospects of a peacekeeping operation. The UN Secretary-General in his report to the UN Security Council supports this point:

> The government's policy of exclusion and harassment of political opponents, as well as systematic abuses of human rights, especially by government militia and security agencies, gravely undermined efforts to promote national reconciliation. This situation, coupled with the absence of effective reform of the security sector, contributed to the resumption of the civil war in Liberia. (UN, September 2003)

We will now examine certain policies of Taylor that led to a resurgence of fighting.

The Taylor Presidency: Politics as Usual?

Charles Taylor achieved his life-long ambition of becoming president following his landslide victory in the July 1997 elections with an estimated 83 per cent of votes. This massive vote count does not however portray a love lust for Taylor. Despite perpetuating years of misery on his countrymen and women, ordinary Liberians came to see him as the only person capable of bringing peace to their land. Taylor had openly threatened a return to war if not voted into power. Following his election victory, he exhibited signs of reconciliation with former enemies. He announced an inclusive cabinet which includes among others, Roosevelt Johnson of ULIMO-J and Alhaji Kromah of ULIMO-K though the latter never accepted the position. However, Taylor soon started showing his true self: a person hungry for total power and weary of opposition. Like Doe before him, Taylor persecuted anyone who dares to oppose his regime. These include former allies like Samuel Dokie who faced gruesome murder with his family under the hands of Taylor's security forces. Another former close ally was Vice President Enoch Dogolea who was beaten to death for opposing Taylor's continued support of the RUF in Sierra Leone. There are many other cases of intimidation of opponents including the attack on former interim president Amos Sawyer. Taylor also tried to neutralise civil society by attempting to co-opt and bribe some of its active members.

During Taylor's presidency, the economic and social conditions of Liberians were appalling. Unemployment rose to an alarming 85 per cent with 75 per cent of the population living below the poverty line. The national debt rose to a record $2.8 billion forcing major financial institutions and bilateral donors to black list the country. Only 26 per cent of the population had access to safe drinking water whilst less than 50 per cent of children of primary age were in school (UN, September, 2003). This was due in part to years of conflict and sanctions. However, the kleptomaniac nature of the Taylor regime owes much of the blame. Like past regimes before him, the state was effectively personalised. In Taylor's own case, this personalisation was legalised with the passing of the Strategic Commodity Act which declared that all 'strategic resources in air, on land, or in the sea are within the right of the President to administer personally' (quoted in ICG, 2002). Most of the proceeds from Liberia's timber and maritime registry went to him. As is the practice in most African states, Taylor used this ownership to keep his patrimonial ties strong. His inner circle of cronies includes unscrupulous Lebanese businessmen, timber dealers and other foreigners interested in illicit diamonds and arms trade. Liberians sarcastically referred to the state as 'Liberia Inc.' as it became the private business of Taylor and his cronies. The Treasury was virtually non-functional as no money passed through it. There was no budget for running ministries. Instead Taylor usually makes 'personal gifts' to ministers and government agencies (ICG, 2002). Taylor and members of his inner circle owned most companies and businesses in Liberia.

One area in which Taylor differs from past regimes is his support for regional dissident groups. These include his support for the RUF in Sierra Leone, Guinean dissidents and MJP and MPIGO fighters in Cote d'Ivoire. This support is partly due to his desire to create a 'Greater Liberia' and his greed for the natural resources of those countries. It was this support that came back to haunt him as Guinea and Cote d'Ivoire in turn supported dissident groups LURD and MODEL respectively. Chapter 2 provides an in-depth analysis of the regional dimension of the conflict as well as the impact of local mercenaries.

The LURD/MODEL Rebellion and Relapse into Full-Scale War

Taylor's intimidation of opponents, corruption and patronage and support for regional instability were bound to stifle democratic opposition and seriously undermine any peacebuilding efforts. That the peace in Liberia unravelled so soon does not come as a big surprise to observers and experts on West African security. For most conflict analysts, the LURD/MODEL rebellion does not represent a new conflict but a continuation of what faction leaders consider an 'unfinished business'. It can therefore be better understood as the second phase of the same conflict.

LURD and MODEL are comprised of diverse anti-Taylor factions dating back to the first phase of the Liberian conflict (1989–1997). A key moment in the formation of LURD was a fire fight between Taylor's forces and former fighters of Roosevelt Johnson's ULIMO-J on 18 September 1998. Fearing intimidation and violence from government forces, these fighters grouped together at Camp Johnson. The government however feared that Johnson was trying to regroup and launch a coup. Taylor ordered the Special Operations Division to break-up the camp and in the process, many fighters were killed. Those that survived the onslaught sought refuge in the American Embassy in Monrovia from where they were evacuated to Sierra Leone and Nigeria. Many other fighters fled to Guinea and Cote d'Ivoire from where they began plotting an invasion of Liberia.

First dissident attacks into Liberia date back to early August 1998 when a group called the Justice Coalition of Liberia (JCL), commanded by a former Taylor associate, General Liberty, attacked Kolahun. Another group, the Organisation of Displaced Liberians (ODL) launched a raid into Liberian territory in April 1999. These raids provided the motivation for the formation of LURD. ICG also claims that the late ECOMOG Task Force Commander in Sierra Leone, Brig. Maxwell Khobe played a key coordinating role (ICG, 2002). There are reasons to believe this claim. Khobe was an outspoken critic of Taylor and does not hide his intention to see him forced out of the West African political and security scene. In meetings held in Freetown in February 2000, the three main anti-Taylor factions, JCL, ODL and Union of Democratic Forces of Liberia (UDL), were amalgamated to form LURD. Efforts to use Sierra Leone as a staging post for incursions into Liberia failed as President Kabbah refused the request and leaked the plan to Taylor. Instead, the LURD attacked from Guinea in July 2000. Guinean support for the LURD intensified following a Taylor-backed RUF incursion into Guinea in September 2000. In March 2003, a faction of LURD that was based in Cote d'Ivoire emerged calling itself MODEL. This became Ivorian President Laurent Gbagbo's proxy force.

What started in 1998 as a series of low level skirmishes characterised by hit and run attacks became full scale war and fight for territory. With support from Guinea and Cote d'Ivoire, the two forces succeeded in overrunning a vast area of Liberia and by June 2003 MODEL had captured Buchanan, Liberia's second port city and LURD was mounting a massive attack on Monrovia. The war had come to Taylor's doorstep.

The Accra Comprehensive Peace Agreement

Following months of intensified LURD/MODEL assault on major towns and the capital, ECOWAS initiated a peace process for Liberia that culminated in the signing of the Comprehensive Peace Agreement in Accra in August 2003. Convened in Ghana under the Chairmanship of President Kufuor, the then ECOWAS chairman, the talks were facilitated by the former Nigerian Head of State, General Abdulsalami Abubakar. In attendance were representatives of the Government of Liberia, LURD, MODEL, 18 registered political parties and civil society groups.

The Agreement calls for the establishment of a National Transitional Government of Liberia (NTGL) that consists of the Executive, the National Transitional Legislative Assembly and the Judiciary. This transitional authority was tasked with implementing the peace accord and conducting elections scheduled for October 2005. Gyude Bryant, a prominent businessman and leader of the Liberian Action Party was selected chairman and inaugurated on 14 October 2003. The 21 cabinet posts were shared between the LURD, MODEL, members of Taylor's former government and political parties and civil society. The 76-member Legislative Assembly was divided between representatives of Taylor's former government (12 seats), MODEL (12 seats), LURD (12 seats), Political Parties (18 seats), Civil Society and other special interest groups (7 seats) and Liberian counties (15 seats). As in previous peace talks, the Accra Talks were dominated by wrangling over jobs. This threatened to stall the process. It took several personal interventions by regional leaders and the ECOWAS Executive Secretary for the talks to resume.

The agreement also calls for the establishment of a number of commissions to oversee compliance of factions to the accord. These include: (1) the Joint Monitoring Commission to supervise the implementation of the cease-fire; (2) the Implementation Monitoring Committee to ensure effective implementation of the accord; (3) the National Commission for Disarmament, Demobilisation Reconstruction, Resettlement and Reintegration (NCDDRRR) to organise and implement the DDR programme; and (4) a Truth and Reconciliation Commission. The delegates also proposed that the Transitional Government offer a general amnesty to perpetrators of war crimes during Liberia's long civil war. Like previous peace agreements in the sub-region, this amnesty provision guarantees impunity for war crimes and encourages a repeat of the past. Considering the level of violence perpetuated by all factions in Liberia, a Truth and Reconciliation Commission alone was not enough to heal the wounds of victims whilst perpetrators are seen in government offices and parastatals.

Although women were represented in the peace talks, men dominated proceedings and the share of positions in the Transitional Government. As a result, women delegates made the Golden Tulip Declaration calling for more inclusion of women in the peacebuilding phase and established a committee to ensure the full participation of women. Although marginalised, women have always been a positive influence on the Liberian peace process. On several occasions when greedy warlords have held the peace process hostage, women have organised demonstrations and sent delegations to force compliance. The Liberia Chapter of the Mano River Women's Peace Network played a key role in bringing the leaders of the Mano River Union together in Rabat in November 2001.

Charles Taylor and War Crimes in Sierra Leone

Following years of involvement in the Sierra Leone conflict, the UN backed Special Court for Sierra Leone indicted Taylor for multiple counts of war crimes and crimes against humanity. This indictment added enormous pressure on an embattled Taylor. There were mounting international calls for him to step down as president and leave the Liberian political scene. On condition that he steps down and refrain from interfering in Liberian politics, President Obasanjo of Nigeria offered him political asylum. As part of the deal, Taylor will escape prosecution from the special court in Sierra Leone. This offer was widely criticised by many human rights organisations and activists. They consider this step as a dangerous precedent. There was also widespread opposition to the offer amongst many Nigerians who consider Taylor as responsible for the deaths of thousands of Nigerian soldiers in Liberia and Sierra Leone. On its part, the Nigeria government defended the deal as the only way to bring lasting peace to Liberia. They argue that saving the lives of millions was far important than prosecuting one man. However, due to external pressure from the US, Obasanjo finally gave in and handed Taylor to the Special Court in Freetown in 2006. The fluid security situation in Freetown led to his transfer to The Hague where he is currently standing trial. The trial of Taylor is sending a very powerful message across the region that the days of impunity are over.

The US and the Liberian Peace Process

The widespread calls for increased US support to the Liberian peace process were predicated on the strong historical ties between the two countries spanning more than a century. Founded with US support as a refuge for freed slaves in 1847, Liberia patterned their flag, constitution, and place names on US models. There has been longstanding commercial and diplomatic relationship between Liberia and the US. US companies have been dominant in exploiting Liberia's timber, rubber and iron ore. Liberia has been a key strategic ally of the US during World War II and the Cold War. Roberts Field, Liberia's only International Airport, was used as a re-supply centre for the North African Campaign and Liberia's Maritime Bureau was created to provide a 'flag of convenience' for US vessels carrying strategic goods. During the Cold War, Liberia was the largest recipient of US foreign aid in Africa.

However, as the Cold War came to an end, Liberia lost its strategic importance. This is evident by the US neglect towards the first phase of the Liberian war which erupted in December 1989. Following French and British intervention in Cote d'Ivoire and Sierra Leone respectively, there were widespread calls from the international community for the US to play a leading role in Liberia. Recognising the potential threat of the Liberian conflict to the fragile peace in Sierra Leone, both Britain and France persuaded the US to play a more direct role. The UN Secretary-General and the AU also repeatedly urged the US to intervene.

Speaking to the House Committee on International Relations Sub Committee on Africa, the Assistant Secretary of State for African Affairs, Walter H. Kansteiner outlined US policy towards Liberia as follows, 'To stop the killing, to facilitate the flow of humanitarian aid, and to achieve a comprehensive, profound change in the way the country was governed' (Kansteiner, 2003). This policy is situated within the Expansive foreign policy of George W. Bush after 11 September in which he focused on failed states as breeding grounds for terrorists. As preconditions for any US intervention, Bush insisted that Taylor depart from the Liberian political scene and the conflicting parties agree a cease-fire. But such an intervention will be very minimal and limited to supporting West African peace initiatives. With both conditions met by mid-August 2003 and increasing international pressure, the US provided limited support to West African ECOMIL troops by providing logistical assistance and paying for the airlift of troops at an estimated cost of US$26 million (Kansteiner, 2003). The US maintained a force of 2300 marines off the coast of Monrovia and authorised few of them to go ashore to facilitate the deployment of ECOMIL troops.

Newspaper reports have indicated that this strategy resulted from disagreements between officials of the State Department and the Pentagon, which the later eventually won (Allen, *Washington Post*, 2003). The State Department have argued for US leadership role in the crisis but the Pentagon resisted a deeper involvement and viewed Liberia as peripheral in its strategic calculations. The fear of overstretching the US Military capabilities was also raised as American troops were heavily involved in missions in Iraq and Afghanistan. But the main factor that convinced the Pentagon to opt for a limited role is the memory of the US fiasco in Somalia in 1993. But Comparing Liberia to Somalia is a misjudgement as the two countries' perceptions of the US are profoundly different. In Somalia, the US faced hostility not only from warring factions but also civilians. On the contrary, Liberians have long regarded the US with affection. Even the warring factions revere them. There are billboards all over Monrovia emphasising the 'special relationship' between the US and Liberia.

Critics of the US role in Liberia have accused the Bush administration of failing to do enough to end the suffering and bring lasting peace to Liberia. They consider this a missed opportunity to demonstrate US commitment towards the fight for human rights and deflect widespread criticism for its war in Iraq. Writing in the *Washington Post*, Mike Allen opined that the Bush administration 'Squandered a chance to show a willingness to keep peace rather than just use war to engineer regime change ... Muscular US involvement also would have bolstered the human-rights justification for the Iraq war that Bush began emphasizing when no unconventional weapons immediately turned up' (Allen, *Washington Post*, 2003). On a similar note, ICG questioned the wisdom of the US policy: 'even from a narrow definition of its national interests, the US missed an opportunity. It had a chance to demonstrate, at a time when Liberia was receiving unprecedented media attention that it could help restore peace and transform the political outlook in a corner of the world where 'Uncle Sam' remains highly popular' (ICG, 2003). This limited role also undermines the US international 'War on Terror' as reports have linked conflicts in West Africa to Al qaeda. However in a bid to silence its critics, the US appears to be doing more towards post war reconstruction efforts as highlighted in Chapter 8.

ECOMIL Intervention in Liberia

With the US unwilling to commit troops to police the Liberian peace process, ECOWAS was again called upon to deploy its peacekeeping force. ECOWAS leaders agreed at a summit held in Dakar, Senegal to deploy a vanguard force to Liberia to help stabilise the situation and facilitate Taylor's departure. UN Security Council Resolution 1497 authorised the deployment of ECOMIL troops to be replaced by a UN force in two months. The deployment of ECOMIL troops started with a vanguard force from the Nigerian contingents serving in UNAMSIL on 4 August 2004. At its peak, the force comprised of 3,600 troops from Nigeria, Guinea Bissau, The Gambia, Ghana, Mali, Senegal, Togo and Benin. This deployment heralded a new phase in UN cooperation with regional organisations primarily for its success in drawing existing UN troops from UNAMSIL in Sierra Leone to start a regional peacekeeping force.

For the second time in 13 years, ECOWAS has been called upon to mount a peacekeeping force in one of the world's most troubled spots. But did ECOWAS learn from its previous experience? Are such lessons being implemented? A comprehensive assessment of the performance of ECOMIL troops is difficult to undertake due to the limited period of deployment – just two months. However, an analysis of the structures put in place and the conduct of ECOMIL troops during their short time in Liberia reveals a significant departure from the problems that beset ECOMOG I, II and III. A useful starting point will be issues of legality that compounded ECOMOG. Many critics have questioned the legitimacy of ECOMOG deployment as it lacks UN approval and a consensus within ECOWAS. As mentioned above, ECOWAS leaders this time sought UN Security Council mandate for ECOMIL. Furthermore, peacekeeping has now been institutionalised within ECOWAS through the adoption of the Mechanism for Peace and Security. Closely related to this is the question of Nigerian hegemony in ECOMOG. Keen to avoid the bitter resentment of Francophone countries towards Nigerian domination of ECOMOG and the Anglophone-Francophone rivalry that followed, Nigeria this time opted for a more inclusive strategy, playing a less domineering role. This can be seen in the composition of the force. Of the eight troop-contributing countries, four are Francophone states, one Lusophone and three Anglophone. An explanation for this change of strategy lies in Nigeria's transition to a democracy. During the days of military rule, the authorities in Nigeria had a free hand in deciding matters of foreign and defence policy as all organised opposition was stifled. It was this same dictatorship that the Nigerian Military authorities extended to the sub-regional stage. But with the democratic dispensation in 1999, foreign and defence policy was now subjected to rigorous internal debate. This new tolerance to debate and inclusion at home was reflected in a dramatic shift of strategy at the sub-regional stage where Nigeria began playing a more coordinating role.

The conduct of ECOMOG troops was also under fire as discussed above due to lack of peacekeeping training and experience. But with years of experience in ECOMOG in Liberia and Sierra Leone, UNAMSIL in Sierra Leone and various training programmes sponsored by the US, France and the UK, the level of professionalism of ECOWAS troops has improved remarkably. In fact most of the troops were taken from the Nigerian Contingent serving in UNAMSIL in Sierra Leone. Although thin on the ground, the force was able to stabilise the fluid security situation in Monrovia, provide protection for hundreds of thousands of civilians and establish safe corridors for the delivery of humanitarian aid. ECOWAS foot patrols and visible presence also resulted in the decline of general lawlessness and restored public confidence. Besides its policing role, the mission also established a weapons-free zone in and around Monrovia. However, as in the previous ECOMOG intervention in Liberia, ECOMIL's failure to deploy outside Monrovia means rebels continued to terrorise defenceless civilians.

The creation of the Office of the Special Representative of the ECOWAS Executive Secretary is also a move in the right direction. In ECOMOG, the Force Commander also doubles as diplomatic and political representative of ECOWAS. The appointment of a civilian head of mission has relieved the Force Commander of additional responsibility – a job he is not trained to perform – giving him time to concentrate on military matters. This also ensures that the ECOWAS Secretariat maintains control over the force rather than the respective troop contributing countries as it used to be. Although ECOMIL is no longer in Monrovia, the office is still maintained to coordinate between ECOWAS and the UN Mission.

With a civilian government in Abuja that is subject to legislative and media scrutiny, Nigeria was no longer prepared to solely bankroll an entire force, as was the case with ECOMOG. It therefore asked for guarantees of funding before committing any troops to the mission. This insistence on funding before deployment produced tangible fruits as the force received support from various sources. The US provided finance and maintained a 2,000 strong contingent off the coast of Monrovia to provide logistical support to ECOMIL. UNAMSIL assisted with airlift facilities. However, this assistance fell well below the financial and logistical needs of the mission. Some troop contributing countries deployed in Monrovia expecting the US logistics firm, PAE to provide all their logistical needs. As a result, there was a shortage of vehicles and communication equipments (Tawiah and Aboagye, 2005). These shortages made it very difficult for the force to deploy out of Monrovia. The logistical constraints and reliance on external support raises serious doubts about the effectiveness of the ECOWAS Security Mechanism.

Conclusion

Liberia's relapse into full scale war barely two years after the withdrawal of ECOWAS peacekeepers is an indication of the fragile nature of transitional societies and the threats and uncertainties they face and underlines the need for continued engagement with countries emerging out of violent conflict. Whilst ECOMOG and the international community's flawed peacebuilding strategies contributed to the resurgence of conflict, however the nature of Taylor's undemocratic and kleptomaniac governance style played a significant role in undermining the fragile peace.

The second ECOWAS intervention in Liberia shows how far the organisation has come from the *ad hoc* days of ECOMOG. The level of training and experience of peacekeeping meant the troops on the ground were more professional. The complimentarity between ECOWAS and the UN also represents a major development in the evolving relationship between the UN and regional organisations. However, logistics and finance continue to hamper the sub-region's efforts at managing and resolving conflicts. Although ECOWAS has been able to minimise Anglophone-Francophone rivalry in peace operations, serious concerns still remain about the commitment of member states to regional security. The support given by Guinea and Cote d'Ivoire to LURD and MODEL respectively seriously undermines any collective sub-regional security and conflict resolution efforts.

Chapter 8
Peacebuilding in Sierra Leone and Liberia: A Comparative Perspective

Introduction

Far from the linear model of transition from civil war to post-war peacebuilding and reconstruction suggested in the conflict resolution literature of the early 1990s, the transitional period between the signing of peace agreements and consolidation of fragile peace has been fraught with difficulties and uncertainties. From Angola to Sierra Leone, Liberia to Cambodia, peace settlements have unravelled few years after coming into effect. There have however been notable success stories in places like Mozambique, Namibia and El Salvador. But what counts as success in a peace process? What are the factors determining such success or failure? What is the role, if any, of regional and international actors in the process? There is a burgeoning body of literature over the past decade focusing on the determinants of a successful peace process and transitional period.[1] But such studies have been hampered by the wide variety of contexts and intervening factors involved. This chapter compares the peacebuilding interventions in Liberia and Sierra Leone after the withdrawal of ECOWAS sub-regional peacekeepers and evaluates the efforts of domestic, regional and international actors in building sustainable peace. Although the focus of this book is on ECOWAS, however an analysis of the transitional period in these countries that does not take into account the contributions of other actors will be severely constrained. By integrating ECOWAS' operations within the wider framework of peacebuilding activities in these countries, this chapter will provide alternative explanations for the difficulties and challenges faced by the sub-regional organisation.

The chapter begins with a review of the literature on peacebuilding to understand the factors that determine its success or failure. Drawing from this literature, we assess peacebuilding in Liberia and Sierra Leone in four different areas: context of implementation, international support, state reform and nature of domestic politics, and transitional justice initiatives. We conclude

---

1   See among others John Darby and Roger Mac Ginty (eds) (2003), *Contemporary Peacemaking: Conflict, Violence and Peace Processes*, Basingstoke: Palgrave Macmillan; Stephen John Stedman et. al. (2002), *Ending Civil Wars: The Implementation of Peace Agreements*, London: Lynne Rienner; Fen Osler Hampson (1996), *Nurturing Peace: Why Peace Settlements Succeed or Fail*, Washington DC: US Institute of Peace.

by looking at the prospects and challenges for durable peace in Liberia and Sierra Leone.

Defining Success in Peace Processes: Theoretical Insights

The definition of success in a peace process has been hotly debated in the theoretical literature and there appears to be no consensus on the subject. Downs and Stedman (2002) use two variables to determine success in peace implementation: (1) the termination of large scale violence while the implementers are present; (2) termination of war on a self-enforcing basis so that the implementers can go home without fear of a resurgence of fighting. This definition classifies a mission as a failure if war resumes in two years after the departure of implementers. These variables however tend to be more focused on short-term measures to halt violence and are mostly focused on the role of international actors, disregarding the key role played by local civil society groups. In his *An Agenda for Peace*, former UN Secretary-General, Boutros-Ghali links peace implementation to peacebuilding which he defines as 'actions to identify and support structures which will tend to strengthen and solidify peace in order to avoid a relapse into conflict' (1992, 11). This broad definition determines success in a peace process in terms of long-term measures to address the political, economic and social underlining causes of war. Miall et al. (2005) distinguish the two different definitions above into two phases: transitional and consolidation. This is also in line with Galtung's (1981) classification of 'negative' and 'positive' peace. The transitional phase involves efforts aimed at preventing a relapse into violence (negative peace), whereas the consolidation phase deals with the removal of structural and cultural violence (positive peace). The transitional phase (negative peace) represents the most urgent tasks facing peacebuilders. As it aims at preventing a relapse into violence, it includes measures such as compromises and trade-offs to factional leaders. In this context, the transitional phase is about who gets what in the post-war period. As Ramsbotham (2000) rightly observes, this short-term aim of preventing violence is often at odds with, and may adversely affect the long-term goal of building sustainable peace. However, despite this dark side, this phase still remains vital to peacebuilding since post-war reconstruction can only be possible in a violence-free environment. On the other hand, the consolidation phase is the most important stage and involves tasks such as strengthening the institutional base, security sector reform, promoting economic development, building social capital and addressing the psychosocial needs of the society. It is only when the necessary political, social and economic structures are in place and there is some notion that the root causes of the original tensions have been eradicated can a fuller and holistic concept of peacebuilding be proclaimed. Drawing from the above analysis, this chapter defines success in a peace process as preventing a relapse into violence and laying of foundations for the achievement of long-term peacebuilding objectives. It therefore adopts a medium-term perspective of success representing a compromise between Stedman's short-term goal and Boutros-Ghali's long-term objectives.

Having adopted a working definition of success in peace process, attention now turns to the factors that determine such an outcome. In the immediate aftermath of the Cold War, most studies of peace processes were limited to the negotiation and signing of peace agreements. Such studies assumed a linear process involving peace agreement, disarmament and peacebuilding. Also the majority of these studies were undertaken by Western academics and based on accounts of peace processes in Northern Ireland, Palestine and Cyprus. This has resulted in the adoption of Western approaches in peacebuilding to non-Western contexts. However since the mid-1990s, there is a growing body of African-based literature focusing on the unpredictable and fragile nature of African peace processes.[2] One of the earliest studies to look into the unpredictable nature of peace agreement implementation is Fen Osler Hampson's *Nurturing Peace* (1996). In this seminal work, he puts forward four determinants for a successful peace process: level of international support, the 'ripeness' of the conflict, systemic and regional power balances and, quality of the peace agreement. International nurturing of peace processes is central to Hampson's argument and considers the 'availability of third parties that can proffer carrots or wield sticks ...' as central to the success of any peace agreement (1996, 11). The need for international support to peacebuilding is premised on the fact that parties to conflicts cannot effectively carry out these tasks due to institutional weakness, limited human and financial resources and economic problems. Since the end of the Cold War, the United Nations has led international efforts in peace processes. Over the years, the UN has developed a standard operating procedure involving power sharing arrangements, a new constitution and regular free and fair elections underpinned by Western liberal market economy (Miall et al., 2005). In most cases, transitional societies have been abandoned after the achievement of these short-term objectives. The international community is very anxious for 'quick-fix' results and as such parties to a conflict are most often pressurised into elections. Whilst accepting the liberalist model, Paris (1997) calls for a longer period of international involvement and different sequencing. Peacebuilding should not be a 'quick fix' affair; on the contrary, the international community should be prepared for a long haul. Closely related to the international third party factor is what Hampson calls 'systemic and regional power balances'. He identified 'the changing dynamics of the East-West competition ... as having a major impact on the possibilities for diplomacy and resolution of regional conflicts' (Hampsons, 1996, 16). Though such a theory has largely been true for

---

2   See for instance, Adebajo Adedeji (ed.) (1999), *Comprehending and Mastering African Conflicts: The Search for Sustainable Peace and Good Governance*, New York: Zed Books and ACDESS, Adekeye Adebajo (2002), *Building Peace in West Africa: Liberia, Sierra Leone and Guinea-Bissau*, Boulder, CO and London: Lynne Rienner.

places like Southern Africa, Southeast Asia, Central America and the Middle East, it does not quite apply to the conflicts in West Africa. Whilst Sierra Leone has never featured prominently in the strategic calculations of the East-West confrontation, the US neglect of Liberia at the end of the Cold War and the limited peacemaking role it played in that country's civil war makes such a theory inapplicable to the cases under study.

In calling for a hurting stalemate, Hampson joins Zartman (2003) and a growing body of analysts advocating for intervention to be timed with 'ripeness' of the conflict. However, as argued in Chapter 1, such an analysis does not take into account the self sustaining nature of violence in today's complex political emergencies and the illegal economy fuelling and sustaining such conflicts. His example of the Cyprus conflict is completely inappropriate to the CPEs which have come to characterise post-Cold War conflicts in Africa and elsewhere in which the scale of human suffering is at alarming proportions. The fourth determinant, quality of the peace agreement, is very much in place. In an attempt to negotiate a 'quick fix' and face saving agreement, most peace agreements have been very ambiguous and failed to address contentious issues that will pose future problems. However, the failure of Hampson to adequately address the challenges posed by the very nature of the conflict and conflicting parties to the success of peacebuilding remains a serious defect of his set of determinants. Downs and Stedman (2002) tried to fill this void by adding the implementation environment. They consider an environment more hostile based on the following factors: the presence of spoilers, disposable natural resources and hostile neighbouring states or networks. Such a determinant will help to explain why some peace processes failed despite the enormous international support and attention they received. It will also help to refocus third party efforts into addressing and neutralising these hostile factors.

Overall, the above literature is very dependent on international/third party role in implementing peace agreements. This reflects the general trend in Western-based literature which tends to neglect the potential role of local agents and indigenous resources in facilitating the implementation of peace agreements. And as Barclay (1999) rightly observes, circumventing domestic grass roots actors in peacebuilding tends to foster dependency, undermine the capacity of civil society and prolong conflict. There are several empirical cases of the constructive role played by indigenous resources and local agents in consolidating fragile peace. In Mozambique, following the failure of the General Peace Agreements (GPA) to punish war crime perpetrators, the local community developed local mechanisms for reconciliation and trauma healing. One of such mechanisms is the cleansing ritual of ex-combatants by traditional doctors for the purposes of reintegrating them into society. This ritual involves the physical cleansing of ex-combatants with steam bath and water plus herbs followed by announcement to death relatives about the return of their 'lost son'. This is climaxed by the ex-combatant's plea for forgiveness and acceptance by the community. In Rwanda, the Gacaca community tribunal system is complimenting the role of the Arusha based international tribunal for Rwanda. With the abundance of local resources in peace processes, analysis of international peacebuilding interventions should therefore emphasise the bottom-up approach which seeks to complement and support initiatives and efforts of the grassroots.

Different conceptual frameworks on peacebuilding have so far emphasised the socio-economic, political and military dimensions whilst paying little attention to the psychosocial aspect of conflict. Due to the nature of post-Cold War conflicts in Africa and elsewhere in which large scale violence has been meted on the civilian population, the need to heal the wounds of war and promote reconciliation is very paramount to the success of peacebuilding. This is where transitional justice initiatives come in as a means of checkmating impunity in human rights abuses and discouraging intransigence on the part of leaders of warring factions. But the literature on transitional justice tends to focus on legalistic approaches to justice based on punishment and retribution. As the examples of Rwanda and Mozambique above indicate, indigenous justice systems, based on reconciliation and fostering community cohesion can play a major role in the search for justice in post-war African societies.

Implementation Environment: Liberia and Sierra Leone in Context

A major defect of international peacebuilding interventions is the uniformity badge given to all post-conflict situations: Liberia is Angola is Bosnia is Cambodia. The need to contextualise the analysis of peace processes cannot be overemphasised. As Downs and Stedman (2002) noted, the success of a peace agreement depends largely on the implementation environment. Both Sierra Leone and Liberia share similar hostile characteristics. In Liberia, Charles Taylor was a key spoiler whilst Sankoh in Sierra Leone was his counterpart. In both contexts, there are thriving war economies: diamonds in Sierra Leone and Timber, rubber and diamonds in Liberia. Hostile neighbours were also present on both sides of the border: Liberia and Burkina Faso in the case of Sierra Leone; Guinea and Cote d'Ivoire in the case of Liberia. Indeed these two countries share a lot in common. In these circumstances, the success of a peace process depends on the strategies used by domestic actors and international third parties to address and neutralise the hostile factors.

In Liberia, following the initial ambivalent approach of the international community towards Taylor, a unified stance was adopted in 2003 that led to his exit in August 2003. His subsequent indictment and trial at the Special Court for Sierra Leone effectively removed him as a factor in the ongoing conflict. In December 2003, the UN Security Council adopted Resolution 1521 which imposed a travel ban on Taylor's associates and in March 2004, the Council froze their assets when it passed Resolution 1532. This no-nonsense approach towards 'spoilers' has had a positive impact on the peace process. However as latter sections of this chapter show, the return of some of Taylor's close allies to key legislative positions in the 2005 elections pose a big threat to the governance reform agenda. In Sierra Leone, civil society played a key role in neutralising Sankoh. Civil society pressure and demonstrations led to the arrest and incarceration of Sankoh in the aftermath of the May 2000 crisis. The UN and the entire international community discredited Sankoh and urged the RUF to choose a new leadership. This uncompromising stance by both domestic and international backers of the peace process tremendously weakened the destructive capacity of the RUF. The poor showing of the RUF Party (RUF-P) at the May 2002 elections virtually confirmed the paralysis of the movement. The British military intervention also neutralised the 'West Side Boys', an offshoot of the AFRC and former Sierra Leone Army, and provided a credible military deterrence to would-be 'spoilers'.

The control of strategic resources is also another key element of the peace process in both countries. In Sierra Leone, the UN set up the *Panel of Experts on Sierra Leone Diamonds and Arms* in response to the May incident to investigate the link between diamonds, small arms and conflict. In its report released in December 2000, the Panel presented a detailed documentation establishing the link between diamonds and arms trafficking in the region and observed that 'President Charles Taylor is actively involved in fuelling the violence in Sierra Leone'. Burkina Faso was also named as a transit point for arms shipped from the Ukraine. In response to this report, the UN introduced a certification scheme for official Sierra Leonean diamonds. To discourage Liberian complicity in fuelling the conflict, sanctions were imposed covering an arms embargo, a ban on Liberian diamonds and travel restrictions on government officials and their families. Although there were reports of sanction-busting, these measures can be credited for weakening the financial base of the RUF and encouraging a rethink in top Liberian government circles. However, the failure to punish Burkina Faso, a country that has been implicated in many of the sub-region's conflicts undermines the international community's efforts to deal with rogue states.

State Reform and Nature of Post-War Politics in Liberia and Sierra Leone

The nature of domestic governance is a key factor in sustaining peace in transitional societies. As most of these conflicts are rooted in unjust and incompetent governance structures and processes, the need for governance reform cannot be overemphasised. This need is often embedded in the provisions of various peace accords. However, as noted above, most attention has been limited to the holding of elections. But governance reform goes beyond the periodic holding of elections to encompass issues such as a genuinely representative government, building of key political institutions, strengthening of civil society and accountability and economic propriety.

Follow-up action and monitoring of the post-agreement governance system must focus on these issues.

Both Sierra Leone and Liberia are failed states that require radical transformation of governance structures and institutions. At various stages, they were effectively UN protectorates. However, the process of state reform is progressing at a steady pace, although there remain major challenges. In Liberia, the Comprehensive Peace Agreement (CPA) signed in August 2003 provided for the establishment of the National Transitional Government of Liberia (NTGL) and a transitional legislature. Made up of representatives of the various rebel groups and civil society representatives, the transitional government was tasked with the responsibility of implementing the peace accord and conducting elections. However the NTGL was made ineffective by lack of capacity and massive levels of corruption. Most of the members of the NTGL were warlords who lack political experience and were more interested in jobs and the wealth and prestige that follow. For instance, arguments over ministerial appointments rendered the NTGL ineffective for most of the period since it was established. The cabinet was only sworn in on 23 March 2004, five months after inauguration of the interim Chairman. The high level of corruption led to the establishment of the intrusive Governance and Economic Management Assistance Programme (GEMAP) by the UN, World Bank, IMF, ECOWAS and the European Union. The programme involves the placement of foreign financial experts in key revenue generating departments.

Elections were held in late 2005 and Ellen Johnson-Sirleaf, a Harvard educated and former World Bank official was elected president. However, a good number of the legislative seats went to the same old guard known for destabilising the country. Key names include Jewel Howard-Taylor, ex-wife of Charles Taylor; Prince Johnson, former leader of the Independent NPFL who was responsible for the brutal murder of President Doe; Adolphus Dolo, a former Taylor Commander also known as 'General Peanut Butter'; Edwin Snowe, a former Taylor associate and son-in-law who became the speaker of the House of Representatives. This outcome is characteristic of post-war elections which tend to empower predatory elites and reinforce the same wartime power structures. Notwithstanding President Johnson-Sirleaf's good image, the composition of the legislature is a negative indicator for the governance reform process. The lack of a government majority in the legislature also means that the government will be forced to make deals and form coalitions with other parties.

Under President Johnson-Sirleaf, Liberia's economy appears to be doing well with a 9 per cent growth rate in 2007 and public revenue amounting to $163 million (UN, March 2008). This is partly due to the lifting of the UN ban on the export of Liberia's diamonds and timber. The country has also benefited from a number of debt cancellations by major financial institutions and bilateral partners. For instance, the World Bank and the African Development Bank have agreed to clear $671 million of the country's $4.8 billion debt arrears whilst the IMF has forgiven $920 million of debt (UN, March 2008). Consequently, the government has been able to undertake a limited programme of rebuilding infrastructure and delivering basic services. For instance, pipe-borne water and mains electricity have been restored to parts of Monrovia. However, unemployment continues to be a major challenge for the government's economic recovery programme. Corruption also continues to be a problem despite efforts by the Johnson-Sirleaf government to curb it. In June 2007, Liberia's independent Auditor-General alleged that the current administration is three times more corrupt than its predecessor (UN, August 2007). Although this allegation was not substantiated, the president herself recently admitted that corruption continues to undermine her government's efforts to respond to the needs of the Liberian people (Butty, 2008).

Consolidation of state authority and the decentralisation process have been hit by lack of funds and capacity. Local council and chieftaincy elections had to be delayed in 2007 because the government could not afford the estimated $19 million to organise them (UN, August 2007). The President had to appoint municipal officials instead. Justice sector reform poses another big challenge to the governance reform process. The judiciary is severely constrained by lack of capacity, adequate infrastructure and poor conditions of service. The government's inability to manage the growing land disputes also poses another threat to the fragile peace. With the return of tens of thousands of refugees, there has been an escalation in the number of violent attacks and community disputes over land. Some returning refugees have found their land and homes taken over. In June 2008, one such incidents resulted in the killing of at least 12 people in a farm some 35 miles south-east of Monrovia (BBC, June 2008).

Since the official end of the war in 2002, Sierra Leone has made significant progress in rebuilding governance structures and consolidating the fragile peace. These include the creation of a National Revenue Authority (NRA) which has developed enhanced revenue collection mechanisms; an ongoing decentralisation process; justice sector reform programme; security forces subject to democratic control, and free and fair elections in 2002, 2004, 2007 and 2008. The economy also appears to be doing well with a reported 7 per cent growth rate over the past two years (ICG, July 2007). With the implementation of the Kimberley Process Certification Scheme, the government's income from diamond exports soared from $10 million in 2000 to $160 in 2004 (Sola-Martin and Kabia, 2007). However, despite the considerable international donor support and impressive macro-economic figures, the country's social and economic indicators make grim reading. Youth unemployment is estimated at around 80 per cent with over 70 per cent of the population living under the poverty line (ICG, July 2007). The 2008 UNDP Human Development Index ranks the country 177th out of 177 countries. Despite the setting up of an Anti-Corruption Commission (ACC), corruption remains high. Whilst the ACC has been able to raise awareness about corruption, it has been hamstrung by political interference and lack of capacity by the judiciary to prosecute those accused of corrupt practices. Public perception of corruption amongst government officials was a key factor responsible for the defeat of the former ruling party in the August 2007 elections. The new president, Ernest Bai Koroma has made the fight against corruption his top priority and has declared zero tolerance. However, it remains to be seen how effective his government will be in tackling this menace.

International Support towards Peacebuilding in Liberia and Sierra Leone

As most post-war countries lack the resources and capacity to implement the terms of peace agreements, the active support of the international community is very critical towards the success of peacebuilding programmes. In addition to the various interventions by UN, NGOs and other bilateral and multilateral agencies, there is an emerging consensus that point to the pivotal role played by so-called 'lead nations' and International Contact Groups in peacebuilding. This section will compare and contrast the UN, international community and 'lead nations' response to peacebuilding in both countries.

UN peacekeeping missions were deployed in both countries with similar Standard Operating Procedures characteristic of post-Cold War peacekeeping missions. The United Nations Mission in Sierra Leone (UNAMSIL) was deployed in October 1999 following the signing of the Lomé Peace Agreement. However, following the near-collapse of UNAMSIL in May 2000 and the constant comparison to international response to the Kosovo and East Timor crises, the peace process received a fresh lease of life from the international community. The humiliation suffered by the UN forces necessitated a critical rethink of the whole concept and practice of peacekeeping in the form of various reviews and reports; the Brahimi Report being the most notable. Consequently, the force was bolstered to 17,500 and given a more robust chapter VII mandate. With additional troop numbers and a robust mandate, the mission was able to deploy country-wide thereby helping the Freetown-hostage government to extend its authority. In Liberia, acting on the recommendation of the Secretary-General, the Security Council on 19 September 2003 adopted resolution 1509 that established the United Nations Mission in Liberia (UNMIL) with mandated troop strength of 15,000 including 1,115 civilian police. The mission replaced the ECOWAS Mission in Liberia (ECOMIL) on 1 October 2003 when the former sub-regional peacekeepers were re-hated. Like UNAMSIL in Sierra Leone, UNMIL was given a robust chapter VII mandate with responsibilities ranging from monitoring the cease-fire, overseeing the DDR programme to restructuring of the Security Sector and extension of government authority. The involvement of troops from developed countries like Sweden and Ireland also bolstered the capability of the force, as is the involvement of a permanent member of the Security Council, China.

Considering the widespread militarisation of the society and the proliferation of arms in both countries, DDR is key to the success of peacebuilding. Following previous half-hearted attempts at disarmament in Sierra Leone, the third phase of the DDR programme started in May 2001 and by January 2002, a total of 72,490 ex-combatants have been disarmed and 42,300 weapons and 1.2 million rounds of ammunition recovered (Kai Kai, 2004). The fact that UNAMSIL was able to disarm a figure far higher than the original estimates is a testimony to the remarkable achievements of the mission. On January 2002, the UN and government of Sierra Leone declared the war over amidst the symbolic burning of disarmed weapons. The success of this programme was highlighted by the unusually violence-free elections conducted in May 2002. However, despite the success of the disarmament and demobilisation phase of the DDR programme, reintegration remains a major doubt. Although most ex-combatants have been given skills training, the continuing economic hardship means there are few jobs available to absorb the thousands of skilled youths. As past experiences in Liberia and Sierra Leone have shown, half-hearted reintegration programmes can lead to a resurgence of conflict.

After stabilising the fluid security situation in Monrovia and its environs, UNMIL embarked on disarming 38,000 estimated ex-combatants. However, the initial attempt to start disarmament in December 2003 failed due to lack of planning, logistics and coordination between the UN and humanitarian agencies. In a bid to impress donors before the February 2004 Donors conference, the UNMIL leadership decided to start disarmament on 7 December 2003. This premature start to the DDR programme did not take into account the low level of troops on the ground and the unavailability of logistics and finance to support the programme. In fact ICG reported that key stakeholders did not meet until few days before the start of the programme. The original plan called for the setting up of cantonment sites targeting 1000 combatants from each faction. But after advise from the military component of UNMIL that it could not cover all the three factions based on its troop strength, it was decided to start with the former government forces. UNMIL cannot cope with the big turn-out – about 12,000. When fighters discovered that there was no cash for weapons, they rioted and erected roadblocks on the streets of Monrovia. At the end of the disturbances, nine people were killed and one UNMIL soldier sustained injuries. UNMIL suspended the programme on 17 December 2003.

The programme restarted in April 2004 and by the end of 2004 had succeeded in disarming over 100,000 ex-combatants. However, despite this high number, there remain serious unresolved problems. The number of weapons surrendered fall far short of expectations and there are worrying signs that they were transported across the border to neighbouring countries (UN, May 2004). The most likely place is Cote d'Ivoire where ex-combatants are paid about US$975 for surrendering their weapons as compared to the US$300 given to Liberians. There are also reports of ex-combatants giving their surplus weapons to civilians for them to collect the $300 on offer. Another problem facing the DDR programme is lack of sufficient funds for reintegration. This is partly due to the discrepancy between the initial estimates of 38,000 and the actual figure of over 100,000. This led to a funding shortfall of $58 million. Furthermore, although disarmament and demobilisation are budgeted for within UNMIL, reintegration is funded through voluntary contributions. However, as in other post-conflict countries, donor countries are very slow in honouring the pledges they made at the Liberian Donor Conference in February 2004. As a result, UNMIL and Liberia's Disarmament and Reintegration Commission are struggling to reintegrate the thousands of ex-combatants who have gone through the disarmament programme. At some point, up to 4000 ex-combatants were expelled from various schools and colleges across Liberia due to UNMIL's failure to pay fees. There is a growing sense of frustration and disappointment amongst ex-combatants and this has caused sporadic unrest in Liberia.

Although Security Sector Reform (SSR) is a key component of post-Cold War UN Peacekeeping missions, there continues to be a funding gap with the UN Security Council expecting so-called 'lead nations' to take the lead in implementing such programmes. In Liberia and Sierra Leone, the UN led on police reform whilst army reform was led by the US and UK respectively. In a joint effort with the Commonwealth, UNAMSIL recruited and trained 3,500 police officers. By 2005 when UNAMSIL withdrew from the country, the strength of the Sierra Leone Police Force stood at 9,500 with 4,000 of that number having gone through basic police training, human rights, computer literacy and middle and senior management training (Sola-Martin and Kabia, 2007). By the end of 2005, the police have deployed country-wide in 74 police stations and 112 posts. The relationship between the police and the public has improved considerably with the introduction of the concept of Local Needs Policing which seeks to involve the community in policing matters. This is a big departure from the pre-war image of the police as corrupt and human rights abusers. However despite the support to the police, the force continues to suffer from logistical constraints and the poor conditions of service threaten to undermine the professional integrity of the force.

In Liberia, the UN police had to start from scratch in rebuilding the Liberian National Police (LNP). Unlike Sierra Leone which had a functioning albeit weak and ineffective police force, the LNP was virtually destroyed after years of conflict. The challenges for UNMIL were therefore enormous. In addition to recruiting, retraining and equipping the force, UNMIL had to work alongside the skeletal LNP in maintaining law and order. The task of rebuilding the LNP was hampered by lack of funds. The US had to provide $500,000 to UNMIL to help with recruiting and training 3,500 officers. By August 2007, a total of 3,522 officers had been trained at the National Police Academy (Malan, 2008). However, the LNP remains ineffective due to a shortage of essential logistics ranging from vehicles, communications equipment to handcuffs and raincoats. There is also a critical shortage of leadership and management skills within the LNP and morale is low and discipline very poor. Consequently, crime continues to be a major problem in Liberia with increasing incidents of robbery and sexual and gender based violence. The inability of the police to tackle the rising crime rate led the Liberian Justice Ministry to urge civilians to organise local vigilante groups to stem the armed robbery.

UNAMSIL withdrew in December 2005. It was replaced in January 2006 by the United Nations Integrated Office in Sierra Leone (UNIOSIL), a political mission tasked with consolidating the gains of UNAMSIL, help the government to strengthen its human rights record, meet the Millennium Development Goals, and hold free and fair elections in 2007. UNAMSIL's exit strategy was successfully linked to meeting the mission's mandate. The mission implemented a phased drawdown plan to enable the Sierra Leone government to take responsibility for security. The government was also assisted in extending its authority including decentralisation, rule of law and judicial reform. To ensure continued engagement with the country, Sierra Leone, was chosen alongside Burundi to become the first beneficiaries of the UN Peacebuilding Fund. Although the role of the international community in reconstructing Sierra Leone is highly commendable, care should be taken to minimise the dependency syndrome gripping the country. Sierra Leone today is effectively a donor driven state with international NGOs and aid agencies providing key amenities. UNMIL on the other hand is in the process of implementing its Consolidation, Drawdown and Withdrawal Plan. By 2010, the troop strength would have been reduced to 9,750. However, although the mission has met some of the indicators in its four benchmarks of security, rule of law and governance, economic revitalisation and basic services and infrastructure, there still remains major challenges. These include reform of the justice and security sectors and human rights (UN, March 2008).

'Lead-Nation' Support: US and UK in Liberia and Sierra Leone

The power and resources that strong and wealthy nations bring into the peace process are very crucial to the success of peacebuilding. Due to their global influence, these countries can help to galvanise international support and commitment to the peace process. Lead nation status is often rooted in a country's historical, political and economic ties with the country in conflict and achieved by the willingness of the country in question to devote significant resources to leading international efforts. Thus as former colonial master, Portugal is expected to play a leading role in conflicts in Angola and Guinea Bissau whilst France is doing just that in Cote d'Ivoire. In the same way, the US and UK were expected to provide the leadership needed to move forward the peace processes in Liberia and Sierra Leone respectively. There are significant differences in the levels of commitment and involvement by both countries.

As discussed in the previous chapter, US-Liberia relationship goes as far back as 1847 when the country was founded as home for freed slaves by the American Colonisation Society. However, despite the close ties during the Cold War, the US did not play an active role towards the resolution of the first phase of the Liberian conflict. Britain's special interest in Sierra Leone stems from the fact that it was that country's colonial power and leader of the International Contact Group. In sharp contrast to the US in Liberia, the British government played a more active role in the Sierra Leone peace process. It is worth pointing out that this role only started in the late 1990s. Before this period, British involvement in the conflict and by extension, its assistance to ECOMOG was minimal. This limited British assistance to ECOMOG can be linked to the Blair government's opposition to the Abacha regime in Nigeria. Direct British assistance of ECOMOG was interpreted as boosting the international standing of Abacha. Following the withdrawal of ECOMOG in May 2000, the British started playing a more active role. In addition to the military stabilisation role discussed in Chapter 5, the UK policy in Sierra Leone set out to maintain momentum of the peace process and build and equip a reformed and accountable military. Such a policy is set against the backdrop of New Labour's 'ethical foreign policy' (Williams, 2001). As leader of the International Contact Group on Sierra Leone, the British government has managed to keep international attention focused on rebuilding the country. The presence of so-called 'over-the-horizon' forces presented a credible deterrent to would-be 'spoilers' whilst making the security situation conducive for security sector reform. The crucial threat to stability posed by the military in Sierra Leone has been highlighted in Chapter 5. As previous attempts to reform the military have ended in failure, British efforts in this respect were of major importance. Working with the International Military Assistance Training Team (IMATT), Britain has trained and equipped a new Sierra Leonean army and also assisted in the UNAMSIL-Commonwealth-led police reform programme (Malan, 2003). The army reform programme in Sierra Leone involves the integration of serving British officers within the Sierra Leone Armed Forces as trainers and advisers. The UK also took a leading role in establishing the Office of National Security and producing a national security strategy and defence policy. In Liberia, the US contracted private security companies, DynCorp International and PAE to recruit, train and equip a 2,000-strong army. In a sub-region where private security companies and mercenaries are notorious for their role in fuelling conflicts, the US decision to use private firms is insensitive. Whilst private companies may be good at providing infantry training, they lack the ethos and values of a professional army. The SSR programme itself has been hit by delays caused by funding problems. Although the figure for reforming the army is put at $210 million, according to Malan, 'the SSR programme in Liberia was never fully funded, that funding to date has fallen far short of this figure, and that money even when forthcoming, has been disbursed in dribs and drabs' (2008, 41). Considering the fact that the failure of SSR was one of the causes of Liberia's relapse into war in 2002, the need to prioritise its implementation cannot be overemphasised. UNMIL has therefore put SSR as one of its benchmarks for the drawdown and withdrawal of the mission and continued delays will not only disrupt that plan but will also undermine the huge efforts to build sustainable peace in Liberia.

Challenges of Transitional Justice in Liberia and Sierra Leone

This section reviews the various transitional justice initiatives undertaken by local and external actors in Liberia and Sierra Leone and assesses their effectiveness within the context of West African sub-regional security. In light of the massive human rights abuses that characterise complex political emergencies, a key concern for post-conflict peacebuilding has been how to address the abuses of the past in order to ensure they are not repeated in the future. This question of transitional justice has received wide attention by legal scholars, conflict resolution practitioners and academics.[3] Transitional justice can be conceptualised as 'the interim legal arrangements which come to the fore as states enter into transition from violent conflict to peace and democracy or undertake profound internal rearrangement ...'.[4]Although there are various models and approaches to transitional justice, there appears to be no consensus on a single model. At the center of this debate are the tensions between reconciliation and justice. Three broad models can be identified: (i) 'Forgive and Forget'; (ii) Tribunals; and (iii) Truth Commissions. The first model, 'Forgive and forget' calls for a general forgiveness and amnesia from both victims and perpetrators for the abuses of the past. By putting the past behind, proponents of this system argue that post-war societies will be able to look to the future and avoid the divisions and hurting of wounds that come with trials and truth commissions. An analysis of several post-conflict societies reveals that this model is widely in use as evidenced by the blanket amnesty in peace agreements. However, an attempt to bury the abuses of the past is counterproductive as it encourages impunity and revenge attacks. Forgiveness itself cannot be forced on victims. The failure to acknowledge the mistakes of the past only serves to undermine the foundations of peace and adds to the pain of victims.

In recognition of the limitations of the above model, human rights groups and conflict resolutions practitioners have been at the forefront of advocating approaches that will bring about accountability for abuses. Since the Nuremberg and Tokyo trials at the end of World War II, international war crimes tribunals have been established to prosecute and punish those responsible for human rights abuses, war crimes, crimes against humanity and other violations of international law. Proponents of this model argue that prosecutions might deter future perpetrators (Rigby, 2001). It also individualises crimes and does not give collective guilt. However, critics of war crimes tribunals argue that whilst

---

3   See for example Andrew Rigby (2001), *Justice and Reconciliation: After the Violence*, London: Lynne Rienner; Robert I. Rotberg and Dennis Thompson (2000), *Truth v. Justice: The Morality of Truth Commissions*, Princetonn NJ: Princeton University Press.

4   Transitional Justice Institute, University of Ulster available online at http://www.transitionaljustice.ulster.ac.uk/, accessed July 2005.

they make victims satisfied that justice has been done, they do not assist in the process of reconciliation and healing. Also due to the combative nature inherent in trials, this model has limitations in unveiling the truth about what happened during the conflict- who does what, where and why. The strongest argument against tribunals is that it represents selective justice, what other people call victor's justice. This is due to the fact that tribunals are most often established after a comprehensive victory over another faction.

The very nature of complex political emergencies often makes war crimes tribunals a very unsuitable model. In most of these conflicts, no single faction has the military capability to comprehensively defeat the enemy. Therefore most of these conflicts end through negotiated peace settlements. Truth Commissions can therefore be seen as a pragmatic approach arising from the compromises and balancing act which characterise the transitional phase. Truth commissions are established to facilitate reconciliation and healing in post-war societies. The tasks of this commission include investigating the truth, providing a forum where victims can tell their stories and perpetrators acknowledge their past abuses, and recommending preventive measures through reforms of security forces, judiciary and other public bodies. The search for truth is also accompanied by recommendations for reparations/compensations for victims. Rotberg and Thompson (2000, 3) therefore concluded that 'truth commissions are intended to be both preventive and restorative'. Opponents of truth commissions argue that this model allows perpetrators of war crimes to go unpunished. This amounts to denial of justice which will be unable to bring about true reconciliation. In response, truth commission proponents argue that this model represents a concept of justice that is survivor or victim centred, not retributive. By trading amnesty for full disclosure of the truth, truth commissions provide a forum for perpetrators to face their victims and the general public. According to Rotberg and Thompson (2000, 4), this act of public testimony is enough to shame the perpetrators, 'exposure is punishment'. On a realist note, proponents of this model consider trials as impracticable due to the high levels of human rights abuses and the number of perpetrators (Rigby, 2001). Other critics accuse truth commissions of further dividing societies by opening up old wounds. However, proponents counter this argument by noting that trials would cause more divisions in society.

Notwithstanding the drawbacks associated with war crimes tribunals and truth commissions, peace processes have been more sustainable where an effective mechanism for addressing abuses of the past is established. Warring factions in both Liberia and Sierra Leone are very notorious for their massive human rights abuses against civilians. Despite this fact, successive peace agreements have called for 'blanket amnesty' for perpetrators of war crimes, the Lomé Accord being the most notable. However, measures to address such abuses differ markedly in both countries. Liberia opted for a Truth and Reconciliation Commission. The Commission started its operations in June 2006 but had to be suspended in early 2007 due to lack of funding and limited capacity. It resumed public hearing in January 2008. Although the TRC represents a bold attempt to establish the truth and address past impunity, Amnesty International (2007) warns that 'it is not a substitute for a court of law. It cannot establish individual criminal responsibility or provide for full reparations to victims'. It therefore calls for the government to pass appropriate legislation to bring to justice all those responsible for human rights abuses in Liberia. However, considering the fact that most of the perpetrators are now holding influential positions in government, the likelihood of passing such legislation remains remote. The poor state of the country's judicial system also makes it difficult to administer local justice. In Sierra Leone, following widespread domestic and international criticism of the blanket amnesty provision of the Lome accord, the government and international community established a Special Court and Truth and Reconciliation Commission. The novelty and impact of these two bodies on the peace process deserve a sub-section.

The Special Court and Truth and Reconciliation Commission of Sierra Leone

By establishing a truth commission and war crimes tribunal, sponsors of the Sierra Leone peace process aim to promote reconciliation whilst at the same time punishing those 'who bear the greatest responsibility for war crimes'. The nature and extent of war crimes against civilians in Sierra Leone makes the establishment of a war crimes tribunal very compelling. Calls for its establishment intensified after the RUF reneged on the terms of Lomé Accord in May 2000. The precedent created by the establishment of the ad hoc International Criminal Tribunals for the former Yugoslavia (ICTY) in 1993 and Rwanda (ICTR) in 1994, and the Rome Statute for the Permanent International Criminal Court (ICC) was also an added impetus. The Special Court for Sierra Leone (SCSL) was established in January 2002 by agreement between the UN and Sierra Leone government with a mandate of brining to justice those 'who bear the greatest responsibility' for war crimes, crimes against humanity, other serious violations of international humanitarian law committed since November 1996 (Sierra Leone Government, 2002). Unlike the ICTR and ICTY, the SCSL is a hybrid court with mixed jurisdiction, combining international law with national Sierra Leonean law. It also has a mixture of personnel: of the eight judges, three are appointed by the Sierra Leone government and five by the UN Secretary-General. Another unique feature of the Sierra Leone Special Court is its location. Unlike ICTR which is based in Arusha, Tanzania and ICTY in The Hague, SCSL is based in Freetown. By locating the court in Freetown, the planners hope to make it accessible to victims and let Sierra Leoneans see that justice is being done. Its location is also intended to send a strong message to would-be war crime perpetrators in the country and the sub-region. The SCSL has also set judicial precedent by classifying the recruitment of child soldiers and forced marriage/sexual offence as war crimes. The court also caused controversy by allowing for the prosecution of juveniles. This issue poses a serious moral dilemma in a country like Sierra Leone where children have been abducted and forced to commit war crimes, making them both victims and perpetrators.

By December 2003, the court had issued 13 indictments including that of Charles Taylor and Sam Hinga Norman. These indictments have been credited for dissuading would-be trouble makers in Sierra Leone from reneging from the peace process. It also severely weakened and neutralised the RUF as most of its senior leadership was indicted. However, the limited jurisdiction given to the court (November 1996) is a major drawback to the quest for justice in a conflict characterised by human right abuses since its outbreak in March 1991. The lack of chapter VII powers also means the court is unable to force member states from handing over suspects. Besides, problems of funding continue to plague the operations of the court. Although its location in Freetown was expected to raise public awareness and support, there appears to be little support for the SCSL amongst Sierra Leoneans. Most locals consider the court as forced upon the country by the international community. They consider it a misplacement of priorities as there are better areas to spend donor funds on. This public perception of the SCSL has been further damaged by the indictment and death in detention of the former CDF Coordinator and Interior Minister, Norman; a person with widespread public support for his role in resisting the RUF onslaught. The effectiveness of the SCSL has also been questioned by the fact that those 'who bear the greatest responsibility' are either dead or have escaped arrest. Foday Sankoh and 'Maskita' Bockarie died in 2003 whilst Johnny Paul Koroma is still evading arrest. There also appears to be a disjuncture between the SCSL and the local justice system. Whilst the SCSL courts and penal system operates at very high standards, the local judiciary appears to be massively under funded.

Unlike the SCSL, the Truth and Reconciliation Commission (TRC) was part of the provisions of the Lomé Accord. However, it only commenced operations in July 2002 due to the fluid security situation and funding problems. The TRC arose out of the impracticability of prosecuting the thousands of ex-combatants and their leaders, and the need to promote reconciliation. The TRC is mandated to 'create an impartial historical record of violations and abuses of human rights and international humanitarian law related to the armed conflict in Sierra Leone,... to address impunity, to respond to the needs of victims, to promote healing and reconciliation and to prevent a repetition of the violations and abuses suffered (Sierra Leone Government, 2000).

The Sierra Leone TRC, unlike its South African counterpart is not mandated to grant amnesty to perpetrators. The TRC's relationship with the SCSL has been very contentious. Although envisaged to work in a complementary manner, public perception of the relationship between the two institutions is quite different. The quality of statements collected by the TRC was hampered by the fear that the SCSL will use TRC material to prosecute suspects. Thus most ex-combatants failed to testify and the trustworthiness of those that testified is questionable. The timing of the two institutions might have contributed to this problem. Confidence of the ex-combatants and the general public would have been boosted if TRC hearings had come after the conclusion of the SCSL. The apparent poor public sensitisation efforts also contributed to this controversy.

Despite the problems associated with both the SCSL and TRC in Sierra Leone, these two institutions managed to send a strong message across the sub-region that war crimes and human rights abuses will not go unaddressed. They challenged the culture of impunity which has been characteristic of conflicts in West Africa. And as noted above, this stance forced compliance from warring factions in Sierra Leone.

Conclusion: Threats to Peace and Stability in Liberia and Sierra Leone

Liberia and Sierra Leone have made remarkable progress in consolidating the fragile peace and put in place structures to ensure its sustainability. Both countries have benefited from substantial international support with the deployment of large UN peacekeeping missions and donor support of peacebuilding programmes. Consequently, significant achievements have been made in rebuilding governance institutions, reviving the economies, disarming and demobilising ex-combatants and reforming the security and judicial sectors.

Despite the achievements discussed above, there still remain considerable threats to peace in Liberia and Sierra Leone. In Liberia, problems with reforming the security sector pose a formidable challenge. The need to prioritise SSR cannot be overemphasised. The failure of SSR after the first phase of the Liberian conflict in 1997 was partly responsible for the country's relapse into conflict. In both countries, problems with reintegration of ex-combatants are posing major threats to peace. Half-hearted reintegration efforts and the prevailing high youth unemployment are causing discontent amongst former combatants and young people in both countries and threaten to unravel the major gains achieved so far. Corruption in both countries also undermines economic recovery efforts and robs the population of the expected peace dividend. Although the macro-economic figures are impressive, however, the pervasive poverty and poor social and economic indicators pose the biggest challenge to peacebuilding.

The situation in neighbouring Guinea and Cote d'Ivoire also pose a significant threat to the peace in Liberia and Sierra Leone. Chapter 2 explored the sub-regional linkages of conflicts in West Africa. Considering the interconnectedness of actors in these countries, conflict in any one is bound to have far reaching security implications for the others. As past experiences have shown, a resurgence of conflict in either Cote d'Ivoire or Guinea risks unravelling the fragile peace in both countries and any long term peacebuilding programme should be cognisant of this.

Chapter 9
Institutionalising Conflict Resolution and Humanitarian Intervention in West Africa

Introduction

The problems encountered and lessons learned in the various ECOWAS peacekeeping operations led to the initiation of a process meant to improve future interventions. In this respect, ECOWAS made moves to institutionalise conflict resolution, security and peacekeeping mechanisms. The revised ECOWAS treaty of 1993 represents the first serious attempt to establish such a permanent mechanism. Besides strengthening economic and fiscal ties to face the challenges of globalisation, the treaty addressed issues pertaining to security, conflict resolution and management. In recognition of the nexus between human rights, good governance and conflicts in the sub-region, ECOWAS in 1991 agreed on the Declaration of Political Principles which committed member states to respect human rights, democracy and the rule of law. This was followed in 2001 by the adoption of the Protocol on Good Governance which addresses the root causes of conflict such as corruption and bad governance. However, the most important security protocols adopted so far are the Mechanism for Conflict Prevention, Management, Resolution, Peacekeeping and Security and the Convention on Small Arms and Light Weapons, their Ammunition and other Related Materials signed in December 1999 and June 2006 respectively. This chapter looks at the provisions of these protocols, analyse the implications for sub-regional security and conflict resolution and discuss their shortcomings. Next we will examine the contribution of extra-regional actors in building the peacekeeping capacity of West African militaries.

The ECOWAS Mechanism for Conflict Prevention, Management, Resolution, Peacekeeping and Security

As its name implies, this mechanism seeks to strengthen the sub-region's conflict prevention, management and resolution capacity as well as build effective peacekeeping, humanitarian support and peacebuilding capabilities. It also addresses cross border crime which is becoming a major problem for the sub-region. In a bid to realise these ambitious aims, the ECOWAS Security

Mechanism (as it is known for short) establishes a number of institutions, arms and strategies which include:

The Mediation and Security Council (MSC)

Comprising Heads of State and Government, Ministers of Foreign Affairs and Ambassadors, this body takes important decisions relating to matters of peace and security and the deployment of peacekeeping/enforcement troops. Membership to the MSC is on a rotational basis and comprises nine states elected for a two-year period with no permanent seats. To facilitate the council's work, a *Committee of Ambassadors (CA)* with dual accreditation to ECOWAS and Nigeria and a *Defence and Security Commission (DSC)* made up of defence chiefs and security technocrats work out the details and technicalities of an operation and make recommendations to the MSC.

An *Early Warning System* (ECOWARN) was also established with regional observation network and observatories. These observatories undertake risk mapping, observation and analysis of social, economic and political situations in the sub-region which have the potential of degenerating into conflict and present appropriate threat perception analysis. To this end, four zones were established as follows:

> *Zone 1*: Cape Verde, The Gambia, Guinea Bissau, and Senegal with Banjul as the capital;
> *Zone 2*: Burkina Faso, Cote D'Ivoire, Mali and Niger with headquarters in Ouagadougou;
> *Zone 3*: Ghana, Guinea, Liberia and Sierra Leone, HQ Monrovia;
> *Zone 4*: Benin, Nigeria and Togo, HQ Cotonou.

The reports coming from these zones will inform the ECOWAS Commission President and the MSC in devising suitable response strategies. Four options are available to diffuse any potential threat to security identified in the various zones and they include: (a) the setting up of a fact finding commission; (b) the use of the good offices of the Commission President; (c) calling on the services of a Council of Elders; and if all else fails (d) the employment of military force. The Council of Elders can be seen as a traditional African conflict resolution mechanism. Made up of 15 eminent persons, one from each member state, this council is charged with the task of facilitating negotiation, mediation and conciliation in a potential conflict.

ECOWAS Standby Force

ECOMOG became formally established as a standby force for the community and, reflecting the changing nature of peacekeeping, its role was expanded to cover conflict prevention, humanitarian intervention, enforcement, peacebuilding and the control of organised crime. In *June 2004*, the ECOWAS Defence and Security Commission transformed ECOMOG into the ECOWAS Standby Force (ESF). The force will be made up of 6500 highly trained soldiers to be drawn from national units. It will include a rapid reaction Task Force of 1,500 troops which will have the capability to be deployed within 30 days whilst the entire brigade could be deployed within 90 days. The ESF will form one of the components of the African Standby Force and will be under the operational control of the African Union. To enhance the force's strategic, tactical and operational readiness, ECOWAS is in the process of implementing a five-year training programme. This involves a series of specialised modules consistent with UN standards to be delivered in three designated Centres of Excellence: Nigerian War College in Abuja, the Kofi Annan International Peacekeeping Centre in Accra, Ghana, and the Ecole du Maintien de la Paix in Bamako, Mali. As of June 2008, ECOWAS has held four military trainings – Command post exercise in Dakar and Accra, June 2006 and December 2007 respectively; the West Battalion Exercise in Thies, Senegal, December 2007 and another Command Post Exercise in Bamako, Mali, June 2008. Such exercises will not only be useful in enhancing the peacekeeping capacity of troops, they will also go a long way in harmonising strategies and equipments. To address the perennial problem of logistics, ECOWAS has also designated two logistics depots – a coastal base just outside Freetown, Sierra Leone and an inland base in Mali.

Small Arms Control

ECOWAS also sought to address the link between small arms and instability in the sub-region when Heads of State adopted the Declaration on the Moratorium on the Importation, Exportation and Manufacture of Light Weapons in October 1998. The Moratorium was extended in July 2001 for further three years. Taking into consideration the devastating effects of small arms and light weapons in the sub-region, any attempt to stem the flow of these arms is a welcome development. Such efforts go as far back as 1992 when the UN imposed an arms embargo on Liberia followed by a similar action on Sierra Leone in 1997. But as clearly shown by the UN Panel of Experts, several states in the sub-region were guilty of busting the sanctions. Burkina Faso for instance used its territory as conduit for arms shipment to Liberia and the RUF. Since then more concrete measures have been taken both regionally and globally. A regional effort to curb the spread of small arms came in the form of the Bamako Declaration adopted by African states on 1 December 2000 designed to harmonise, standardise and codify national norms and coordinate and enhance sub-regional and regional arms control measures. At the global level, there are two main instruments to control weapons spread and transfer. The first of which is the UN Protocol against the Illicit Manufacture of and Trafficking in Firearms, Their Parts and Components and Ammunition adopted on 21 May 2001. The next is the Programme of Action (PoA) adopted in the 2001 UN conference on Illicit Trade on Small Arms and Light Weapons.

At the sub-regional level is the ECOWAS Moratorium on Importation, Exportation, and Manufacture of Light Weapons. Building on the success achieved in ending the Tuareg rebellion in the North of Mali, President Omar Konare proposed a moratorium on small arms. This proposal received the backing of ECOWAS leaders. Signed by all ECOWAS member states on 31 October 1998, the Moratorium was renewed in 2001 for a further three year period ending October 2004. The Moratorium is not legally binding but an expression of shared political will. The Programme for Coordination and Assistance for Security and Development (PCASED), based in Bamako and administered by the UNDP, is the implementation arm of the Moratorium. Among other things, the PCASED is tasked with the following:

- establishing a civilian culture;
- establishing National Commissions in each Member State;
- training for military, security and police forces;
- enhancing weapons controls at border posts;
- establishing a small arms and light weapons register;
- collecting and destroying surplus and unauthorised weapons;
- facilitating dialogue with producers/suppliers;
- reviewing and harmonising national legislative and administrative procedures;
- enlarging membership of the moratorium.

Since coming into effect in 1998, the Moratorium has achieved some success as reflected in the harmonisation of arms control legislation among member states, enhanced border control, improved arms registration and effective arms control schemes. The Moratorium has also facilitated a number of arms collection and destruction schemes across the sub-region. However, a major drawback of the Moratorium is the fact that it is voluntary and not legally binding. As such there are no sanctions to be imposed on any defaulter. Contrary to the numerous Summits, Communiqués and Speeches by leaders in the sub-region, the actions of various countries clearly contravenes the spirit and purpose of the ECOWAS Moratorium. Critics also contend that the Moratorium is heavily state-centric and fails to address the role of non-state actors. Although it calls for the inclusion of Civil Society representatives in the various National Commissions, these representatives are often marginalised and chosen not on the basis of objective criteria but depending on links to national government (Ebo, 2003). Notwithstanding the marginalisation by government authorities, civil society organisations across West Africa are heavily involved in raising awareness and lobbying governments for greater action. One such group is the West African Action Network on Small Arms (WAANSA). Launched in 2002, WAANSA is an umbrella body comprising civil society groups in 10 West African states involved in arms control issues. Although the combined efforts of governments, International Governmental Organisations, NGOs and Civil Society groups have raised awareness of the dangers of small arms, there remains much to be done to address this problem.

In View of the above limitations, ECOWAS leaders adopted the *ECOWAS Convention on Small Arms and Light Weapons, their Ammunition and other Related Materials* on 14 June 2006. This effectively transformed the Moratorium into a legally binding convention. The lack of a specialised unit within ECOWAS responsible for implementing the Moratorium had been a major weakness. In recognition of this fact, a Small Arms Unit has been established within ECOWAS to oversee the implementation of the convention. However, the failure of member states to ratify the convention is a negative indication of their commitment to the problem of small arms. It requires ratification by nine member states to come into effect. As of June 2008, only six countries have ratified it. This means until the ninth ratification, the convention will not come into force.

Extra-Regional Actors and Humanitarian Intervention in West Africa

Over the past decade, P-3 countries (US, UK and France) have initiated programmes intended to strengthen the capacity of African militaries to respond to humanitarian disasters and conflict. These programmes vary in terms of levels of political commitment, finance and logistics. Although these initiatives cover the entire African continent, West Africa has considerably shaped their design and implementation. This section will examine the various policies prescribed for African peacekeeping and humanitarian intervention and assess their effectiveness and relevance to the West African context.

The US African Crisis Response Initiative (ACRI)

The Somalia fiasco of 1993 necessitated a rethink in top US policy circles regarding peacekeeping in Africa. This led to the declaration of Presidential Decision Directive 25 (PDD-25) of 1994 that effectively restricted the deployment of US troops in African conflicts. In place of direct US military involvement, military, intelligence and diplomatic policy makers in Washington developed a pragmatic initiative that involves providing indirect support to African militaries whilst maintaining the global role of the US. The programme became known as the African Crisis Response Initiative. In 1996, the then Secretary of State, Warren Christopher toured several African states to discuss the idea of creating an African Crisis Response Force (ACRF) that can be rapidly deployed in a major humanitarian crisis. Launched in 1997, this initiative draws heavily on existing programmes of the UN (UN Standby Arrangement System) and the

OAU (Standby Rapid Deployment Force). The programme involves training of a contingent of about 5,000 to 10,000 peacekeepers recruited from amongst African countries to be selected by the US. Based on common peacekeeping doctrines used by the US, UN, UK and Nordic countries, the curriculum includes human rights training, refugee protection, civil-military relations and international law of armed conflict. Training is conducted by the 3rd and 5th US Special Forces in joint exercises on a 60-day training circle. Follow-up sustainment training is conducted twice a year. In addition to training, the programme also involves the provision of non-lethal equipment to African militaries. Requests for deployments of the force can come from the UN, OAU and sub-regional organisations. Battalion size units have been trained in Senegal, Uganda, Malawi, Mali, Ghana and Ethiopia.

The ACRI can be credited for taking the radical move from providing military aid to African dictators to a more proactive approach that addresses Africa's humanitarian disasters. By providing training and logistics to potential African peacekeepers and humanitarian interveners, this programme has attempted to solve a major problem hampering the success of African peacekeepers. However, the programme has been criticised for failing to take into consideration local dynamics and the nature of African conflicts by focusing their training on 'conventional peacekeeping doctrine and techniques rather than on doctrines and techniques relevant to the difficult conflict environment in which African armed forces now find themselves, including operations against guerrilla forces in difficult terrain' (Ebo, 2003). The ACRI has also been criticized for contradicting the very notion it seeks to promote: African solutions to African problems. By failing to engage in a broad consultative process, the initiative ended up duplicating peacekeeping efforts in the region. Besides, the proposal also suffers from lack of ownership (Francis, 2001). The selection of participating countries is also very problematic as it appears to be dictated by US national interests. In theory, membership is open to functioning democracies where the military is under civilian control. But the inclusion of Uganda, a country with a de facto one party system raises serious doubts about the selection criteria. The fact that the selected states are all strong US allies further reinforces this doubt. In the West African context, any peacekeeping programme that does not include Nigeria is doomed to fail. Some of the shortcomings of the ACRI have been recognised as the US is now actively consulting with the AU, France and the UK with a view to harmonising the various peacekeeping strategies in the sub-region. In 2000, the US launched 'operation focus relief' to train Nigerian peacekeepers in Sierra Leone. To address West African conflicts, the US has also established the West African Stabilisation Programme. ACRI has since been renamed African Contingency Operations Training Assistance (ACOTA). However, since events of 9/11, US capacity building efforts have tended to shift more towards counter terrorism measures as evidenced by its Pan-Sahelian Initiative which is designed to capacitate countries in the Sahel region to combat terrorism.

The French Renforcement des Capacites Africaines de Maintien de la Paix (RECAMP)

As the French government was reviewing its defence agreements with Francophone states in Africa and also down scaling its troop commitment in the region, there was need for strengthening the capacity of African militaries to fill the void left by departing French troops. The proposal to create a Standing African force under OAU control was first presented by the French during the 1994 Franco-African Summit in Biarritz. The proposal was accepted in the 1998 Franco-African summit in Louvre, France and became known as RECAMP. The programme revolves around the notion of partnership between France and African countries. It calls for the establishment of Peacekeeping Training Centres. The Zambakro Peacekeeping Training School was established in Cote d'Ivoire in 1999 to train officers from across Africa. Training is also done through regular exercises conducted in African countries. The first was the multinational training exercise in Togo (Nangbeto Exercise) in March 1997, followed by the Guidimakha Exercise conducted in Senegal in February 1998. However, by focusing exclusively on Francophone states, RECAMP is further deepening the Francophone-Anglophone divide that is endemic in West Africa and undermining the sub-region's security efforts.

British Military Advisory and Training Teams (BMATT)

The UK's peacekeeping training programme involves cooperation between the Departments of Defence, Foreign and Commonwealth Office and International Development. The programmes are delivered by the British Military Advisory and Training Teams (BMATT). BMATT grew out of bilateral military cooperation agreements between Britain and individual African countries. The first BMATT was established in Ghana in 1976 followed in 1980 in Zimbabwe and 1994 in South Africa. Responding to the need to build sub-regional peacekeeping capacity, BMATT is developing national staff colleges into centres of excellence for sub-regional peacekeeping training. In 1996, the centres in Ghana and South Africa were renamed BMATT West Africa and BMATT Southern Africa respectively. Unlike the French who focus on multinational field exercises, the UK's peacekeeping capacity building programme is primarily focused on training officers. Due to its relatively smaller size, the programme is designed to train officers who will in turn train large number of troops; in other words, 'training the trainer'. BMATT West Africa is conducting training courses for senior military staff at the Ghanaian Armed Forces Command and Staff College. Military personnel are drawn from across West Africa. In addition to BMATT, the UK also has small scale training programmes. In 2000, the International Military Assistance Training Team (IMATT) was established in collaboration with the Commonwealth to assist with security sector reform programmes in Sierra Leone. The role of IMATT in transforming the renegade Sierra Leone army has already been noted in Chapter 7.

Conclusion

ECOWAS deserves commendation for institutionalising peacekeeping and incorporating conflict prevention and peacebuilding into its security mechanism. As argued in the Chapter 3, humanitarian and peace support operations in today's complex political emergencies call for a coherent and effective peacebuilding component to prevent a relapse into violence. The experiences in Liberia and Sierra Leone are indicative of the importance of incorporating peacebuilding into humanitarian intervention. The emerging policy shift within ECOWAS towards issues of human security is also encouraging. The Protocol on Good Governance, which is closely linked to the Security Mechanism, addresses the root causes of the sub-region's security crisis and sought to shift attention towards the well being of the individual. The focus on conflict prevention and early response is another step in the right direction. However, the placement of one of the observatories in Burkina Faso, a country notorious for supporting insurgencies in the sub-region, is misguided. The ability of the observatory to gather and disseminate critical information on this government will be adversely affected, as the government in question will definitely restrict the system's work. The institutional and financial incapacity of its secretariat also poses an obstacle in realising the aims embodied in this mechanism. Ebo (2003) noted the lack of personnel as provided for in the mechanism. The problem of funding is not new to the organisation. The organisation's financial crisis is characteristic of the weak economic status of its member states. Perhaps the major threat towards the realisation of the sub-region's peace and security aspirations is the fact that ECOWAS leaders are known to be making high sounding declarations and policies which they hardly implement. For example, as of June 2008, only 6 countries had ratified the Convention on small arms.

The various capacity building programmes of the P3 countries are meant to support the sub-region in overcoming the problems discussed above. However, these programmes are incoherent, uncoordinated and pose a threat to sub-regional ownership. Besides, the funding remains inconsistent and unpredictable. Recognising the need to anchor any peacekeeping training within a sub-regional foundation, members of the P-3 have entered into agreement with ECOWAS wherein a representative from each of these countries will be based in the ECOWAS secretariat on an advisory and coordinating capacity. In the context of sub-regional security, these initiatives represent a big boost to West African humanitarian and conflict response capacity. However, these programmes also risk eroding local ownership of security structures and encourage a disproportionate dependence on outside prescriptions.

Conclusion

The ECOWAS interventions in West Africa have far reaching implications for humanitarian intervention and Africa's international relations. Faced with unprecedented scale of human suffering and Western disengagement from African conflicts, ECOWAS peacekeepers were forced to take on both forcible and non-forcible humanitarian roles by default. The dynamics and unpredictability of conflicts in the sub-region have posed significant challenges to the traditional conceptualisation of humanitarian intervention and have consequently led to ongoing efforts to re-conceptualise the practice to meet the challenges of post-Cold War conflicts. State collapse, which can be both a cause and consequence of complex political emergencies, have expanded the remits of humanitarian interveners from the 'fire brigade' mentality to efforts aimed at rebuilding collapsed states. Besides providing the first opportunity for the UN to cooperate with regional organisations, ECOWAS interventions also necessitated a rethinking of the traditional OAU principles of sovereignty and non-interventionism in the internal affairs of states. These principles have for so long been major obstacles to the OAU's capability of resolving conflicts. Dictators and warlords alike have often exploited this loophole to perpetuate misery and untold suffering on the African people. The ECOWAS intervention in Liberia provided the impetus for the OAU's establishment of the Mechanism for Conflict Prevention, Management and Resolution. The AU (the successor to the OAU) has also learned from the OAU's weaknesses and ECOWAS' experience. In its Constitutive Act, the AU has enshrined the right to intervene in member states 'in respect of grave circumstances, namely war crimes, genocide and crimes against humanity'.[1] AU Defence and Security Ministers' meeting in January 2004 concluded the framework document for an establishment of an African Standby Force and a Common Defence and Security Policy. At the sub-regional level, ECOWAS operations also inspired peacekeeping and humanitarian intervention initiatives of various other African sub-regions. The SADC intervention in Lesotho and the Democratic Republic of the Congo are key examples. General Malu, ECOMOG's last Force Commander in Liberia observes, 'I think ECOMOG is a good example of how this can be done, and I believe we have something to give to the world to copy from'.[2]

But what lessons can the world learn from ECOWAS peacekeeping experiences? For analytical purposes, we will divide ECOWAS missions into

---

1   African Union (2000), *Constitutive Act of the African Union*, Lome: AU, Article 4 (h).

2   Victor Malu (General), Interview with *West Africa Magazine* (March 1997), 466.

three periods: pre-1999 period include missions in the Mano River Union countries of Liberia and Sierra Leone; the intermediate period covers the intervention in Guinea Bissau; and the post-1999 period represents the institutionalisation of peace and security mechanisms in the sub-region and cover ECOMICI in Cote d'Ivoire and ECOMIL in Liberia. The pre-1999 period represents the organisation's first foray into peacekeeping and all the uncertainties and challenges it brings. These missions are characterised by Nigerian domination and ECOMOG's constant shift between peacekeeping and peace enforcement. Considering the nature of complex political emergencies and the fluidity of the security situation and actors involved in Sierra Leone and Liberia, this flexibility represents an effective response. This duality resulted in the establishment of *de facto* safe havens, sharing of the limited military supplies with starving civilians and securing humanitarian relief corridors. It also comes with its own challenges and setbacks. These include the force's lack of capacity to effectively safeguard civilians under their control, poor human rights record of troops, lack of neutrality and complicity in exploiting the natural resources of the host countries. The missions in both countries were also hampered by financial, military and political difficulties. The endemic funding and logistical constraints suffered by ECOMOG severely limited the capacity of the force. Another crucial factor that adversely affected ECOMOG's operations in both countries was the rivalry and lack of political consensus between French and English speaking West Africa. For the greater part of the operations, French-speaking states were less cooperative with some even supporting rebel groups against ECOMOG. This lack of political consensus on the part of the mandating body complicated an already complex situation and further derailed efforts to resolve both conflicts. Even amongst troops on the ground, there were differences of approach and strategy. Whilst Ghana favoured traditional peacekeeping strategies, Nigeria adopted more robust enforcement action. This difference of strategy led to problems with inter-contingent coordination and chain of command. These tensions were exacerbated by the lack of effective ECOWAS oversight of both forces and the sub-regional resentment of Nigeria's hegemonic position. Relations between ECOMOG and aid agencies were also tense.

The peace processes in both countries were also seriously flawed as they attempted to reward political violence. In Sierra Leone, the Lomé accord soon disintegrated and without the timely intervention of the United Kingdom, the country would have relapsed into full scale war in May 2000. Chapter 7 reveals how regional appeasement to Charles Taylor contributed to a resurgence of fighting in that country. Furthermore, the failure of peace processes in both countries can be linked to the inability of ECOWAS to understand the nature and dynamics of conflicts and actors involved. Despite the widely held view that regional/sub-regional bodies have a better understanding of the conflict and the actors involved, the evidence in both countries suggests the contrary. By relying on the goodwill and commitment of warlords for the success of peace accords, ECOWAS failed to understand the zero sum nature of CPEs and therefore set the stage for intransigence and 'spoiler' tactics. Its association with different warring parties in both countries also undermined its impartial status as a third party mediator. The peacebuilding process was equally flawed. In Liberia, whilst ECOMOG achieved qualified success in disarming thousands of combatants, the demobilisation and reintegration programme were problematic as lack of international support derailed the achievements of the disarmament phase. Security sector was never implemented as Taylor reneged on his earlier commitments. Peacebuilding by ECOMOG in Sierra Leone was a total failure. The fighting between ECOMOG and AFRC/RUF rebels never allowed DDR and security sector reform programmes to kick off as planned. The haphazard manner in which the force withdrew from the country further threatened to unravel the limited gains made. However, although ECOMOG was not successful in addressing the root causes of both conflicts and preventing a relapse into war in Liberia, the force can be credited for linking humanitarian action to peacemaking and rebuilding collapsed states through programmes such as security sector reform, DDR and elections. And as Chapter 7 argues, the failure of peacebuilding cannot be blamed on ECOMOG alone but also the wider international community. The Sierra Leone case has demonstrated the importance of international actors, working in concert with regional/sub-regional countries and local civil society to the success of peacebuilding.

The ECOWAS intervention in Guinea Bissau adds a new dimension to the analysis of West African security. Besides being the first non-Anglophone country in which ECOWAS intervened, it is also notable for the absence of Nigeria, a country responsible for over 75 per cent of troops and funding for previous interventions. The subsequent humiliation and total collapse of ECOMOG III underlines the indispensability of Nigeria in West African security and the need for a regional hegemon.

The challenges and opportunities faced in the above operations have led to a process of institutionalising peacekeeping, conflict prevention and management as manifested by the adoption of the ECOWAS security mechanism discussed in Chapter 9 and the signing of good governance and arms control conventions. Less than three years after its adoption, the ECOWAS security mechanism faced its first major test when an army mutiny on 19 September 2002 plunged Cote d'Ivoire into turmoil. Liberia also relapsed into full scale civil war in the summer of 2003. What role, if any, did the ECOWAS Security mechanism play in diffusing these crises? Has ECOWAS learned from its previous experiences? Are such lessons being implemented? Unlike earlier missions in Liberia and Sierra Leone where the legality of interventions was questionable, ECOWAS this time requested and was granted prior Security Council authorisations for both forces through resolution 1464 and 1497 in Cote d'Ivoire and Liberia respectively. Closely related to this is the question of Nigerian hegemony in ECOMOG. Keen to avoid the bitter resentment of Francophone countries towards Nigerian domination of ECOMOG and the Anglophone-Francophone rivalry that followed, Nigeria opted for a more inclusive strategy, playing a less domineering role. This can be seen in the composition of both forces. In Cote d'Ivoire, Ghana was the only Anglophone country out of five whilst in Liberia, four were Francophone states, one Lusophone and three Anglophone. One possible explanation for this change of strategy lies in Nigeria's transition to a democracy. During the days of military rule, the authorities in Nigeria had a free hand in deciding matters of foreign and defence policy as all organised opposition was stifled. It was this same dictatorship that the Nigerian Military authorities extended to the sub-regional stage. But with the democratic dispensation in 1999, foreign and defence policy was now subjected to rigorous internal debate. This new tolerance to debate and inclusion at home was reflected in a dramatic shift of strategy at the sub-regional stage where Nigeria began playing a more coordinating role. However, despite this new found regional cooperation, serious concerns remain about the commitment of member states to regional security. The retaliatory support given by Guinea, Liberia, Burkina Faso and Cote d'Ivoire to each other's insurgents seriously undermine any collective sub-regional security and conflict resolution efforts.

The conduct of ECOMOG troops in previous missions came under fire due to poor human rights record, complicity in exploiting the war economies and lack of peacekeeping training and experience. In Cote d'Ivoire and Liberia, there were no reports of excesses or human rights abuses by ECOMICI and ECOMIL forces. One explanation can be the favourable conditions for troops in these missions. Unlike Liberia and Sierra Leone where ECOMOG troops faced bitter opposition by rebel forces, ECOMICI and ECOMIL were accepted by all the parties to the conflicts. Both missions therefore assumed traditional peacekeeping roles without the need to engage in enforcement action. Notwithstanding the benign conditions, the improved professionalism can be attributed to years of experience in ECOMOG in Liberia and Sierra Leone, UNAMSIL in Sierra Leone and various training programmes sponsored by the US, France and the UK. The creation of the Office of the Special Representative of the ECOWAS Executive Secretary in both countries also represents a move in the right direction. In ECOMOG, the Force Commander also doubles as diplomatic and political representative of ECOWAS. The appointment of a civilian head of mission relieved the Force Commander of additional responsibility – a job he is not trained to perform – giving him time to concentrate on military matters. This also ensures that the ECOWAS Secretariat maintains control over the force rather than the respective troop contributing countries as it used to be. Although ECOMICI and ECOMIL are no longer in theatre, the offices are still maintained to coordinate between ECOWAS and the respective UN Missions. The relationship between the UN and ECOWAS also appears to have matured considerably. After the re-hating of the former ECOMICI troops into the new UN Operation in Cote d'Ivoire (UNOCI), ECOWAS continued to lead efforts aimed at facilitating a negotiated settlement to the conflict. In Liberia, this cooperation led to the first case of a regional body drawing troops and resources from an existing UN force. ECOWAS, through its designated mediator, the former Nigerian military ruler, Abdusalami Abubakar, worked with UNMIL in implementing the fragile peace.

Unlike ECOMOG, there was a relatively high level of international support to both missions. In Cote d'Ivoire, Memoranda of Understanding were signed between the various troop contributing countries and a Western partner to assist with logistics and communication equipment. The UK supported Ghana, Belgium assisted Benin whilst France channelled its support to Senegal, Togo and Niger. The US provided support towards strategic transportation within the mission area and two-thirds of the force's food requirements (Faye, 2004). The Liberian case was not so straight forward. With a civilian government in Abuja that is subject to legislative and media scrutiny, Nigeria was no longer prepared to solely bankroll an entire force, as was the case with ECOMOG. It therefore asked for guarantees of funding before committing any troops to the mission. This insistence on funding before deployment produced tangible fruits as the force received support from various sources. The US provided finance and maintained a 2000 strong contingent off the coast of Monrovia to provide logistical support to ECOMIL. UNAMSIL assisted with airlift facilities. However this assistance fell well below the financial and logistical needs of the mission. These difficulties made it very difficult for the mission to deploy out of Monrovia. In Cote d'Ivoire, despite the substantial international support highlighted above, the mission also suffered from shortages of equipment and logistics (Gberie and Addo, 2004). These logistical constraints and over reliance on external support raises serious doubts about the effectiveness of the ECOWAS Security Mechanism. Considering the weak state of the economies of West African states, this reliance on western financial and logistical aid is bound to continue. However, with the US and other Western states shifting attention to the 'war on terror', less attention will be paid by developed nations in assisting African countries tackle the continent's intractable conflicts.

If regional peacekeeping and humanitarian intervention is problematic and extra-regional peacekeeping capacity building programmes are incoherent and unsustainable, what then is the future of humanitarian intervention in West Africa? Co-deployment has been put forward as a credible alternative (Francis et al., 2005). But can this evolving relationship between the UN and regional/sub-regional organisations provide an effective alternative to traditional UN peacekeeping and sub-regional efforts? With sharp contrast to the Cold War era in which regional organisations were regarded as threats to the universalistic approach espoused by the UN, changes in the post-Cold War international political order have rendered cooperation between the UN and such organisations as not only desirable but necessary if international peace and security is to be maintained. The strategic overstretch of the UN has become common knowledge. This has been made even worse by the growing lack of big power support to UN peacekeeping. US PDD 25 is a clear indication that the US is no longer willing to commit itself to UN peacekeeping. But with conflicts raging in Africa, the Middle East and Eastern Europe, the only other option will be for the UN to cooperate with regional organisations. As experiences in West Africa demonstrate, regional organisations have greater interest in responding to conflicts since they are directly affected. But being close to the conflicting parties also means that members of a regional body often have vested interests and may find it difficult to remain neutral. This lack of neutrality often robs them of the credibility which is key to the success of any third party intervention. With the exception of NATO and the EU, most regional institutions lack effective peacekeeping capacity, financial, human and military resources to undertake an effective peacekeeping and humanitarian operation. These limitations therefore meant regional organisations still need the UN in managing conflicts. The later has the credibility, capacity, access to resources and neutrality required. This underlines the need for task sharing between regional organisations and the UN.

But this cooperation is not without its shortcomings. Poor working relationship continues to plague such operations. The UN is still not able to take the lead role in some of these missions and as Alagappa rightly notes, the UN will continue to play second fiddle '... where the security concerns of major powers, especially those of the Permanent Five members of the Security Council are concerned ...' (1998, 22). The then US deputy Secretary of State, Strobe Talbott makes no secret of this when he cautioned that 'we must be careful not to subordinate NATO to any other international body or compromise the integrity of its command structure ... the alliance must reserve the right and freedom to act when its members, by consensus, deem it necessary' (quoted in Chandler, 2001, 15). Closely linked with this is the regional hegemon factor. Such dominant powers will continue to dictate the pace and operations of peacekeeping as are the cases of Nigeria in ECOWAS, the US in NATO and OAS and Russia in the CIS. Nevertheless, cooperation between the UN and regional organisations will continue to be the most viable alternative to an overburdened UN and regional organisations in dire need of credibility, resources and capacity. And as Alagappa (1998, 26) recommends, the success of future co-deployment greatly depends 'on a good understanding of the possibilities and limitations of each, an effective division of labour, and accountability of the various institutions involved in managing a specific conflict'. In West Africa, the emerging complimentarity model between the UN and ECOWAS is consistent with this suggestion. Already experimented in Liberia and Cote d'Ivoire, this model is based on ECOWAS providing a rapid reaction force to stabilise a volatile conflict situation and handing over to a larger, well resourced UN mission whilst leading peacemaking efforts. This represents the most viable option aimed at maximising each organisation's comparative advantage.

Whilst this book has been able to cover substantial issues surrounding ECOWAS conflict management and resolution mechanism, there still remain vast areas for further research. Firstly, there is need to further study the link between local mercenaries and conflicts in the sub-region and how this impacts on the operations of peacekeeping and humanitarian intervention missions. Secondly, there is need for further research into the evolving concept of co-deployment between the UN and regional/sub-regional organisations with a view to developing an effective framework to guide such operations. And finally, further research is needed to study the emerging broader concept of human security and how this relates to ECOWAS.

References

Adebajo, A. (2000), 'Nigeria: Africa's New Gendarme?', *Security Dialogue*, Vol. 31, No. 2.

Adebajo, A. (2002), *Liberia's Civil War: Nigeria, ECOMOG and Regional Security in West Africa*, London: Lynne Rienner.

Adebajo, A. (2002), *Building Peace in West Africa: Liberia, Sierra Leone and Guinea Bissau*, Boulder, CO: Lynne Rienner.

Adedeji, A. (1999), 'Comprehending African Conflicts' in Adedeji, Adebayo (ed.), Comprehending *and Mastering African Conflicts: The Search for Sustainable Peace and Good Governance*, New York: Zed Books and ACDESS.

Adeshina, R.A. (Brig. Gen.) (2002), *The Reversed Victory: Story of Nigerian Military Intervention in Sierra Leone*, Ibadan: Heinemann Educational Books (Nigeria) plc.

Adibe, C. (1998), 'The Liberian Conflict and the ECOWAS-UN Partnership' in Weiss, Thomas G. (ed.), *Beyond UN Subcontracting: Task Sharing with Regional Security Arrangements and Service-Providing NGOs*, London: Macmillan Press Ltd.

Adibe, C. (2002), 'Muddling Through: An Analysis of the ECOWAS Experience in Conflict Management in West Africa' in Liisa Laakso (ed.), *Regional Integration for Conflict Prevention and Peacebuilding in Africa*, University of Helsinki.

Adler, E. and Michael B. (eds) (1998), *Security Communities*, Cambridge: Cambridge University Press.

Africa Confidential (March 1994), 'Liberia: Problematic Peacekeeping', Vol. 35, No. 5.

Africa Confidential (March 1998), 'Sierra Leone: Freetown Fracas', Vol. 39, No. 5.

Africa Confidential (1998), The Freetown Fall-out' Vol. 39 No. 10.

Africa Confidential (January 1999), 'No Surrender, No Deal', Vol. 40, No. 2.

African Union (July 2000), *Constitutive Act of the African Union*, Lomé: AU available online at http://www.au2002.gov.za/docs/key_oau/au_act.htm accessed July 2003.

Akinrinade, S. (1998), 'The Re-democratisation Process in Africa: Plus ca Change, Plus c'est la Meme Chose?' in Sola Akinrinade and Amadu Sesay (eds), *Africa in the Post-Cold War International System*, London: Pinter.

Alao, A., J. Mackinlay and F. Olonisakin (1999), *Peacekeepers, Politicians and Warlords: The Liberian Peace Process*, Tokyo: United Nations University Press.

Allen, M. (August 2003), 'Critics Assail Bush's Strategy of Restraint in Liberia', *Washington Post*.

Amnesty International (1998), *Sierra Leone: 1998 – A Year of Atrocities Against Civilians*.

Amoako, K.Y. (1999), 'Address delivered at the 21st Session of the Assembly of Heads of State and Government of ECOWAS', Lomé, Togo, 9 December 1999.

Anderson, M. (1999), *Do No Harm: How Aid can Support Peace – or War*, Boulder, CO: Lynne Rienner.

Annan, K. (1997), 'Address to the Annual Assembly of Heads of State and Government of the Organisation of African Unity', Harare, 2 June 1997, New York: UN Document SG/SM/6245 AFR/9.

Annan, K. (1998), *The Causes of Conflict and the Promotion of Durable Peace and Sustainable Development in Africa*, New York: United Nations.

Aning, K. (1994), *Managing Regional Security in West Africa: ECOWAS, ECOMOG and Liberia*, Copenhagen: Centre for Development Research.

Aning, K. Emmanuel (2000), 'War to Peace: Dilemmas of Multilateral Intervention in Civil Wars', *African Security Review*, Vol. 9, No. 3.

Anste, B. (March 1997), 'The ECOMOG Miracle', *West Africa Magazine*.

Arend, A. and Beck, R. (1993), *International Law and the Use of Force*, London: Routledge.

Asante, S.K.B. (1986), *The Political Economy of Regionalism in Africa: A Decade of Economic Community of West African States*, New York: Praeger.

Azar, E.E (1990), *The Management of Protracted Social Conflict, Theory and Cases*, Aldershot: Dartmouth.

Bach, D.C. (1999), *Regionalism in Africa: Integration and Disintegration*, Oxford: James Currey.

Bank of Sierra Leone (2004), Annual Report and Statement of Account: 2004, available online at http://www.bankofsierraleonecentralbank.org/pdf/, accessed June 2005.

Barclay, A. (1999), 'Consolidating Peace through Governance and Regional Co-operation: The Liberian Experience' in Adebayo Adedeji (ed.), *Comprehending and Mastering African Conflicts: The Search for Sustainable Peace and Good Governance*, New York: Zed Books and ACDESS.

BBC Africa Online (June 2000), 'EU Suspends Liberia' Aid, 13 June 2000, available online at http://news.bbc.co.uk/1/hi/world/africa/789128.stm, accessed March 2005.

BBC Africa Online (2000), 'Nigeria: Sack UN Force Commander', 10 September 2000, available online at http://news.bbc.co.uk/1/hi/world/africa/917962.stm, accessed August 2005.

BBC Africa Online (2004), 'Ivory Coast Backed Burkina Coup', available online at http://news.bbc.co.uk/2/hi/africa/3604315.stm, accessed April 2004.

BBC Africa Online (2005) 'Liberia's Peacekeeping Legacy', available online at http://news.bbc.co.uk/2/hi/africa/4195459.stm, accessed January 2005.

BBC Africa Online (2008), 'Liberians Killed in Farm Massacre', available online at http://news.bbc.co.uk/1/hi/world/africa/7448970.stm, accessed June 2008.

Berdal, M.R. (1996), 'Disarmament and Demobilisation After Civil Wars: Arms, Soldiers and the Termination of Armed Conflict', *Adelphi Paper* No. 303.

Biguzzi, Bishop G. (2000), 'Role of Religious Leaders in Conflict Situations and Peacebuilding', paper presented at Havard University, 16 October 2000.

Black, P.W. (2003), 'Identities' in Cheldelin, Sandra et al. (eds), *Conflict*, London: Continuum.

Blair, T. (1999), 'Doctrine of the International Community', speech by the British Prime Minister to the Economic Club of Chicago, USA, 22 April 1999, available online at http://www.globalpolicy.org/globaliz/politics/blair. htm, accessed July 2004.

Boafo-Arthur, K. (2001), 'ECOWAS: Between Balkanization and Integration', paper presented at the 13th Biennial Congress of AAPS, Yaounde, Cameroon, June 2001.

Boutros-Ghali, B. (1992), *An Agenda for Peace*, New York: United Nations.

Boutros-Ghali, B. (1995), *Supplement to an Agenda for Peace*, New York: United Nations.

Boutros-Ghali, B. (1998), 'Peacemaking and Peacekeeping for the New Century' in A. Otunu, Olara andMichael W. Doyle (eds), *Peacemaking and Peacekeeping for the New Century*, Oxford: Rowman and Littlefield.

Brahimi, L. (2000), *Report of the Panel on United Nations Peace Operations,* New York: United Nations.

Brooks, D. (2000), 'Messiahs or Mercenaries? The Future of International Private Military Services', *International Peacekeeping*, Vol. 7 No. 4.

Bundu, A. (2002), *Democracy by Force? A Study of International Military Intervention in the Conflict in Sierra Leone from 1991–2000*, Parkland, FL: Universal Publishers.

Burton, J.W. (1997), *Violence Explained*, Manchester: Manchester University.

Butty, J. (2008), 'Liberia's President Sirleaf Asks Cabinet to put Corruption Fight in Writing', *Voice of America,,* available online.

Buzan, B. (1991), *People, States and Fear: An Agenda for International Security Studies in the Post-Cold War Era* (2nd edn), Harlow: Longman.

Callaghy, T.M. (2000), 'Africa and the World Political Economy' inJohn W. Harbeson and Donald Rothchild (eds), *Africa in World Politics: The African State System in Flux*, London: Westview Press.

Carment, D. (2001), 'Anticipating State Failure', paper presented to the Conference on 'Why Sates Fail and How to Resuscitate Them', available online at http://www.carleton.ca/cifp/docs/anticipatingstatefailure.pdf, accessed November 2003.

Carnegie Commisiion on Preventing Deadly Conflict (1997), *Report of the Carnegie Commission on Preventing Deadly Conflict*, New York: Carnegie Corporation.

Chalmers, M. (2000), *Security Sector Reform in Developing Countries: An EU Perspective*, London: Safe World and the Conflict Prevention Network.

Chambers, M.I. (2002), *Fostering Regional Integration Through NEPAD Implementation: ECOWAS Annual Report 2002*, Abuja: ECOWAS Secretariat.

Chandler, D. (2001), 'The People-Centred Approach to Peace Operations: The New UN Agenda', *International Peacekeeping*, Vol. 8, No. 1, pp. 1–19.

Chandler, D. (2004), 'The Responsibility to Protect? Imposing the 'Liberal Peace', *International Peacekeeping*, Vol. 11, No. 1.

Chazan, N. et al. (1999), *Politics and Security in Contemporary Africa* (3rd edn), Boulder, CO: Lynne Reinner.

Clapham, C. (1982), 'Clientelism and the State' in Christopher Clapham, *Private Patronage and Public Power*, London: Pinter.

Clapham, C. (1998), 'Rwanda: The Perils of Peacemaking', *Journal of Peace Research*, Vol. 35, No. 2, pp. 193–210.

Clarke, A. (2001), 'Research and the Policy-making Process', in Nigel Gilbert (ed.), *Researching Social Life* (2nd edn), London: SAGE Publications Ltd.

Clark, I. (1998), *Waging War: A Philosophical Introduction*, Oxford: Clarendon.

Cliff, L. and R. Luckham (1999) 'Complex Political Emergencies, State: Failure and the Fate of the State', *Third World Quarterly*, Vol. 20 No. 1.

Cocker, P. (2003), 'The Role of the Media and Public Information' in Mark Malan et al. (eds), *Sierra Leone: Building the Road to Recovery*, Monograph No. 80, Pretoria: ISS.

Collier, P. (2000), 'Doing Well Out of War' in M. Berdal and D. Malone (eds), *Greed and Grievance: Economic Agendas in Civil Wars*, Boulder, CO: Lynne Rienner.

Commission for Africa (2005), *Our Common Interest: Report of the Commission for Africa, London: Commission for Africa*, available online at http://www.commissionforafrica.org.

Conciliation Resources (1997), 'Nigerian Intervention in Sierra Leone', available online at http://www.c-r.org/pubs/occ_papers/briefing2.shtml, accessed 15 March 2005.

Creative Associates (1997), *Assessment of the Demobilisation and Disarmament Process in Liberia, Final Report*, United States Agency for International Development (USAID).

Da Costa, P. (July 1991), 'Towards the ECOWAS Ideal of Collective Security: The Liberian Lessons' , *West Africa Magazine*, p. 1077.

Darby, J. and R. Mac Ginty (eds) (2003), *Contemporary Peacemaking: Conflict, Violence and Peace Processes*, Basingstoke: Palgrave Macmillan.

De Cuellar, J.P. (1991), *Report of the Secretary-General of the UN*, New York: United Nations.

Deutsch, Karl W. et al. (1957), *Political Community and the North Atlantic Area: International Organisation in the Light of Historical Experience*, Princeton, NJ: Princeton University Press.

DFID (2005), *Why We Need to Work More Effectively in Fragile States*, London: DFID.

DFID (2005), *Fighting Poverty to Build a Safer World: A Strategy for Security and Development*, London: DFID.

Diamond, L. (1995), 'Promoting Democracy in Africa: US and International policies in Transition', in John W. Harbeson and Donald Rothchild (eds), *Africa in World Politics: Post Cold War Challenges*, London: Westview Press.

Dokken (2002), 'Regional Conflict Management in West Africa', paper for the XIII Nordic Political Science Association meeting, Aalborg, 15–17 August 2002.

Downs, G. and S.J. Stedman. (2002), 'Evaluation Issues in Peace Implementation' in Stephen John Stedman et al. (eds) (2002), *Ending Civil Wars: The Implementation of Peace Agreements*, London: Lynne Rienner.

Duffey, T. (2000), 'Cultural Issues in Contemporary Peacekeeping' in Tom Woodhouse and Oliver Ramsbotham (eds), *Peacekeeping and Conflict Resolution*, London: Frank Cass Publishers.

Duffield, M. (1994), 'Complex Emergencies and the Crisis of Developmentalism', *IDS Bulletin,*, Vol. 25, No 4.

Duffield, M. (2001), *Global Governance and the New Wars: The Merging of Development and Security*, New York: Zed Books.

Dunn, E. (1999), 'The Civil War in Liberia' in Taisier M. Ali and Robert O. Matthew (eds), *Civil Wars in Africa, Roots and Resolution*, Montreal: McGill-Queen's University Press.

Ebo, A. (2003), *Small Arms Control in West Africa*, London: International Alert.

ECOWAS (1975), *Treaty of the Economic Community of West African States*, Lagos: ECOWAS Secretariat.

ECOWAS (1978), *Non-Agression Treaty*, Lagos: ECOWAS Secretariat.

ECOWAS (1981), *Mutual Assistance on Defence Treaty*, Freetown: ECOWAS.

ECOWAS (1990), *Standing Mediation Committee Decision*, A/DEC/1/8/90.

ECOWAS (1993), *Revised Treaty of the Economic Community of West African States*, Abuja: ECOWAS Secretariat.

ECOWAS (1993), *Cotonou Agreement*, Contonou: ECOWAS.

ECOWAS (1996), *Accra Agreement*, Accra: ECOWAS.

ECOWAS (1997), *Foreign Ministers Final Communique*, 26 June, 1997, available online www.sierra-leone.org, accessed March 2005.

ECOWAS (1997), *Decision on Sierra Leone*, 29 August 1997, available online www.sierra-leone.org, accessed March 2005.

ECOWAS (1998), *ECOWAS Six-month Plan for Sierra Leone*, Conakry, 23 October 1998.

ECOWAS (1998), *Declaration on the Moratorium on the Importation, Exportation and Manufacture of Light Weapons*, Abuja: ECOWAS.

ECOWAS (1998), *Final Communiqué of the Extraordinary Meeting of the Committee of Five on Sierra Leone*, Abidjan, 28 December 1998.

ECOWAS (1999) *Mechanism for Conflict Prevention, Management, Resolution Peacekeeping and Security*, Abuja: ECOWAS Secretariat.

ECOWAS (2000), *1975–2000: Achievements and Prospects*, available online: www.ecowas.int accessed July 2005.

El-Agraa, A.M. (1999), *Regional Integration*, London: Macmillan.

Ero, C. (2000), *Sierra Leone's Security Complex*, London: King's College.

Farah, D. (November 2001), 'Al Qaeda Cash Tied to Diamond Trade', *Washington Post*.

Farer, T. J. (2003), 'Humanitarian Intervention Before and After 9/11: Legality and Legitimacy' in J.L. Holzgrefe and Robert O. Keohane (eds), *Humanitarian Intervention: Ethical, Legal, and Political Dilemmas*, Cambridge: Cambridge University Press.

Fawcett, L. and A. Hurrel (eds) (1995), *Regionalism in World Politics: Regional Organisations and International Order*, Oxford: Oxford University Press.

Faye, A. (2004), 'ECOWAS Mission in Cote d'Ivoire: Partnerships for Peace', available online at http://mandela.inwent.org/ef/military/fall.htm, accessed October 2005.

Ferreira, P.M. (2004), 'Guinea Bissau: Between Conflict and Democracy', *African Security Review*, Vol. 13 No. 4.

Fetherston, A.B. (2000), 'Peacekeeping, Conflict Resolution and Peace building: A Reconstruction of Theoretical Frameworks' in Tom Woodhouse and Oliver Ramsbotham (eds), *Peacekeeping and Conflict Resolution*, London: Frank Cass Publishers.

Fetherston, A.B. (1993), *Towards a Theory of United Nations Peacekeeping*, Peace Research Report Number 31, Dept of Peace Studies, University of Bradford.

Francis, D. (2000), 'ECOMOG: A New Security Agenda in World Politics' in Tswah Bakut Bakut and Sagarika Dutt (eds), *Africa at the Millennium: An Agenda for Mature Development*, London: Palgrave.

Francis, D.J. (1999), 'The Economic Community of West African States, the Defence of Democracy in Sierra Leone and Future Prospects', *Democratisation*, Vol. 6, No. 4.

Francis D.J. (2000), 'The Fire Next Door: Regional Diplomacy and Conflict Resolution in West Africa', *African Review of Foreign Policy*, Vol. 2, No. 2.

Francis, D.J. (1999), 'Mercenary Intervention in Sierra Leone: Providing National Security or International Exploitation?', *Third World Quarterly*, Vol. 20, No. 2, pp. 319–38.

Francis, D.J. (2001), *The Politics of Economic Regionalism: Sierra Leone in ECOWAS*, Aldershot: Ashgate.

Francis, D.J., 'Torturous Path to Peace: The Lomé Peace Agreement and Post-war Peacebuilding in Sierra Leone', *Security Dialogue*, Vol. 3, No. 3, pp. 357–73.

Francis, D.J. et al. (2005), *The Dangers of Co-deployment: UN Co-operative Peacekeeping in Africa*, Aldershot: Ashgate.

Francis, D.J. (2005), 'Introduction' in David Francis (ed.), *Civil Militia: Africa's Intractable Security Menance?*, Aldershot: Ashgate.

Frank, T. and N. Rodley (1973), 'After Bangladesh: The Law of Humanitarian Intervention by Military Force', *American Journal of International Law*, 67, pp. 275–305.

G8 (2005), *Progress Report by the G8: African Personal Representatives on the Implementation of the African Union Plan*, London: G8, available online at http://www.dfid.gov.uk/pubs/files/98-africa-progress-report.pdf.

Galtung, J. (1981), 'Cultural Violence', *Journal of Peace Research*, Vol. 27, No. 3, pp. 291–305.

Gambari, I. (1991), *Political and Comparative Dimensions of Regional Integration: The Case of ECOWAS*, London: Humanities Press International.

Gberie, L. (2001), *Destabilising Guinea: Diamonds, Charles Taylor and the Potential for Wider Humanitarian Catastrophe*, Ottawa: Partnership Africa Canada.

Gberie, L. and P. Addo (2004) *Challenges of Peace Implementation in Cote d'Ivoire: Report on an Expert Workshop by KAIPTC and ZIF*, Monograph 105, Pretoria: Institute of Security Studies, available online at http://www.iss.co.za/pubs/Monographs/No105/4UN.htm, accessed October 2005.

Global Witness (2002), *Logging Off: How the Liberia's Timber Industry Fuels Liberian Humanitarian Disaster and Threatens Sierra Leone*, London: Global Witness.

Goodhand, J. (1999), 'Research in Conflict Zones: Ethics and Accountability', *Forced Migration*, Review 8.

Goodhand, J. and D. Hume (1999), 'From Wars to Complex Political Emergencies: Understanding Conflict and Peacebuilding in the New World Disorder', *Third World Quarterly*, Vol. 20, No. 1, pp. 13–26.

Government of Sierra Leone (1997), *The Conakry Peace Plan – Report of the Meeting of the Ministers of Foreign Affairs of the Committee of Five on Sierra Leone*, 23 October 1997, Conakry.

Government of Sierra Leone (1999), *The Lomé Agreement: Peace Agreement Between the Government of Sierra Leone and the Revolutionary United Front*, 7 July 1999, Lomé: GOSL.

Government of Sierra Leone (1996), *The Abidjan Agreement: Peace Agreement Between the Government of Sierra Leone and the Revolutionary United Front*, 30 November 1996, Abidjan: GOSL.

Government of Sierra Leone (2002), *Agreement Between the United Nations and the Government of Sierra Leone*, available online at http://www.sierra-leone.org/Laws/2002-9.pdf, accessed July 2004.

Government of Sierra Leone (2000), *The Truth and Reconciliation Act of 2000*, available online at http://www.sierra-leone.org/Laws/2000-4.pdf, accessed July 2004.

Graduate Institute of International Affairs (2003), *Small Arms Survey 2003*, Oxford: Oxford University.

Hampson, F.O. (1996), *Nurturing Peace: Why Peace Settlements Succeed or Fail*, Washington DC: US Institute of Peace.

Harbeson, J.W. (1995), 'Africa in World Politics: Amid Renewal, Deepening Crisis' in John W. Harbeson and Donald Rothchild (eds), *Africa in World Politics: Post-Cold War Challenges*, London: Westview Press.

Harvey, P. (1997) 'Rehabilitation in Complex Political Emergencies: Is Rebuilding Civil Society the Answer?', *IDS Working Paper*, No. 60.

Hass, E. (1958), *The Uniting of Europe*, Stanford, CA: Stanford University Press.

HMSO (1995), *Wider Peacekeeping*, London: HMSO.

Holzgrefe, J.L. (2003), 'The Humanitarian Intervention Debate' in J.L. Holzgrefe and Robert O. Keohane (eds), *Humanitarian Intervention: Ethical, Legal, and Political Dilemmas*, Cambridge: Cambridge University Press.

Hoogvelt, A. (1997), *Globalisation and the PostColonial World: The New Political Economy of Development*, Basinngstoke: Macmillan.

Howe, H. (1996/97), 'Lessons of Liberia, ECOMOG and Regional Peacekeeping', *International Security*, Vol. 21, No. 3, pp. 145–76.

Hugh, M. et al. (1999), *Contemporary Conflict Resolution*, Cambridge: Polity Press.

Human Rights Watch (1997), 'Nigeria's Intervention In Sierra Leone', available online at http://www.hrw.org/reports/1997/nigeria/Nigeria-09.htm, accessed 15 March 2005.

Human Rights Watch (1993), *Waging War to Keep the Peace: The ECOMOG Intervention and Human Rights*, Vol. 5, Issue No. 6.

Human Rights Watch (2002), *Back to the Brink: War Crimes by Liberian Government and Rebels*, Vol. 14, No. 4.

Human Rights Watch (1999), *The Price of Oil: Corporate Responsibility and Human Rights Violations in Nigeria's Oil Producing Communities*.

Human Rights Watch (2005), *Youth, Poverty and Blood: The Lethal Legacy of West Africa's Regional Warriors*, available online at http://hrw.org/reports/2005/westafrica0405/, accessed July 2005.

Human Security Centre (2005), *Human Security Report 2005: War and Peace in the 21st Century*, Oxford: Oxford University Press.

Human Security Network (2004), *Mapping of Non-State Armed Groups in the ECOWAS Region Preliminary Report*, presented at the 6th Ministerial Meeting of the Human Security Network, Bamako, Mali, 27–29 May 2004.

IANSA/Biting the Bullet (2004), *International Action on Small Arms 2004: Examining the Implementation of the UN Programme of Action*, London: IANSA.

ICG (April 2002), *Liberia: The Key to Ending Regional Instability*, Africa Report No. 43, Freetown/Brussels: ICG.

ICG (2003), *Tackling Liberia: The Eye of the Regional Storm*, Africa Report No. 62, Freetown/Brussels: ICG.

ICG (2003), *Sierra Leone: The State of Security and Governance*, Africa Report No. 67, Freetown/Brussels: ICG.

ICG (November 2003), *Liberia: Security Challenges*, Report No. 71, Freetown/Brussels: ICG.

ICG (January 2004), *Rebuilding Liberia: Prospects and Perils*, Africa Report No. 75, Freetown/Brussels: ICG.

ICG (2007), *Cote d'Ivoire: Can the Ouagadougou Agreement bring Peace?*, Africa Report No. 127, Dakar/Brussels: ICG.

ICG (July 2007), *Sierra Leone: The Election Opportunity*, Africa Report No. 129, Dakar/Brussels: ICG.

ICG (April 2008), *Cote d'Ivoire: Ensuring Credible Elections*, Africa Report No. 139, Dakar/Brussels: ICG.

International Commission on Intervention and State Sovereignty (ICISS) (2001), *The Responsibility to Protect: Report of the International Commission on Intervention and State Sovereignty*, Ottawa: International Development Institute.

IRIN (nd), 'Mauritania: Government Accusses Burkina Faso and Libya of Backing Coup' available online at http://www.irinnews.org.

IRIN News (2004), 'Liberia: Bryant appeals for $44m to Complete DDR and Send IDPs Home', 14 September 2004, available online: http://www.irinnews.org/report.asp, accessed September 2004.

Isaac, E. (1993), 'Humanitarianism Across Religions and Cultures' in Thomas G. Weiss and Larry Minear (eds), *Humanitarianism Across Borders: Sustaining Civilians in Times of War*, Boulder, CO: Lynne Rienner.

Jackson, R. (2000), *The Global Covenant: Human Conduct in a World of States*, Oxford: Oxford University Press.

Jakobsen, P.V. (2001), 'UN Peace Operations in Africa Today and Tomorrow', paper presented at the 26th Annual BISA Conference, Edinburgh, 17–19 December 2001.

Jetley, V. (Maj. Gen.) (2000), *Report on the Situation in Sierra Leone*, available online at www.sierra-leone.org.

Jonah, J.O.C. (October 2005), 'Letter to the UN Secretary-General', available online at www.sierra-leone.org, accessed March 2004.

Jonah, J. O.C. (1993), 'Humanitarian Intervention' in Thomas G. Weiss and Larry Minear (eds), *Humanitarianism Across Borders: Sustaining Civilians in Times of War*, Boulder, CO and London: Lynne Rienner.

Jordan, R.S. (1969), *Government and Power in West Africa*, London: Faber and Faber.

Kabia, J.M. (2002), *Co-operative Peacekeeping: UN and ECOWAS in Liberia and Sierra Leone*, University of Bradford unpublished Masters thesis.

Kaikai, F. (2004), 'Executive Secretariat Report', Freetown: NCDDR, available online at http://www.dacosl.org/encyclopedia/5, accessed September, 2004.

Kansteiner, W.H. (2003), Assistant Secretary of State for African Affairs, 'Testimony to the House Committee on International Relations Sub Committee on Africa', 2 October 2003.

Kaldor, M. (2001), *New and Old Wars*, Cambridge: Polity Press.

Kandeh, J. D. (1999), 'Ransoming the State: Elite Origins of Subaltern Terror in Sierra Leone', *Review of African Political Economy*, Vol. 26, pp. 353–4.

Kaplan, R. (1994), 'The Coming Anarchy', *Atlantic Monthly*, February, pp. 44–76.

Keen, D. (2005), *Conflict and Collision in Sierra Leone*, Oxford: James Currey Ltd.

Kegley, C. and E. Wittkopf (2004), *World Politics: Trend and Transformation* (9th edn), Belmont: Wadsworth/Thomson Learning.

Khobe, M. (2000), 'The Evolution and Conduct of ECOMOG Operations in West Africa', *Boundaries of Peace Support Operations*, available online at http://www.iss.co.za, accessed March 2002.

Koroma, A.K. (1996), *Sierra Leone: The Agony of a Nation*, London: Andromedra Publications.

Koromah, J.P. (November 1997), 'Statement on the ECOWAS Six Month Plan', 4 November 1997, available online at www.sierra-leone.org, accessed April 2005.

Koromah, J.P. (July 1997), 'Statement by Major Johnny Paul Koroma', 30 July 1997, available online at www.sierra-leone.org, accessed April 2005.

Koromah, J. P. (August 1997), 'Letter from AFRC Chairman Major Johnny Paul Koromah to ECOWAS Chairman Sani Abacha', available online at www.sierra-leone.org, accessed 18 March 2005.

Kuyateh, L. (1999), *ECOWAS Annual Report*, Abuja: ECOWAS.

Lamb, David (1984), *The Africans*, New York: Random House.

Le Roux, L., J. Ricardo Dornelles and R. Williams (2004), 'Establishing a Common Understanding for Security Sector Transformation' in Ann Fitz-Gerald and Anicia Lala (eds), *Networking the Networks: Supporting Regional Peace and Security Agendas in Africa*, Shrivenham: Global Facilitation Network for Security Sector Reform.

Lewer, N. (1999), 'International Non-Governmental Organisations and Peacebuilding – Perspectives from Peace Studies and Conflict Resolution',

Working Paper Series, Centre for Conflict Resolution, Department of Peace Studies, University of Bradford.

Lilich, R. (1967), 'Forcible Self-help by States to Protect Human Rights', *Iowa Law Review*, Vol. 53, pp. 325–51.

Lord, D. (2000), *Paying the Price: The Sierra Leone Peace Process*, Conciliation Resources: London: Accord.

Luttwak, E. (1999), 'Give War A Chance', *Foreign Affairs*, Vol. 78, No. 4, pp. 36–44.

Mackinlay, J. and A. Alao (1995), *Liberia 1994: ECOMOG and UNOMIL Response to a Complex Emergency,,* Occasional Paper Series 2.

Malan, M. (2003), 'Security and Military Reform' in Mark Malan et al. (eds), *Sierra Leone: Building the Road to Recovery*, Monograph No. 80, Pretoria: ISS.

Malan, M. (2004), 'ECOWAS Peace Operations: Lessons from 1990 to 2004', paper presented at the ECOWAS Lessons Learned Workshop, Kofi Annan International Peacekeeping Training Centre, Acrra, 18–19 November, 2004.

Malan, M. (2008), *Security Sector Reform in Liberia: Mixed Results from Humble Beginings*, Carlisle: Strategic Studies Institute.

Maresko, D. (2004), 'Development, Relief Aid, and Creating Peace: Humanitarian Aid in Liberia's War of the 1990s', *The Online Journal of Peace and Conflict Resolution*, Vol. 6 No. 1, pp. 94–120.

Mburu, N. (2003), 'African Crisis Response Initiative: Its Workability as a Framework for Conflict Prevention and Resolution', *OJPCR: The Online Journal of Peace and Conflict Resolution*, Vol. 5, No. 1, pp. 77–89, available online www.trinstitute.org/ojpcr/5_1mburu.htm, accessed March 2005.

Mitrany, D. (1996), *A Working Peace*, Chicago: Quadrangle Books.

Mortimer R.A. (1996), 'ECOMOG, Liberia and Regional Security in West Africa' in Edmund J. Keller and Donald Rothchild (eds), *Africa in the New International Order: Rethinking State Sovereignty and Regional Security*, Boulder, CO: Lynne Rienner Publishers.

Mortimer, R. (1996), 'Senegal's Role in ECOMOG: The Francophone Dimension in the Liberian Crisis', *Journal of Modern African Studies*, Vol. 34, No. 2.

Musah, A. and J. Kayode Fayemi (2000), *Mercenaries: An African Security Dilemma*, London: Pluto Press.

Musah, A. (2002), 'Small Arms: A Time Bomb under West Africa's Democratization', *The Brown Journal of World Affairs*, Vol. 9, No. 1.

Muthiah, A. (1998), 'Regional Arrangements, the UN, and International Security: A Framework for Analysis', in Thomas G. Weiss (ed.), *Beyond UN Subcontracting: Task Sharing with Regional Security Arrangements and Service-Providing NGOs*, London: Macmillan Press Ltd.

Nicholls, B. (1987), 'Rubber Band Humanitarianism', *Ethics and International Affairs*, Vol. 1.

Nordstrom, C. (1992), 'The Backyard Front' in Carolyn Nordstrom and JoAnn Martin (eds), *The Paths to Domination, Resistance, and Terror*, Oxford: University of California Press.

Obasanjo O. (1999), 'Address to UN General Assembly, September 1999', New York: United Nations.

Observatoirie de l'Afrique (2008), 'Security Sector Reform in Guinea Bissau', *Africa Briefing Report*, Brussels: Observatoirie de l'Afrique.

Ofodile, A.C. (1994), 'The Legality of ECOWAS Intervention in Liberia', *Columbia Journal of Transnational Law*, Vol. 32, No. 2 pp. 381–418.

Ofuatey-Kodjoe, W. (1994), 'Regional Organisations and the Resolution of Internal Conflict: The ECOWAS Intervention in Liberia', *International Peacekeeping*, Vol. 1, No. 3, pp. 261–301.

Ojo, O. (1980), 'Nigeria and the Formation of ECOWAS', *International Organisation*, Vol. 34, No. 4.

Olonisakin, 'F. (1996), 'UN Co-operation with Regional Organisations in Peacekeeping: The Experience of ECOMOG and UNOMIL in Liberia', *International Peacekeeping*, Vol. 3, No. 3, pp. 33–51.

Olonisakin, 'F. (1999), 'Humanitarian Intervention and Human Rights: The Contradictions in ECOMOG', *International Journal of Human Rights*, Vol. 3, No. 1, pp. 16–39.

Olukoshi, A. (2001), 'West Africa's Political Economy in the Next Millennium: Retrospect and Prospects', *CODESRIA Monograph Series*, No. 2.

Omeje, K. (2005), 'The Egbesu and Bakassi Boys: African Spiritism and Mystical Re-Traditionalisation of Security' in David J. Francis (ed.), *Civil Militias: Africa's Intractable Security Menance?*, Aldershot: Ashgate.

Oudraat, C.J. (2001), 'UN Sanction Regimes and Violent Conflict' in Chester A. Crocker et al. (eds), *Turbulent Peace: The Challenges of Managing International Conflict*, Washington: United States Institute of Peace.

Pape, R. (1997), 'Why Economic Sanctions Do Not Work', *International Security*, Vol. 22, No. 2, pp. 90–136.

Paris, R. (1997), 'The Perils of Liberal International Peacebuilding', *International Security*, Vol. 22, No. 2, pp. 54-89.

Paris, R. (2004), *At War's End: Building Peace After Civil Conflict*, Cambridge: Cambridge University Press.

Pearce, J. (1999) 'Peace-building in the Periphery: Lessons from Central America', *Third World Quarterly*, Vol. 20, No. 1.

Pham, J. Peter (2004), 'Lazarus Rising: Civil Society and Sierra Leone's Return from the Grave', *The International Journal of Not-for-Profit Law* , Vol. 7, Issue 1.

Pugh, M. (2004), 'Peacekeeping and Critical Theory' , *International Peacekeeping*, Vol. 11, No. 1.

Pugh, M. and N. Cooper with J. Goodhand (2004), *War Economies in a Regional Context: Challenges of Transformation*, Boulder, CO and London: Lynne Rienner.

Putnam, R. (1993), *Making Democracy Work: Civic Traditions in Modern Italy*, Chichester: Princeton University Press.

Quentin, O. (1997), 'Cruel Wars and Safe Havens: Humanitarian Aid in Liberia 1989–1996', *Disasters*, Vol. 21, No. 3, pp. 189–205.

Ramsbotham, O. and T. Woodhouse (1996), *Humanitarian Intervention in Contemporary Conflict*, Cambridge: Polity Press.

Ramsbotham, O. and T. Woodhouse (1999), *Encyclopaedia of International Peacekeeping Operations*, Oxford: ACC-CLIO.

Ramsbotham, O. (2000), 'Reflections on UN Post-Settlement Peacebuilding' in Tom Woodhouse and Oliver Ramsbotham (eds), *Peacekeeping and Conflict Resolution*, London: Frank Cass.

Ramsbotham, O. and T. Woodhouse (2005), 'Cosmopolitan Peacekeeping and the Globalisation of Security', *International Peacekeeping*, Vol. 12, No. 2, pp. 139–56.

Reisman, M. and M. McDougal (1973), 'Humanitarian Intervention to Protect the Ibos', in R. Lilich (ed.), *Humanitarian Intervention and the United Nations*, Charlottesville, VA: University of Virginia Press, pp. 167–96.

Reno, W. (1998), *Warlord Politics and African States*, London: Lynne Rienner.

Richards, P. (1996), *Fighting for the Rain Forest: War, Youth and Resources in Sierra Leone*, Oxford: The International African Institute.

Richards, P. (2003), *The Political Economy of Internal Conflict in Sierra Leone*, Working Paper 21, The Hague: Netherlands Institute of International Relations 'Clingendael'.

Richmond, O.P. (2004), 'UN Peace Operations and the Dilemmas of the Peacebuilding Consensus', *International Peacekeeping*, Vol. 11, No. 1.

Rigby, A. (2001), *Justice and Reconciliation: After the Violence*, London: Lynne Rienner.

Roberts, A. (1993), 'The Road to Hell: A Critique of Humanitarian Intervention', *Havard International Review*, Vol. 16, No. 1.

Robson, C. (1993), *Real World Research*, Oxford: Blackwell Publishers.

Rogers, P. and O. Ramsbotham (1999), 'Peace Research – Past and Future', *Political Studies.*

Roper, J. (1998), 'The Contribution of Regional Organisations in Europe' in O. Otunnu and W.D. Michael (eds), *Peacemaking and Peacekeeping for the New Century*, Oxford: Rowman and Littlefield.

Rotberg, R.I. and Dennis Thompson (2000), *Truth v. Justice: The Morality of Truth Commissions*, Princeton, NJ: Princeton University Press.

Saliu, H.A. (2000), 'Nigeria and Peace Support Operations: Trends and Policy Implications', *International Peacekeeping*, Vol. 7, No. 3, pp. 105–19.

Sandline International (1998), 'Comment by Sandline International', available online http://www.sandline.com, accessed April 2004.

Sapsford, R. and V. Jupp (1986), *Data Collection and Analysis*, London: SAGE Publications Ltd.

Scott, C. (1994), *Humanitarian Action and Security in Liberia 1989–1994*, Occasional Paper No. 20, Thomas J. Watson Jr Institute for International Studies.

Scott, J. (1990), *A Matter of Record*, Cambridge: Polity Press.

Sebahara, P. (1998), 'The Creation of Ethnic Division in Rwanda', *Voices from Africa: Conflict, Peacekeeping and Reconstruction*, Vol. 8, pp. 93–100.

Secretary-General's High-Level Panel on Threats, Challenges and Change (2004), *A More Secure World: Our Shared Responsibility*, New York: United Nations.

Security Council (2000), *Report of the Security Council Mission to Sierra Leone*, New York: United Nations.

Sellstrom, T. and L. Wohlgemuth (1996), 'Study 1: Historical Perspective: Some Explanatory Factors' in *The International Response to conflict and Genocide: Lessons from the Rwanda Experience*, Steering Committee of the Joint Evaluation of Emergency Assistance to Rwanda.

Sesay, M. (1996), *The Liberian Peace Process*, London: Conciliation Resources.

Sesay M.A. (1999), 'Collective Intervention or Collective Disaster? Regional Peacekeeping in West Africa', *Security Dialogue*, Vol. 26, No. 2, pp. 205–22.

Shaw, T.M. and J.E. Okolo (1994), 'African Political Economy and Foreign Policy in the 1990s' in Timothy M. Shaw and Julius Emeka Okolo (eds), *The Political Economy of Foreign Policy in ECOWAS*, Basingstoke: St Martin's Press.

Sierra Leone Web News Page Available on line http://www.sierra-leoneweb.org.

Silverman, David (1993), *Interpreting Qualitative Data: Methods for Analysing Talk, Text and Interaction*, London: SAGE Publications.

Smillie, I. et al. (2000), *The Heart of the Matter: Sierra Leone, Diamonds and Human Security*, Ottawa: Partnership Africa Canada.

Smith, M.L.R. (2003), 'Guerrillas in the Mist: Reassessing Strategy and Low Intensity Warfare', *Review of International Studies*, Vol. 29, No. 1, p. 34.

Sola-Martin, A. and J.M. Kabia (2007), *UNAMSIL Peacekeeping and Peace Support Operations in Sierra Leone*, Bradford: University of Bradford Press.

Stedman, S.J. et al. (eds) (2002), *Ending Civil Wars: The Implementation of Peace Agreements*, London: Lynne Rienner.

Stedman, S. (1993), 'The New Interventionists', *Foreign Affairs*, Vol. 73, No. 6, pp. 34–46.

Steven, S. (1984), *What Life Has Taught Me, Abbotsbrook*, Bourne End: Kensal Press.

Swift, J. (1989), 'Why are Rural People Vulnerable to Famine?', *IDS Bulletin*, Vol. 20, No. 2.

Tawiah, T and F.B. Aboagye (2005), 'Synergies of Regional and UN Interventions: The ECOWAS Mission in Liberia and the Protection of

Civilians' in F.B. Aboagye and A.M.S. Bah (eds), *A Torturous Road to Peace: The Dynamics of Regional, UN and International Humanitarian Interventions in Liberia*, Pretoria: Institute for Security Studies.

Taw, J.M. and A. Grant-Thomas (1999), 'US Support for Regional Complex Contingency Operations: Lessons from ECOMOG', *Studies in Conflict and Terrorism*, Vol. 22, pp. 53–77.

Teson, F.R. (2003), 'The Liberal Case for Intervention' in J.L. Holzgrefe and Robert O. Keohane (eds), *Humanitarian Intervention: Ethical, Legal, and Political Dilemmas*, Cambridge: Cambridge University Press.

Thompson, A. (2004), *Introduction to African Politics*, London: Routledge.

UN (March 1993), *Report of the Secretary General on the Question of Liberia*, New York: United Nations.

UN (November 1995), *Report of the Secretary-General on the Situation in Sierra Leone*, New York: United Nations, S/1995/975.

UN (September 1997), *Final Report of the Secretary-General on the United Nations Observer Mission in Liberia*, New York: United Nations, S/1997/712.

UN (February 1998), *Third Report of the Secretary-General on the Situation in Sierra Leone*, New York: United Nations, S/1998/103.

UN (March 1998), *Fourth Report of the Secretary-General on the Situation in Sierra Leone*, New York: United Nations, S/1998/249.

UN (June 1998), *Fifth Report of the Secretary-General on the Situation in Sierra Leone*, New York: United Nations, S/1998/486.

UN (August 1998), *First Progress Report of the Secretary-General on the United Nations Observer Mission in Sierra Leone*, New York: United Nations, S/1998/750.

UN (October 1998), *Second Progress Report of the Secretary-General on the United Nations Observer Mission in Sierra Leone*, New York: United Nations, S/1998/960.

UN (December 1998), *Third Progress Report of the Secretary-General on UNOMSIL*, New York: United Nations, S/1998/1176.

UN (March 1999), *Co-operation Between the United Nations and Regional Organisations/Arrangements in a Peacekeeping Environment: Suggested Principles and Mechanisms*, New York: UN DPKO/Lessons Learnt Unit, available online at www.un.org/dept/dpko/lessons/regcoop.htm, accessed August 2002.

UN (March 1999), *Fifth Report of the Secretary-General on UNOMSIL*, New York: United Nations, S/1999/237.

UN (June 1999), *Sixth Report of the Secretary-General on UNOMSIL*, New York: United Nations, S/1999/645.

UN (January 2000) *Second Report of the Secretary-General on UNAMSIL*, New York: United Nations, S/2000/13.

UN (March 2000), *Third Report of the Secretary-General on UNAMSIL*, New York: United Nations, S/2000/186.

UN (2000), *Final Report of the UN Panel of Experts on Violations of Security Council Sanctions Against UNITA* ('The Fowler Report'), New York: United Nations, S/2000/203.

UN (May 2000), *Fourth Report of the Secretary-General on the United Nations Mission in Sierra Leone*, New York, United Nations, S/2000/455.

UN (December 2000), *Eighth Report of the Secretary-General on the United Nations Mission in Sierra Leone,* New York: United Nations, S/2000/1199.

UN (2000), *Report of the Panel on United Nations Peace Operations*, New York: UN.

UN (March 2001), *Ninth Report of the Secretary-General on the United Nations Mission in Sierra Leone*, New York: United Nations, S/2001/228.

UN (June 2001), *Tenth Report of the Secretary-General on the United Nations Mission in Sierra Leone*, New York: United Nations, S/2001/627.

UN (2001), *Report Of The Panel Of Experts Appointed Pursuant To UN Security Council Resolution 1306 (2000), Paragraph 19 In Relation To Sierra Leone*, New York: United Nations.

UN (September 2001), *Eleventh Report of the Secretary-General on the United Nations Mission in Sierra Leone*, New York: United Nations.

UN (December 2001), *Twelfth Report of the Secretary-General on the United Nations Mission in Sierra Leone*, New York: United Nations, S/2001/1195.

UN (March 2002), *Thirteenth Report of the Secretary-General on the United Nations Mission in Sierra Leone*, New York: United Nations, S/2002/267.

UN (2003), *Lessons Learned from United Nations Peacekeeping Experiences in Sierra Leone*, New York: UNDPKO.

UN (September 2003), *Report of the Secretary-General to the Security Council on Liberia*, New York: United Nations, S/2003/875.

UN (September 2004), *Fourth Progress Report of the Secretary-General on UNMIL*, New York: United Nations, S/2004/725.

UN (May 2004), *Third Progress Report of the Secretary-General on UNMIL*, New York: United Nations, S/2004/430.

UN (August, 2007), *Fifteenth Progress Report of the Secretary General on the United Nations Mission in Liberia*, S/2007/479.

UN (March, 2008), *Sixteenth Progress Report of the Secretary General on the United Nations Mission in Liberia*, S/2008/183.

UN (April 2008), *Sixteenth Progress Report of the Secretary General on the United Nations Operations in Cote d'Ivoire*, S/2008/250.

UN, Charter of the United Nations, Chapter VIII, available online at http://www.un.org/aboutun/charter/, accessed March 2005.

UN DPKO, Peacekeeping Operations: Facts and Figures available online at www.un.org/dept/dpko.

UNDP (2003), *Human Development Report 2003*: *Millennium Development Goals: A Compact among Nations to End Human Poverty*, New York: UNDP.

UNDP (2005) *Human Development Report 2005: International Co-operation at a Crossroads: Aid, Trade and Security in an Unequal World*, New York: UNDP.

UNDP (2004), *Human Development Report 2004: Cultural Liberty in Today's Diverse World*, New York: UNDP, available online at http://hdr.undp.org/reports/global/2004/pdf/hdr04.

UN (2004), *Report of the Secretary-General's High-Level Panel on Threats, Challenges and Change, A More Secure World: Our Shared Responsibility*, New York: United Nations, available online at http://www.un.org/secureworld/report3.pdf.

Utterwulghe, S. (1999), 'Rwanda's Protracted Social Conflict: Considering Subjective Perspective in Conflict Resolution Strategies', *The Online Journal of Peace and Conflict Resolution*, Issue 2:3.

Verwey, W. (1992), 'Legality of Humanitarian Intervention After the Cold War' in E. Ferris (ed.), *The Challenge to Intervene: A New Role for the United Nations?*, Uppsala: Life and Peace Institute.

Vincent, R.J. (1974), *Non-intervention and International Order*, Princeton, NJ: Princeton University Press.

Vincent, R.J. (1986), *Human Rights and International Relations*, Cambridge: Cambridge University Press.

Vincent, R.J. and P. Watson (1993), 'Beyond Non-Intervention' in I. Forbes and M.J. Hoffmann (eds), *Political Theory, International Relations and the Ethics of Intervention*, London: Macmillan.

Walraven, K.V. (1999), *Containing Conflict in the Economic Community of West African States: Lessons from Intervention in Liberia, 1990–97*, The Hague: Project Conflict Prevention in West Africa.

Walter, M. (1999), *The Logic of Regional Integration: Europe and Beyond*, Cambridge: Cambridge University Press.

Walzer, M. (1992), *Just and Unjust Wars: A Moral Argument with Historical Illustrations* (2nd edn), London: Basic Books.

WANEP (2002), 'Crisis in Cote d'Ivoire', *WARN Policy Brief*.

West Africa Magazine (October 1990), 'Interview with Salim A. Salim'. p. 2691.

West Africa (October–November 1990), 'The Forgotten Victims', p. 2741.

West Africa (December 1990), 'Interview with Dauda Jawara', p. 2894.

West Africa (March 1997), 'A No-nonsense Commander', p. 466.

West Africa 1–16 August 1998, p. 606.

Wheeler, N.J. (2000), *Saving Strangers: Humanitarian Intervention in International Society*, Oxford: Oxford University Press.

Wheeler, N.J. and A.J. Bellamy (2004), 'Humanitarian Intervention in World Politics' in John Baylis and Steve Smith (eds), *The Globalisation of World Politics* (3rd edn), Oxford: Oxford University Press.

Willett, S. (2005), 'New Barbarians at the Gate: Losing the Liberal Peace in Africa', *Review of African Political Economy*, No. 106, pp. 569–94.

Williams, P. (2001), 'Fighting for Freetown: British Military Intervention in Sierra Leone', *Contemporary Security Policy*, Vol. 22, No. 3, p. 145.

Wipmann, D. (1993), 'Enforcing the Peace: ECOWAS and the Liberian Civil War' in Lori Fisler Damrosch (ed.), *Enforcing Restraint*, New York: Council on Foreign Relations Press.

Witchell, N. (1998), 'Labour, One Year on: Ethical Foreign Policy', available onlinehttp://news.bbc.co.uk/2/hi/special_report/1998/04/98/, accessed November 2005.

Woodhouse, T. and O. Ramsbotham (2001), *Hawks and Doves: Peacekeeping and Conflict Resolution*, available online: http://www.berghofcenter.org/handbook/woodhouse/s8.htm, accessed March 2005.

World Bank (1989), *Sub-Saharan Africa: From Crisis to Sustainable Growth*, Washington DC: World Bank.

World Bank (1993), *Demobilisation and Reintegration of Military Personnel in Africa: Evidence from Seven Country Case Studies*, Working Paper, Washington: Africa Technical Department, World Bank.

World Bank (2005), *African Development Indicators 2005*, Washington DC: The World Bank.

Yoroms G.J. and E.K. Aning (1997), *West African Regional Security in the Post Liberian Conflict Era: Issues and Perspectives*, Copenhagen: Centre for Development Research.

Zartman, W. (ed.) (1995), *Collapsed States: The Disintegration and Restoration of Legitimate Authority*, Boulder, CO and London: Lynne Rienner Publishers.

Zartman W. (2003), 'The Timing of Peace Initiatives: Hurting Stalemates and Ripe Moments' in John Darby and Roger Mac Ginty (eds), *Contemporary Peacemaking: Conflict, Violence and Peace Processes*, Basingstoke: Palgrave Macmillan.

Index